Published by the Comedy Council of Nicea LLC.

266 West 37th Street, 12th floor, New York, NY 10018, U.S.A.

First published in the United States of America,

First Edition, 2013

10 9 8 7 6 5 4 3

Library of Congress Control Number: 2013941789

ISBN

0989387801

978-0-9893878-0-4

Written By:

Matt Besser
Ian Roberts
Matt Walsh

Edited by: Joe Wengert
Illustrations by: David Kantrowitz
Layout and Design by: Camille Bugden

Special Thanks to:

Amy Poehler
Alex Sidtis
Alex Berg
Julie Brister
Owen Burke
Chad Carter
Chelsea Clarke
Michael Delaney
Drew DiFonzo Marks
Alex Fernie
Chris Gethard
Ian M. Gibbs
David Harris
Kevin Hines
Will Hines
Anthony King
Will McLaughlin
Billy Merritt
Shannon O'Neill
Danielle Schneider
Amanda Sitko
Matt Whitaker

TABLE OF CONTENTS

INTRODUCTION

This book will be dealing with comedic improvisation. More specifically, it will outline guidelines and techniques for Long Form improvisation as it is taught at the Upright Citizens Brigade Training Centers and performed at the Upright Citizens Brigade Theatres in New York and Los Angeles.

There is a common misconception that improvisation is a whimsical or lazy art form. Since improvisers don't use costumes or scripts, it often seems that preparation does not have a place in improvisation. The style of improvisation performed at the Upright Citizens Brigade Theatres is not just comprised of funny jokes and clever bits of dialogue. The fun that you see great improvisers having when they perform can be misleading and help spread this misconception.

In reality, the role of the improviser is one of responsibility. In reality, no matter how much fun they are having onstage, great improvisers are working together while adhering to a set of clear guidelines. Every improviser who starts a scene with another improviser is entering into a tacit agreement to use these guidelines to build a comedic scene with his or her scene partner. **There are two major styles of comedic improv: Short Form improvisation and Long Form improvisation.**

Short Form improvisation revolves around the performance of short "games" with predetermined rules or gimmicks. Performers go into each performance knowing the set rules of each of these "games." For example, in the "emotion game," two or more improvisers will perform a scene. During the course of the scene, a third improviser will shout out emotions. As each new emotion is shouted, the improvisers in the scene will have to change their behavior and dialogue to reflect the suggested emotion. The humor in this "game" is derived from its predetermined gimmick.

Long Form improvisation is compromised of Long Form scenes. In a Long Form scene, the **Game** of the scene is not predetermined. Long Form improvisers create Games and their rules in the moment, during the course of the scene. The concept of the Game of the scene is the linchpin of the Upright Citizens Brigade Theatre's teaching and performance of Long Form improvisation.

The Game of the scene, in the simplest terms possible, is the single specific idea that makes a scene funny. This text will help you learn how to work together with other new improvisers to discover that specific idea, and then explore it throughout the course of one improvised scene. You will be introduced to exercises and techniques that will help develop the necessary skills for you to become a successful Long Form improviser.

A performance of Long Form improvisation is referred to simply as a **longform**. A longform is any structure that incorporates two or more scenes into one performance derived from a **single suggestion**.[1] A suggestion is any piece of information provided by the audience to inspire improvisation (e.g., a word, an object, a song lyric, etc.). The audience suggestion verifies that everything an ensemble does is being made up on the spot. Longforms open up opportunities for connections between the scenes. This book will teach you how to perform a few specific longforms.

Just reading this book alone will not make you a great improviser, but should, however, be a companion to constant practice and performance. As with any other art form, you will not become a competent improviser by just reading about how to do it. Experience will be your best teacher, so you must find the time to practice as much as possible.

A Long Form improv scene is comprised of two parts. The first part of a Long Form scene is called the **base reality**. This is the world you create that grounds or provides context for the comedy of your scene. The second part of the scene is "the Game," the comic spine of the scene.

There are essential principles that you must follow in a Long Form scene in order to make it successful. These basics will be introduced in the first section of this book on the "beginning of the scene."

The diagram below is a visual representation of a Long Form scene centered around the Game.

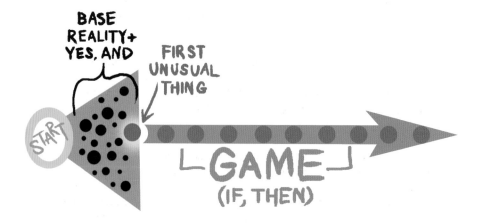

[1] An exception to this definition is the Monoscene, which is simply one extended scene.

SECTION I:
THE BEGINNING OF THE SCENE

Establishing a base reality at the outset of a scene is an essential first step in the creation of a successful Long Form scene. Once you have established this reality, you will be able to easily identify the unusual, which is the starting point of playing the Game of the scene.

You should feel no pressure to make the base reality part of your scene funny. The emphasis in the base reality section should be making strong choices and playing them realistically.

Starting a scene with agreement is like building the basement of a house. It's never the most decorative part of the structure, but the basement is certainly the sturdiest. It holds the essential materials to make the rest of the house function, and it must support all of the weight you build on top of it.

It is important to note that the beginning of the scene often will be much, much shorter than the part of the scene in which the Game will be explored. In comedic improv, your goal should be to establish your base reality as efficiently as possible so that you have something against which you can recognize the first unusual thing. You can't start the comedy of your scene until you find the first unusual thing.

CHAPTER 1

What is a Base Reality?

Yes And

▸DEFINITION

Yes And. These two simple words are the building blocks of every Long Form improv scene. "Yes" refers to the idea that you should be agreeing with any information your scene partner gives you about your reality. "And" refers to the adding of new information that relates to the previous information. Yes And is very important at the beginning of every scene, since it will allow you and your scene partner to discover the base reality in which your characters exist.

When we speak to people in real life, we move the conversation forward by adding new information in response to what has already been communicated. Imagine that you are talking with a group of friends. If everybody else is telling stories about their dog, and you start talking about how good you are at basketball out of the blue, you haven't added to the conversation already in progress. In order to successfully participate in this conversation, you should offer another dog story. Yes And is how we mirror this process in our **scene work**.

At the very start of a Long Form scene, you and your scene partner will have absolutely no information about who your characters are, what they are doing, and where they are. By following the principle of Yes And, you can work together to quickly determine the base reality of the scene. By continually agreeing with what has been established and adding new, related information, you will establish a base reality against which you will be able to recognize the *first unusual thing* when it happens. This is important because the first unusual thing is the beginning of the Game, or comedy, of the scene.

In general, make Yes And choices that add details about the present moment or the people in the scene. Do not add information about the past, the future, or people who aren't there.

Think of a Long Form scene as a painting. If you were going to paint your idea in blue, you wouldn't want to start with a blue canvas. You wouldn't be able to differentiate between the foundation and your art. Blue doesn't show up well on blue. Starting scenes with a clearly communicated and specific base reality is like starting your scenes with a white canvas on which the blue paint of what is funny will show up vibrantly.

THE FIRST LINE OF YOUR SCENE

To begin Yes And–ing, you need a first line for your scene. The first line of an improv scene is called the **initiation**. Although you could conjure this out of nothing, the initiation is usually inspired by a **suggestion** provided by someone other than the performers. A suggestion is taken for two reasons. First, the suggestion serves as inspiration for the improvisers. Second, it proves that they are indeed improvising and that the scene has not been scripted.

When you get a suggestion, you want to notice the connection you immediately make to it in your mind, and then use that connection to fashion an initiation. The suggestion may or may not be used in the initiation, depending on the connection you have made.

Example Suggestion: balloon

If "balloon" made you think of how your mother used to tie balloons to your wrist so you didn't lose them, you might offer the following initiation:

Initiation One: "I'm going to tie the balloon around your wrist so you don't lose it, honey."

If "balloon" made you think of a birthday party, you might offer the following initiation:

Initiation Two: **"Okay, blow out the candles and make a wish."**

In both of these examples, the audience should see the connection between the suggestion and your initiation.

Make sure that your initiation line starts the scene "in the middle of things." You want an initiation that allows you to get to the important part of an interaction as quickly as possible. Avoid any extraneous dialogue leading up to this moment.

Notice that in our first example, we didn't need to start with the characters noticing the balloon vendor or the transaction of buying the balloon. In the second example, we didn't need to start with people arriving at the party or people placing gifts on the gift table. In both examples, we cut to the chase by starting "in the middle."

You should initiate off of your suggestion immediately. If you hesitate, it shows that you are planning and not improvising.

YES AND, IN OTHER WORDS

YES	AND
AGREEING	ADD TO

YES AND EXAMPLES

It is important to point out that Yes And–ing does not mean literally saying the words "Yes And" before you add new information.

EXAMPLE 1

Suggestion: **balloon**

Player 1 mimes knocking on a door. Player 2 answers the door.

PLAYER 1:   "Hi, I'm the magician for the birthday party."

PLAYER 2:   "Yes, and the kids are all in the rec room having cake and ice cream."

For the sake of example, we have used the words "Yes" and "And" in Player 2's response. However, in performance, Yes And–ing will look something more like this:

EXAMPLE 2

Suggestion: **balloon**

Player 1 mimes knocking on a door. Player 2 answers the door.

PLAYER 1:   "Hi, I'm the magician for the birthday party."

PLAYER 2:   "Great! The kids are all in the rec room having cake and ice cream."

The same information is conveyed in Example 2 as was conveyed in Example 1. While the words "Yes" and "And" weren't literally said, the rule of Yes And (agreeing and adding new information) was still employed.

EXERCISE: FIND YES AND IN A REAL CONVERSATION

INSTRUCTIONS

- As we have already mentioned, Yes And naturally occurs in most conversations all of the time.

- The next time you are on public transportation, in a restaurant alone, or at a crowded party, try to zero in on a conversation and listen for Yes And–ing. Are these people Yes And–ing each other? Is their ability to Yes And each other having an effect on the conversation? In good conversations, you will notice that people are constantly Yes And–ing without being conscious of doing so.

- Also try to look for conversations in which an absence of Yes And ruins the conversation. These will be conversations in which one speaker changes topics without segue, doesn't listen, or only talks about themselves. These behaviors are to be avoided in conversation and should also be avoided in scene work.

PURPOSE

- This exercise allows you to practice Yes And outside of the classroom or rehearsal studio. Recognizing how Yes And naturally occurs will make you better at using this concept in your scene work.

HONOR THE REALITY OF THE SCENE

New improvisers often look to force something "crazy" or "wacky" at the beginning of scenes, or they will rush to a conflict (an argument) with their scene partner instead of adding information through Yes And–ing. New improvisers do this because they are worried about being funny and do not yet have faith in the rules of improv.

Agreement

▸DEFINITION

In order to create a Long Form scene with another improviser, the very first thing you must do is come to an agreement with each other about the basic context of the scene you are performing. Imagine that you are going to dance with someone. Are you going to waltz or salsa? You would be able to tell almost immediately from the first action your dance partner takes. Joining in with this first choice (whether it is waltz or salsa) may seem very obvious and simple, but it is undoubtedly essential if dancing is to happen at all. A failure to come to a basic agreement about the context of the scene stops a scene from succeeding before it even starts.

Two improvisers should be looking to agree from the very start of the scene. It is important to note that even though you are in the pursuit of comedy, you are not "going for laughs" at this point in a scene. You are going for the establishment of a reality. Normally, what we find to be "funny" in a scene is a break from the expected norms of reality. For the unusual to stand out from the commonplace, it is important that you and your partner start the scene in agreement about a normal reality. If you start off a scene in which everything is crazy or funny, it will be difficult to determine what is unusual.

CHARACTER OF THE SPACE

The most basic form of agreement involves the *character of the space*. As soon as two improvisers walk onstage—before they even begin talking—they are more likely to find success if they can come to a basic agreement about the physical and/or emotional state of their characters.

As you enter a scene, your first job is to acknowledge any choice about the character of the space that your scene partner has made. (Your scene partner will do the same if you are the one to step out first.) You should then find a way to fit into that same physical space.

For example, if your scene partner steps out and is shivering, you could mirror or match this action and shiver as well. You are agreeing that it is cold. You are allowing your characters to start off in the same environmental condition.

AGREEMENT

Maybe your scene partner has stepped out, sighed, and mimed mopping their brow with a handkerchief. If you enter the scene fanning your face, you have acknowledged the character of the space without matching your partner's exact physical choice. You are showing that your character is also hot in a different way.

You can also come to agreement about the character of the space through the physical environment of the scene or an activity your characters might be engaged in. If your scene partner starts the scene hunched over to signify that they are inside of a cave, the best thing for you to do is to simply hunch over as well. If your scene partner steps out and picks an apple off of a tree, you could match them and pick an apple for yourself as well. If your scene partner starts a scene by skeet shooting, you could load a gun or pull a pair of earphones down around your neck. Both of these actions acknowledge and agree with the choice your partner has made about the character of the space.

Failing to come to basic agreement with regard to the character of the space can start your scenes out with implicit conflict.

A physical choice made by either improviser helps ground your scene from the start and can give you valuable information about the reality of your scene. When your scene partner initiates with a choice about the physical environment, you want to take this opportunity to connect with him or her immediately by starting your scene with some sort of physical agreement. Acknowledge their choice by doing something that mirrors or complements it. If they establish something about the environment, be in that environment as well, and establish something else about it if possible.

For example, if you start by washing dishes, we can assume that you are in a kitchen. Your scene partner doesn't necessarily have to mirror this choice, but they must acknowledge it. If they choose to start drying dishes, they have established basic physical agreement. Both characters exist in this kitchen.

Or, if your scene partner initiates by tearing off an order slip and flipping a burger, you can come to physical agreement with them by choosing to be another short-order cook lowering some fries into oil or a waitress picking up dishes.

Most Long Form shows will involve a few chairs onstage. Through basic nonverbal cues and the manipulation of these chairs, important choices about the physical environment can be made, and you will have an opportunity to start your scene with physical agreement.

If your scene partner sets two chairs close together facing the audience, sits down, and mimes holding a steering wheel, you can come to physical agreement by simply sitting down in the passenger seat he or she has created. If your scene partner sets two chairs facing each other and points to the other chair, you can come to physical agreement with them simply by sitting in that other chair.

You want to be aware of these physical cues so that you can always start off your scenes in agreement. If you choose to simply watch the activity of your scene partner instead of doing something that fits with that activity, you're missing your first opportunity to Yes And, thereby beginning to build the base reality of your scene.

EXERCISE: CHARACTER OF THE SPACE

One improviser will, in silence, make a choice that establishes one of the following aspects of the character of the space: **activity** (playing pool, fishing, stretching, etc.), **location** (automobile, prison cell, supermarket, etc.), or **environmental condition** (zero gravity, hot/cold, bright lights, etc.).

A second improviser will join the scene and nonverbally agree with the choice that has been made.

Example: Activity
Player 1 *steps out into the scene and begins folding laundry.*
Player 2 *joins in by putting dirty laundry into a washing machine.*

Example: Location
Player 1 *steps out and mimes holding onto prison cell bars.*
Player 2 *stands next to him and holds out a mirror to see down the row of cells.*

Example: Environmental Condition
Player 1 *steps out squinting with his hand in front of his face.*
Player 2 *simply mirrors this behavior.*

WHO, WHAT, AND WHERE

Before you can get to the Game, in which you play with what is funny about the scene, you and your scene partner must agree on **WHO** your characters are, **WHAT** your characters are doing, and **WHERE** your characters are. The Who, What, and Where are essential to determining the foundation or base reality of the scene. Agreeing on who you are, what you are doing, and where you are at the top of the scene gives your scene a realistic context from which a first unusual thing can be discovered.

The sooner you establish the Who, What, and Where at the top of the scene, the better. It will be very difficult for you to determine what is unusual about your scene if you are a minute into the scene and still haven't determined this base reality. For example, bullets flying by your head would be very unusual if you are a teacher in a classroom but not if you are soldiers in the battlefield. Once again, the first unusual thing will be the beginning of your Game, the funny part of your scene.

Don't be precious about the Who, What, and Where of your scene. Just get it out there. You need to "write in your head" and invest a lot of energy into making these choices since the real comedy of the scene will come from what you do with them. Don't worry about making this part of the scene funny. You will be able to find the comedy in any Who, What, and Where. You just need to make sure that these essential elements of the scene are clear to you, your scene partner, and your audience so that you can all discover what is funny about those choices together.

Please note that while it is completely valid for a performer to establish the Who, What, and Where in a single line, it is not imperative that scenes must start this way. Remember that scenes are always built by both performers.

Let's look at some examples of the very start of three different scenes in which the improvisers successfully establish the Who, What, and Where.

WHO, WHAT, AND WHERE EXAMPLES

EXAMPLE 1

PLAYER 1:   "The chicken's done."

PLAYER 2:   "Oh good, honey. The Jensens will be here soon."

PLAYER 1:   "Can you finish up the vegetables? I'm gonna go tidy up the living room."

Player 1 starts the scene with a very simple initiation, but one that still establishes the What. (This person is cooking chicken.) Player 2 Yes Ands this choice by making the Who of the scene clearer.

(By referring to Player 1 as "honey" and referring to the arrival of another couple, we can assume that this scene is about a married couple.) Player 1 then establishes a specific Where with the next line. (We can assume that this couple is currently in their kitchen.)

Now let's see a bad example in which two improvisers fail to establish a strong Who, What, and Where in the first three lines.

EXAMPLE 2

PLAYER 1:	**"The chicken's done."**
PLAYER 2:	**"Great, I love chicken!"**
PLAYER 1:	**"Let's eat it right now."**

Player 1 still establishes the What, but the next two lines fail to expand on this information. (They "Yes" but do not "And.") We never discover anything about who or where these people are. All we know is that they have cooked and are now going to eat chicken.

Let's look at another example in which an improviser successfully establishes the Who, What, and Where in a single line.

EXAMPLE 3

PLAYER 1:   **"Alright class, take your seats for the test."**

From this initiation, Player 1 is able to clearly establish the Who (Player 1 is a teacher addressing a group of students), What (the students are taking a test), and Where (a classroom). Now that the context of the scene has been set up so clearly, the improvisers can begin to look for the first unusual thing that breaks from this base reality.

Let's take a look at two more examples of establishing the Who, What, and Where, one good and one bad.

EXAMPLE 4

Player 1 walks onstage, miming a coffee cup in his hand.

PLAYER 1: "Thompson, get out of your cubicle...the Quarterly Report you submitted is only half finished!"

Player 1 has once again established the Who, What, and Where in his initiation. Note that there are multiple cues establishing information, both verbal and physical. Player 1 has communicated the Who through both naming his scene partner and how he has addressed them. Using the other character's last name and speaking in an angry tone about this report being unacceptable communicates to Player 2 that Player 1 has a higher status. We can assume that Player 2 works for Player 1. Player 1 communicates the What by making it clear that this scene is about a boss reprimanding his employee. Finally, Player 1 communicates the Where by using the word "cubicle." Now we can assume that the characters are in an office.

Here is an example of a weak initiation attempting to convey the same information established in Example 4.

EXAMPLE 5

Player 1 walks onstage neutrally.

PLAYER 1: "Thompson, I need to speak to you."

This initiation from Player 1 is clearly lacking. First, we don't know much about the Who. We know nothing about Player 1, and we only know that Player 2 is named Thompson. Player 1 could be a coach, sergeant, or teacher at this point because we have established status without establishing a specific relationship. We don't know anything about the Where and we know very little about the What. Player 1 wants to talk to Thompson about something, but we don't know what about.

Statements are the best way to efficiently establish the Who, What, and Where at the start of a scene. Avoid asking questions during the base reality section of a scene, since questions will only delay you from determining the context of your scene. In fact, asking questions will place the burden on your scene partner to provide this information. The rule of not asking questions only relates to the base reality section of the scene. Asking questions in the Game section of the scene is acceptable and often necessary to play the Game of the scene.

Your top priority in establishing the Who, What, and Where of a scene is to be clear. You should also look to be specific and personal whenever possible. Specificity will help your scenes stand out. Specific choices are always funnier than generic ones. Making choices based on your own opinions and life experiences will make your choices personal. Being specific and personal will make your scenes engaging and relatable. Doing so will also often result in getting to your Game in less time.

NAME YOUR CHARACTERS

It is good to include the specific names of the characters at the start of the scene. That way, they will be easy to identify as the longform progresses.

Novice improvisers are sometimes hesitant to quickly and clearly establish the Who, What, and Where. Instead, they remain vague out of deference to their scene partner. They erroneously feel that by establishing the Who, What, and Where, they are forcing their ideas onto their scene partner. This is not the case. In fact, there is nothing wrong with one improviser establishing the Who, What, and Where in one line. Establishing the Who, What, and Where quickly is not selfish. It is equivalent to priming a canvas before you paint. By providing as many details about the Who, What, and Where as you can early on, you are serving the scene and eliminating confusion. Make choices and be specific.

Conversely, don't cut off your scene partner as they are initiating a scene. Give them a chance to get their idea out.

SHOW, DON'T TELL

Sometimes nonverbal choices made at the top of the scene will help you to establish the Who, What, and Where for your scene. "Show, don't tell" is the phrase improvisers use to describe instances in scenes when an improviser establishes information through action and physical choices instead of speaking. When you "show" instead of "telling," information is conveyed as clearly as it would be if spoken. Sometimes opting to follow the principle of "show, don't tell" will actually make the start of your scene seem smoother and more natural. "Show, don't tell" also often allows you to make your scene work more visually engaging.

Long Form is more than smart ideas and verbal gymnastics. You want to constantly remind yourself that the visual and physical aspects of your scene work are very important parts of the overall theatrical experience that your audience is having.

Instead of initiating a scene by saying, "I'm unloading the dishwasher," you can simply start unloading it. This will allow you to establish the What and Where without being unnatural. Starting a scene by saying, "I'm a doctor and we are in an operating room, let's get started with this surgery" is "telling." Getting yourself engaged in the environment by washing up or putting on some surgical gloves is "showing." Now you can focus on what is going on between the characters in the scene.

"Show, don't tell" can also refer to starting scenes verbally but in an organic, realistic way. For example, initiating a scene by saying, "As your mother, I think you're watching too much TV," would be unrealistic. In real life, people don't speak in exposition. An example of verbal "show, don't tell" would be to say anything you might expect to hear from a mom (e.g., "What have your father and I told you about watching so much TV?").

Even though examples of "show, don't tell" will often closely resemble what you do in real life, this skill will take time to develop. With practice, you and your scene partners will become better at communicating with each other subtly and realistically without overstating the reality of the scene.

Object Work

Since in Long Form improvisation there are no actual objects onstage (beyond chairs), the improvisers must mime those objects that would exist in a given reality. This is called **object work**. Handling and interacting with the objects in your scene's fictional physical environment helps the improviser commit to their reality, and helps the audience buy into that same reality. For example, if it is established that you are playing a secretary, sitting down and miming a computer or a telephone will help ground your scene in a believable, physical reality. Additionally, object work can add another degree of theatricality to your performance.

After an environment has been established verbally, you can use your imagination to determine what else is there. By physically touching and using objects in that environment, you will be able to share your vision of your surroundings with your scene partner and the audience. We don't want our Long Form scenes to be nothing more than a pair of "talking heads" exchanging ideas; we want them to be theatrical. Through object work, we can create the illusion of a visual setting for the scene. The audience will "see" the environment you are creating through object work. Object work helps you to make each scene scenic or visually engaging. In other words, object work offers your audience more of a "full experience" in terms of the Who, What, and Where of your scene. Sometimes object work can be employed before any lines are even spoken, in order to establish the context of the scene quickly and nonverbally.

Object work can also act as a grounding force for you as a performer if you find yourself in a scene environment that is not completely familiar to you. Just as a wig or a costume might help a sketch performer to "get into character," object work can be a great way to immerse yourself in a performance and start feeling more like the character you are portraying. If your scene takes place on a ranch, it's not imperative that you know everything about ranching to do the scene. You may have never worked on a ranch, but you've seen ranches on television or in movies. You could probably list several items you would find in a barn or out in a field. By miming one of these objects, you should find it easier to ground yourself in your performance as a ranch-hand.

Another benefit of object work is that it allows you to more closely mirror what happens in real life. When you visit the doctor, he or she usually doesn't stand in front of you and trot out all of the medical information they have at their disposal. Chances are they probably will grab a chart or place an X-ray on a lighted screen—things that any of us are capable of miming in a scene. In this way, simple object work can help you to play a scene at the top of your intelligence.

Object work also allows you to use your environment as a way to slow down and think about what you are doing. Many beginning improvisers get laughs in a scene without immediately understanding how or why they are making the audience laugh. If you stop and think about why you are getting those laughs, you won't run past the unusual thing. You will identify it so that you know what to build on. Object work gives the audience something to watch while you are doing this thinking. If you start washing dishes, the audience can watch your character do this while you (the improviser) can take a few seconds to process what is happening in the scene. The importance of those few seconds shouldn't be underestimated. Novice improvisers often find it hard to be comfortable in the silence. They will try to fill the "empty space" with chatter until something catches because they feel uncomfortable not talking onstage.

Object work allows you to analyze what has been established in your scene while giving the audience the impression that the fiction of the scene has continued unabated. Rather than standing there motionless, looking like an improviser who is at a loss for the next thing to say, you will look like a character who has taken a natural pause in their conversation while continuing to do their activity. As an improviser, you shouldn't feel exposed as you do this thinking because the audience isn't really watching you; they are watching a character.

Let's say you're in a scene where you are playing a mechanic. You and your scene partner have just gotten a huge laugh from the audience that you feel could be your first unusual thing, but you aren't quite sure how to build on the moment. There are any number of object work choices you could make at this moment to keep your audience engaged in the scene. Open the hood of a car and take a look at the engine. Check the tire pressure. Pick up a wrench and work on an exposed engine block. All of these moves could easily be made while you think of your response, and your audience will feel that they're watching a mechanic behave exactly as a mechanic does. If you don't do anything, the audience will quickly lose confidence in you and most likely "see" you thinking. If you are doing object work confidently, the audience will have patience.

Note: The objects that you create during the base reality portion of the scene may become useful later in the Game portion of the scene when you can use them as vehicles to explore the comedy of your scene.

One additional note: Sometimes your object work may get unintentional laughs. Do not get seduced by those easy laughs and make object work the only funny aspect of your scene. Use your object work as another way to make everything except your single comedic idea seem real.

COMMON OBJECT WORK MISTAKES

When miming objects, your goal should be to make them as real as possible. Remember that whenever you mime, your hand isn't becoming the object; it is holding the object. If your character is holding a gun, don't extend your index finger and raise your thumb like the "play guns" you made as a kid. Instead, you should actually pretend to hold a gun in your hand. Give it mass. If you don't need it, put it in its holster.

The same goes for phones. Don't hold out your thumb and pinky finger; pretend to hold an actual phone in your hand. Ask yourself what kind of phone you are holding. How big is it? Is it a cell phone or a desk phone? Do you have to flip it open? Does it have a touch screen?

In general, you want to make all of your object work, just like every other aspect of your scene outside of your single comedic idea, seem realistic and normal. Don't cartoonishly bang your hands up and down if your character is using a typewriter. Don't just abruptly stand up if your character is in a car. Open the door and step out.

Be consistent; mime all of the objects you use onstage. This includes objects you might have with you, such as keys, phones, wallets, clothing, and shoes. You don't want to use both real and mimed objects in your scenes (e.g., a robber using a mimed gun to take a real wallet). It's jarring. Once you see one real object in the space, it sets up the expectation that everything should be real, which is an expectation that you cannot fulfill as an improviser. Imagine if an actor in a play where props are being used suddenly pulled out a mimed gun. This would be very distracting. An improviser using an actual object in a scene has the same effect.

Another reason not to use actual objects is that doing so can paint you into a corner. While you could take off your actual jacket, you could not hang it on an imaginary coatrack.

The one exception to not using actual objects onstage is chairs, as some scenes will require you to sit.

Taking these aspects of your objects into consideration will help you to better commit to your reality. It will make your acting more realistic and help you to visualize your environment.

BAD OBJECT WORK

Here are some frequent object work mistakes:

- Constantly steering back and forth while driving instead of just holding onto a steering wheel

- Driving a car while sitting cross-legged in a chair

- Holding a beer one moment and then dropping it without putting it down on a surface

- Walking through a table or desk

BASE REALITY: IN REVIEW

SUMMARY

The establishment of a **base reality** is the first task to be accomplished when starting a Long Form scene. At the start of the scene, you should be ready to use the principle of **Yes And**. Find ways to "say yes" to or agree with anything that your scene partner establishes, and then add to the choices that they've made. The process of Yes And starts from the second you step out onstage by coming to basic physical **agreement** with your scene partner about the **character of the space**. Then your goal is to establish the **Who**, **What**, and **Where** as soon as you possibly can.

ADDITIONAL POINTS

Before we move on, please keep in mind these two additional points that are important to the beginning of any Long Form scene.

First, it is important for you to maintain the environment that has been established during the base reality section throughout the rest of the scene. Many new improvisers will "drop" their environment once they begin talking. Keeping your characters grounded in the world established at the start of the scene will help you to keep your audience engaged in the reality you have created. Also remember, you will later be able to use this environment as a vehicle through which you can explore the comedy of your scene.

Additionally, while establishing the base reality of your scene is very important, you want to be sure to avoid simply talking about whatever it is that you and your scene partner are doing. Once you start speaking, you don't want to just speak about your physical environment. In order to more closely mirror real life, you should push yourself to determine the Who, What, and Where of the scene by talking about something else as you remain engaged in the physical choices you've made. If you think about it, this is how we usually behave in real life. Your goal should be to simply exist in your Who, What, and Where.

EXERCISE: TALK ABOUT SOMETHING ELSE

INSTRUCTIONS

- Two improvisers take the stage.

- One improviser will initiate with some sort of physical activity that can be done continuously throughout the scene (sorting mail, washing dishes, having dinner, playing golf, setting up a campsite, etc.).

- The other improviser should immediately join in with this activity.

- When either improviser starts speaking, they must talk about something other than what they are doing.

PURPOSES

- In real life, you are usually doing one thing and talking about another. For example, if you're folding laundry, you are most likely not talking about folding laundry. This exercise will help you to better mirror this reality of life in your scenes.

CHAPTER 2:

How to Create a Base Reality

Listening

▸DEFINITION

When building a Long Form improv scene with someone else, there is nothing more important than **listening**. The beginning of the scene is built through Yes And, and you cannot Yes And something if you haven't heard it. It is important to listen because you are going to have to agree with and add to what your scene partner has just said. The last thing said onstage is either going to make your base reality more detailed and specific, or it will be the first unusual thing, the start of your Game.

We have already compared starting a scene to building the basement of a house. The start of the scene, like a basement, needs to be strong enough to support everything else that will be built upon it. Listening needs to happen so that you and your scene partner are on the same page about what *kind* of house you are building. If you don't actively listen at the beginning of a scene, you may think that you are building a house out of straw, while your teammate thinks you are building it with bricks.

The goal of the beginning of the scene is to establish a relatable reality from which an unusual or absurd thing can be recognized. None of this will be possible if you are not actively listening. A great improviser is a good listener.

GIVE AND TAKE

To be able to communicate effectively and build a Long Form scene with another improviser, you have to learn when to speak and when to listen. This is called *give* and *take*.

One improviser shouldn't be doing all of the work in a scene. By giving and taking focus, you share the burden of discovery and creation. Giving and taking are equally important. It is important that you stop talking and *give* focus to your scene partner when they want to add to the scene. It is equally important that you begin speaking and *take* focus from them when you have something to contribute to the scene.

There is nothing more awkward to watch onstage than two improvisers fighting for focus. An ability to give and take focus is necessary for good listening.

EXERCISE: COCKTAIL PARTY

INSTRUCTIONS

- The participating improvisers split into groups of three and then spread out. Another improviser acts as a "conductor."

- Each group is assigned a number.

- Each group of improvisers should commit physically to the idea that they are different parts of the same cocktail party.

- All three groups are given the same suggestion to inspire three different conversations. For example, if the suggestion was "gun," one group may talk about gun control, another group may talk about Guns N' Roses, and the third group may talk about video games.

- The conductor calls out the number of the group that will have focus.

- While one group is speaking, the others should mime a conversation while listening to what is being said.

- When the conductor calls out a new number, the previous group *gives* focus by stopping their conversation. The new group *takes* focus by starting or resuming their conversation.

- After a few rounds of calling out numbers, the conductor falls away and the three groups begin giving and taking focus on their own. The improvisers should look for natural pauses in conversation and take focus by loudly and clearly restarting their conversation.

- Each group should take the passage of time into consideration as they return to their

conversation. You are not "pausing" your conversation and picking it up exactly where you left off; it should be assumed that your characters have been talking while you have been miming and the other group has had the focus in the scene.

VARIATION

- Use the same basic setup, but this time each group should listen carefully to the group currently speaking.

- After each group has had at least two opportunities to speak, you should look for ways to make connections between your conversation and the other conversations happening.

- When your group retakes focus, try to incorporate specifics, details, ideas, and themes that you heard mentioned by the other groups.

PURPOSE

- The purpose of this exercise is to allow improvisers to practice taking and giving focus in group scenes.

- This variation of the exercise gives new improvisers another opportunity to practice listening.

- If you are really listening to the other conversations, you should be able to find ways for themes and ideas to overlap naturally. This is a skill you will use often when performing Long Form.

EXERCISE: "YES...AND" SCENE WORK

INSTRUCTIONS

- At least three improvisers are needed for this exercise.

- Two improvisers perform a scene from a single suggestion given by the third. The third improviser watches the scene.

- One improviser will initiate, or give the first line of the scene.

- The improvisers will then literally say "Yes... And" at the start of each successive line. The "Yes And" will come in this form:

    - "Yes" [repeat the information from the last line]

    - "And" [add new information to the scene]

- Statements are necessary for this exercise. Questions won't add new information; they will only force your scene partner to add information. Imperatives (e.g., "Come here!") also fail because they often force your scene partner to do something without adding new information about the Who, What, and Where. Statements allow you to more quickly establish a reality and find something unusual to explore in that reality.

- Make sure that your Yes And statements add information to the present moment and the characters in the scene. Avoid Yes And statements that refer to the past, the future, or characters not in the scene.

- Resist the urge to "Yes...But." Someone else in your group should stop the scene every time a scene partner says "But" instead of "And" to give them a chance to deliver a different line without "But." "Yes…But" shows a desire to argue instead of building the scene together.

PURPOSE

- One purpose of this exercise is to practice listening in a Long Form scene. You must be listening carefully in this exercise since you will have to repeat what was just said. Repeating the information from the previous line proves that you have been listening.

- When you add new information in your line, you are showing that you understand your partner's contribution to the scene.

- Yes And scenes usually feel a little stilted. However, this exercise is essential for getting the behavior of Yes And–ing into your muscle memory. Before things become second nature, we need to practice them consciously.

- This exercise will make it glaringly obvious whether or not you are listening. This exercise prevents you from skipping this important scene work step.

"YES...AND" SCENE EXAMPLES

EXAMPLE 1

PLAYER 1: "I baked you an apple pie."

PLAYER 2: "Yes, you baked me an apple pie, and I'm so happy you remembered our wedding anniversary."

(Player 2 has established the Who and What with this "Yes And." We now know that the characters are a married couple celebrating a wedding anniversary.)

PLAYER 1: "Yes, you're happy I remembered our wedding anniversary, and let's eat this tonight when we come home from dinner."

(Player 1 has started to establish the Where with this "Yes And." We now know that the couple is in their house, getting ready to go to dinner.)

EXAMPLE 2

PLAYER 1: "I baked you an apple pie."

PLAYER 2: "Yes, you baked me an apple pie, and everyone else in the office is going to be jealous of me."

(Player 2 has established the Where with this "Yes And." We now know that the characters are at their workplace.)

PLAYER 1: "Yes, everyone in the office will be jealous of you, and you just tell them that if their sales were as high as yours, I'd bake them an apple pie too."

BAD "YES...AND" SCENE EXAMPLES

EXAMPLE 1

PLAYER 1:   "I baked you an apple pie."

PLAYER 2:   "Yes, you baked me an apple pie, and it is on a plate."

(Player 2 has not really offered an "And" for the scene in this example. You want to go beyond the obvious of what you probably already know or could assume when you Yes And. No new information has been established with the "And" in this example.)

EXAMPLE 2

PLAYER 1:   "I baked you an apple pie."

PLAYER 2:   "Yes, you baked me an apple pie, and I used to have apple pie every Sunday when I was a kid."

(Player 2 has made this scene about the past.)

EXAMPLE 3

PLAYER 1:   "I baked you an apple pie."

PLAYER 2:   "Yes, you baked me an apple pie, and I'll eat this tomorrow with my lunch."

(Player 2 has made this scene about the future.)

EXAMPLE 4

PLAYER 1:   "I baked you an apple pie."

PLAYER 2:   "Yes, you baked me an apple pie, and my brother Mike loves apple pie."

(Player 2 has made the scene about a character not in the scene.)

EXAMPLE 5

PLAYER 1: "I baked you an apple pie."

PLAYER 2: "Yes, you baked me an apple pie, but I'm not hungry."

(Player 2 has done "Yes But" instead of "Yes And." Doing so will start your scenes off with unnecessary conflict.)

EXERCISE: THREE-LINE SCENES

INSTRUCTIONS

- Have any number of improvisers form two single-file lines on opposite sides of the stage. The line on the left side of the stage will be the "*initiation*" line. The line on the right will be the "*response*" line.

- One improviser from each line will step forward to perform a scene inspired by a suggestion offered by someone else in the group.

  - Left Side will initiate.

  - Right Side will respond to the initiation.

  - Left Side will respond to the response.

- After the three lines, each improviser should go to the end of the opposite line. The next two improvisers in line then step out, get another suggestion, and do a new three-line scene.

- These three-line scenes will not be complete scenes. They will end after the third line. These scenes don't have to reach any sort of resolution. You should still make strong choices and commit as if these are going to be full-length scenes.

- Continue until everyone has had a chance to initiate and respond.

PURPOSE

- The purpose of this exercise is to practice establishing the Who, What, and Where as quickly and clearly as possible. It will be easier for you to establish this information if you make strong choices at the top of your scenes.

EXERCISE: CONDUCTED STORY

INSTRUCTIONS

- Three or more improvisers stand in a line.

- Another improviser will stand in front of them and act as the "conductor" for a story that they will tell together.

- The conductor points at an improviser, who begins telling a story.

- The conductor will then randomly point at a different improviser. The improviser currently speaking will abruptly stop telling the story. Then, the new improviser being pointed at will pick up telling the story at the exact moment where the previous improviser left off. The same rule will apply each time the conductor points to a new improviser.

- The conductor can point to a new improviser at any time.

- Caution: Don't try to be funny. Don't try to add absurd twists for laughs. Your only goal is to tell a simple story with a clear plot and consistent tone throughout, as if written by a single author.

PURPOSE

- This exercise will improve your listening by forcing you to be in the moment. You don't know when you are going to be called on to speak. You could have to continue telling the story at any point—the end of a sentence or in the middle of a word. This means that you must be listening intently to know both what has been said just before you are called upon to speak, AND what has happened so far in the story as a whole.

- If you do a good job of listening, they will be able to tell a seamless story that sounds as if it is coming from one person.

COMMITMENT

There is a need for reality in Long Form improvisation. All elements of a scene outside of the Game (or funny part of the scene) should be grounded in the reality that the performers have agreed upon. Obviously, this includes your performance. You could be following all of the rules we have presented and still not draw an audience into your reality if you do not commit.

In simplest terms, *commitment* is good acting. A Long Form improviser is expected to invest in the reality of the scene in such a way that the audience doesn't see an improviser, but a believable character onstage. Good actors in movies or television disappear into their roles. Bad actors "take you out of the movie." Good acting and commitment to the choices you make in a scene will help your audience become engaged in the reality you are creating.

A commitment to the reality of the scene does not mean that every scene you perform has to take place in our reality. It means that you can do scenes about vampires, pirates, or truckers in deep space, as long as you are committing to the specific reality in which we might find these sorts of characters. You must make choices about how to portray these characters and then remain consistent with your portrayal of the characters for the entire scene.

Focusing on commitment will prevent you from forcing an "unusual thing." If you commit to your characters and portray them as real people, it will make it easier for you to recognize the unusual when it happens organically.

Commitment allows your audience to suspend disbelief and fully experience a fictional reality. The antithesis of commitment is *detachment*. Detachment makes the audience aware of the artifice of the scene, drawing attention to the fact that you are a comedian performing a scene as opposed to a character within the fictional reality of a scene.

Detachment generally comes in one of two forms: unintentional detachment and ironic detachment.

Unintentional detachment is the result of improvisers making choices, but playing them in a halfhearted way. It often comes down to bad acting. Generally, improvisers guilty of this form of detachment are simply "telling" and not "showing" an audience their ideas. One example of unintentional detachment would be a man playing a petite little girl without adjusting his voice or demeanor. The improviser "says" he is a little girl but he fails to "be" a little girl. Another example would be an improviser saying that they just broke their leg in three places, but failing to limp or show any emotional response to their injury.

Ironic detachment means consciously not committing to the reality of the scene in order to get a laugh. Again, this will take the audience out of the reality of the scene. This is also referred to as *commenting*. The examples from the previous paragraph would be examples of ironic detachment if the lack of commitment was intentional. Below are some other examples of ironic detachment:

- You are in a courtroom scene and choose to comment on the fact that there are only two chairs in the room. (You are not committing to the fictional reality of the Where.)

- Your male scene partner is playing a woman and you make a "Boy, you're an ugly woman" remark. (You are not committing to the fictional reality of the Who.)

- You are playing Paul Revere and say something like, "It's a shame that there isn't some sort of mobile device that would allow me to contact my fellow colonists remotely." (You are not committing to the fictional reality of the What.)

While commenting will often allow a performer to get a quick laugh, that laugh will come at the expense of establishing a base reality, which ultimately will undermine the integrity of the scene. Even a momentary lapse in commitment can make it difficult for your audience to stay engaged in the base reality of the scene.

The best improvisers completely commit themselves to their scenes. You must commit to the character you are playing and your reality, and never sell it out for a laugh or out of fear of not getting a laugh. The more you commit to your character and the reality of the scene, the more engaging the scene will be and the more likely it is that you will discover what is truly funny about the scene.

TOP OF YOUR INTELLIGENCE

In simplest terms, "top of your intelligence" refers to responding truthfully to any stimulus within a scene. It is about allowing yourself to have a true, honest emotional response. "Intelligence," in this case, is your knowledge of how a human being would react to a given situation. This requires emotional and social intelligence. Playing at the top of your intelligence means responding the way a real person would in a given situation.

The principle of "show, don't tell" comes into play here. It is not enough to simply react verbally. In order to truly play at the top of your intelligence, you will need to react emotionally as well. Marry your verbal response with an emotional one.

For example, when another character pulls out a gun in a scene and you are scared of it, you are playing at the top of your intelligence. When you lovingly embrace your girlfriend upon hearing the news that she is pregnant, you are playing at the top of your intelligence. When your character touches something hot and you recoil in pain, you are playing at the top of your intelligence. When you resentfully get coffee for your mean boss or a rude elderly woman, you are playing at the top of your intelligence. It is important to note the above responses are not the only valid responses to each given scenario. Any real or truthful response that a person might have in any of these situations would also be considered a "top of intelligence" response. For instance, in the case of hearing the news that your girlfriend is pregnant, it is equally valid to respond in shock or despair.

What Top of Your Intelligence Is Not

Top of your intelligence is often misunderstood. Top of your intelligence does *not* mean that you should have your character rattle off trivial or obscure facts. It does not mean that your character has to be "smart." It does not mean that you should quip cleverly or show off how well-educated you may be in real life. It also does not mean that every character you play has to know everything that you know. If you are playing a character dumber than you are, your character will not know everything that you do.

Commitment and playing at the top of your intelligence helps you to create a rich base reality for your scene.

EXERCISE: GIVE THE SETUP

INSTRUCTIONS

PART 1

- Two improvisers take the stage.

- Instead of receiving a suggestion, every scene will start with the two improvisers having a conversation as their actual selves. The improvisers in this scene should focus on playing the scene in a grounded, realistic, and truthful way. The scene should have a casual or conversational tone.

- A third improviser will stop them if he or she feels that either improviser is "performing" or not acting realistically in any way. This third improviser should be asking him or herself, "Is this really what either of these people would say?" in order to find those moments that are not realistic or genuine.

- Once the "unreal" moment has been discussed, the improvisers should back up and play the moment again in a way that is more realistic.

- Stop and repeat this process if the scene again becomes unrealistic.

PART 2

- Now each pair of improvisers will be given a simple, specific, and relatable scenario or "setup" to start with (e.g., two parents watching their kids in a little league game, a second date at a familiar chain restaurant, etc.).

- Again, the improvisers should play close to themselves in these scenes. Their focus should once again be on playing themselves in a grounded, realistic, and truthful way.

- A third improviser should look to stop the scene any time either performer in the scene is not acting realistically.

- Once the "unreal" moment has been discussed, the improvisers should back up and play the moment again in a way that is more realistic.

- Stop and repeat this process if the scene again becomes unrealistic.

PART 3

- Now each pair should be given the suggestion of two character archetypes that will be different from their actual selves, but within the realm of possibility in real life (e.g., two astronauts, the Pope and a Cardinal, the President and the First Lady, etc.).

- The goal of both players in these scenes is to play these character archetypes in the same grounded, realistic, and truthful manner that they played themselves in Part 1.

- The third improviser looking to stop the scene can judge the success of this part of the exercise by considering how closely these scenes resemble the tone and execution of those scenes in Part 1. Again, the third improviser should stop the scene any time either performer in the scene is not acting realistically.

- Once the "unreal" moment has been discussed, the improvisers should back up and play the moment again in a way that is more realistic.

- Stop and repeat this process if the scene again becomes unrealistic.

PART 4

- For the final section of this exercise, each pair should be given the suggestion of two character archetypes that are so fundamentally different from their actual selves that they could not "be" them in real life. These character archetypes should require the improvisers to alter their voices and physicality (e.g., two elderly people, two Russian immigrants, two characters of opposite gender of the improvisers in the scene, etc.).

- Again, the goal of both players in these scenes is to play these characters in the same grounded, realistic, and truthful manner that they played themselves in Part 1.

- While the improvisers will need to adopt a character voice or different way of moving in these scenes, they should make these traits as realistic as they can.

- The third improviser can once again judge the success of this part of the exercise by looking for how closely these scenes resemble the tone and execution of those scenes in Part 1. This third improviser should now be asking, "Is this really what either of these types of people would say or do in real life?" in order to find those moments that are not realistic or genuine.

- Once the "unreal" moment has been discussed, the improvisers should back up and play the moment again in a way that is more realistic.

- Stop and repeat this process if the scene again becomes unrealistic.

ADDITIONAL TIPS

- Start your scenes "in the middle." That means initiating with a specific statement and assuming or labeling a relationship from the start. Starting your scenes "in the middle" is a good idea in general.

- Remember the lessons from the "TALK ABOUT SOMETHING ELSE" exercise. In real life, you usually don't just talk about whatever it is that you are doing as you are doing it. You usually talk about lots of other things: work, your family, your friends, interests, etc. Use the scenes in this exercise as an opportunity to practice doing this. The third improviser watching these scenes should stop the scene if the improvisers get trapped into talking about what they are doing.

PURPOSE

- The purpose of this exercise is to give you a chance to focus on playing the reality of the scene in a believable way. If you are able to successfully portray characters and situations that feel real and grounded, the absurd element of the scene will stand out better in contrast. It is easier to recognize the unusual in a scene if we begin our scenes with a familiar situation or recognizable reality.

- This exercise also reinforces that our ideas for scenes do not have to be crazy, wacky, forced or complicated at the start. In fact, starting with the familiar increases our odds of finding a first unusual thing.

EXERCISE: WOULD YOU?

INSTRUCTIONS

- Have two improvisers take the stage.

- Do a series of two-person scenes where the suggestion must be an emotionally charged scenario (e.g., finding out you have cancer, being involved in a robbery, going on a first date, etc.).

- Video-record these scenes.

- As a group, watch each scene.

- Stop line by line and ask the improviser in the scene variations on the question, "Would you?..." in relation to their action and dialogue (e.g., "Would you have really reacted that way to a person in real life?")

- Each answer should be an honest assessment of whether or not they were successful in giving their character realistic human behavior.

- Whenever the question is answered with some version of "No," discuss other options this improviser had in that scene.

PURPOSE

- This exercise is a great way to consider how you are reacting in scenes.

- Analyzing your scene work in the moment is extremely difficult. Watching scenes on videotape after the fact allows you to step outside of your own performance and really focus on your tendencies as a performer.

Denial

▸**DEFINITION**

Denial means failing to agree with any aspect of the reality established by your scene partner. You should look at every contribution that your scene partner makes to the scene as a gift. If you acknowledge and build upon these gifts, your job of finding a scene will be easier.

Failing to agree with whatever your partner is trying to establish about your scene can happen in many different ways at the beginning of a scene. When it does, it puts you and your scene partner in a very difficult position in terms of building a successful, funny scene.

PULLING THE RUG OUT

There are many different forms of denial. One classic example of denial is the *pulling the rug out* denial. Let's look at an example:

Player 1 steps out and mimes opening a medical file.

PLAYER 1:   "Your test results have come back. I have some good news for you."

PLAYER 2:   "You're not a doctor! Why are you acting like a doctor?"

Player 2 has done something worse here than failing to add information to the start of the scene. Player 2 has "pulled the rug out" from under Player 1 and actively destroyed the information he has just been given (the idea that he is a patient and that Player 1 is a doctor). This is the antithesis of Yes And, wherein information is created. Not only are the improvisers back at square one, but they must now also deal with the fact that Player 1 must be crazy or a liar for pretending to be a doctor. Player 2 has denied himself and his scene partner the chance to organically discover something unusual in their scene. The worst thing about this denial is that it ruins what could have been a great idea from Player 1. Denying your scene partners will make it impossible for you to build trust with them.

Out of nervousness, many new improvisers will force something unusual to happen at the start of a scene to get a laugh. One of the quickest, cheapest, and easiest ways to make your audience laugh is to make your scene partner seem crazy. Playing like this will make the rest of your scene more difficult to perform, and it will turn you into an improviser with whom nobody wants to play.

BEING INATTENTIVE

Being inattentive is a more mild form of denial. It involves poor listening and a failure to acknowledge what your scene partner has established about the scene. "Being inattentive" denials are less intentional than "pulling the rug out," but they are just as damaging to the start of the scene.

When you are inattentive, you can miss important details, such as the gender, age, or name of the character your scene partner is playing. You could also miss important information about the character of the space.

For instance, if your scene partner steps out shivering and you fail to acknowledge that it is cold, you are denying an aspect of your reality (that it is cold) being provided to you by your scene partner. This will likely force some sort of explanation and take your focus away from establishing the base reality of your scene.

DUELING INITIATIONS

Another common form of denial is referred to as *dueling initiations.* In this form of denial, one of the improvisers refuses to let go of his or her preconceived idea. They are unnecessarily forcing a new element into the scene instead of building upon what their scene partner has offered up.

Dueling Initiations Example:

Two improvisers doing a two-person scene off of the suggestion "office."

Player 1 walks onstage, miming a coffeepot in his hand.

PLAYER 1: "If you finish the break room coffee, you need to start a new pot."

PLAYER 2: "Look, I'll get to that. We need to bring in a ringer for the company softball team or else we're gonna get destroyed."

In this example, Player 2 has acknowledged the information established by Player 1 while also adding in new information. The problem is that this new information does not build upon anything established by the scene initiation. Instead, Player 2 has rejected Player 1's idea in favor of his own. Instead of steamrolling with a new idea, Player 2 should be looking to Yes And the specific base reality offered in the first line.

DENIAL'S EFFECT ON THE AUDIENCE

If you deny the contributions of your scene partner, you run the risk of confusing your audience. Remember that in Long Form, we are starting each scene in a blank space, a void without costumes or a set. Given the lack of visual information, the audience is logically going to latch onto and invest in whatever the improvisers establish as the reality of the scene. A denial at the start of a scene is confusing because it creates competing realities instead of a single reality that you have built together.

The danger of denial extends beyond the obvious, practical pitfall of confusing your audience. Denial that flies in the face of information established by an initiation is often the product of a conscious choice. Conscious choices like these often feel pushed or forced, especially at the beginning of the scene. They are also usually just not as interesting as the unusual thing that you would eventually discover with your scene partner. An unusual thing that you discover with someone else will always be more satisfying and much more fun to play with.

Don't be tempted by the quick, easy laughs that you will sometimes get from denial. You will be distinguishing yourself as a bad teammate in exchange for these laughs. An improviser that relies on the sort of cheap laughs you might get from a denial is like a basketball player that does nothing but score by taking the ball away from the point guard on his own team. When you deny your scene partner, you make them feel cheated and unsupported. Single laughs coming from a denial will be at the expense of consistent laughs later in the scene.

Making the Game of your scene a denial is not the same as building a scene with your scene partner. If you try to make every scene like this, you have nothing more than a gimmick.

AVOIDING DENIAL

If your scene partner establishes the Who, What, or Where before you do so in a scene, always drop your idea and go with theirs. Holding onto your own ideas about the context of the scene could lead you to deny your scene partner. Holding onto your own idea is also likely to create confusion and disconnect between you and your fellow improviser. Simply agreeing about the base reality of the scene is far more important than the specifics of the reality itself. In the end, the memorable part of the scene is not going to be the base reality of the scene (the Who, What, and Where). The memorable part of the scene will be the funny thing you discover that breaks from this base reality you and your scene partner have created.

There is never a good reason to deny any aspect of the reality that your scene partner has established. Denying your scene partner may occasionally get a laugh, but it ultimately prevents you from finding a strong, successful, funny scene.

TAKE A BREATH & HANG IN THERE

We are now ready to move on to the "funny" part of the scene. As you can see, an awful lot goes into the base reality of any scene. In many ways, the success of a Long Form scene as a whole rides on what happens in those first few lines.

You may feel overwhelmed at this point. Realize that this is a natural part of the learning process. The only way you will ever own these concepts is through lots of practice and repetition. You shouldn't have a disregard for the rules as you learn them; you should look to practice them so much that you no longer find them overwhelming.

The many "rules" discussed for the beginning of the scene tend to overwhelm new improvisers who are attempting to follow them all, in the moment, while creating a scene. According to Del Close, to be an improviser, one must be a juggler. Improvisers have to be actors, directors, and editors all at once. You are handling all of these skills simultaneously and you must also have a sense of where your scene could be going. Inevitably, you are always carrying a little bit of baggage in some part of your brain while you are improvising.

The challenge is to never let this baggage block the moment you're in. With repeated practice, the rules and instructions described as being essential to the beginning of the scene do start to become second nature. As this happens, you should find it easier and easier to truly "be in the moment."

Think back to when you first learned to ride a bike. Learning how to ride was originally quite daunting. New bike riders are making constant minor adjustments just to keep from falling over, and in spite of these constant adjustments, new bike riders can expect to fall over many times. However, once you finally learn how to ride, doing so becomes—and usually remains—effortless. Keeping all of the rules straight when doing your first Long Form scenes is very much like those first bike rides, in which you had to consciously think about steering, pedaling, and keeping balanced all at once. Right now, it is just important to realize that time and practice will eventually make following the rules more automatic.

SECTION II:
THE GAME OF
THE SCENE

Think of your favorite written comedy sketch. Now try to sum up what is funny about that sketch in just a few words. That is "the Game" of that particular sketch. Let's distill two classical sketches from the influential late '60s–early '70s British comedy troupe Monty Python down to their Games. In the "Cheese Shop" sketch, a befuddled patron attempts to buy cheese from the proprietor of a cheese shop who, while claiming to have cheese, literally has no cheese for sale. The Game of this sketch could be described as "specialty shop that does not sell what it claims to sell." In "The Parrot Sketch," an angry customer attempts to return a dead parrot to the owner of a pet shop who refuses to acknowledge that the parrot is dead. The Game of this sketch could be described as "refusal to acknowledge an irrefutable fact."

Let's imagine a sketch in which a woman comes home to find her husband in bed with another woman. The husband refuses to admit that he is cheating in spite of the obvious evidence to the contrary. This sketch would essentially have the same Game as "The Parrot Sketch" (refusal to acknowledge an irrefutable fact).

Notice that in both of the previous examples, the Games were described without either of the specifics one would be most likely to associate with each sketch ("cheese" and "parrot," respectively). We did not describe the Game of "The Parrot Sketch" as "man returns a dead parrot," because that description resembles a plot synopsis. Comedic Improv is not achieved by creating a plot or story. It is achieved by creating a Game.

The Who, What, and Where are the elements that make up the plot of the scene. The plot is not what is funny about the scene. Our style of Long Form improvisation is not about plot or story. What is funny is the Game, a pattern that is played within the context of that Who, What, and Where. If you strip away the specifics (the Who, What and Where) of any successful sketch or scene, you should still be able to describe the Game of a scene, and you'll probably be able to set it in a new context, as we have done with "The Parrot Sketch." This is because the Game of the scene is not beholden to the specifics of the scene. The specifics are there to support the Game.

CHAPTER 3:

What is a Game?

AN ABSTRACT EXPLANATION

Once you and your scene partner have established the base reality of
your scene, you are ready to find and play the Game of the scene. Again,
the Game is what is funny about your scene. It is a consistent pattern of
behavior that breaks from the expected patterns of our everyday lives.
You and your partner will work together to discover "the funny" of your
scene. Once it is found, you will heighten and explore "the funny" for
the rest of the scene.

The key to finding and playing the Game is identifying the first unusual thing in
a scene, the first piece of information that breaks from the pattern of normal life.
Once this has been discovered, the improvisers will shift away from "Yes…And"
and move onto "If…Then" (asking the question "If this unusual thing is true, then
what else is true?"). With Yes And, we were agreeing with information presented
and adding new information to develop a base reality. Once the unusual thing has
been found, we no longer need to develop a base reality; we need to be funny.
Repeatedly answering the question "If this unusual thing is true, then what else
is true?" creates a comic pattern. Each answer to this question (or similar, related

versions of this question) is called a "Game move." A combination of game moves forms a pattern that we call a "Game."

The Game of the scene requires building funny patterns of behavior in scenes. To help you understand how Game helps improvisers to build scenes, think of forming a pattern with numbers.

Let's say you started a series of numbers like this:

3…

Three will represent the first unusual thing in a scene.

Then imagine the first Game move is the number 6.

3, 6…

At this point, the Game is still not cemented because we have still not clearly established a pattern. Imagine that the next Game move is 9.

3, 6, 9…

At this point, if you are going to successfully follow this pattern, you are going to have to "Add 3 to the previous number." We have already agreed that "Add 3" is what is funny. The audience also expects to see you "Add 3." If you "Add 2" or "Add 5," it is going to confuse your audience and it will destroy what you have established.

You can think of the 9 move as "locking" your pattern. From this point on, we know that we are only going to "Add 3." Anything else would fall outside of our pattern or Game. Once this pattern has been established, it must stay the same in order to focus what is funny about the scene.

3, 6, 9, 12, 15…

Now let's start over:

3, 6…

Now, instead of 9 being the next Game move, let's imagine that the next Game move is 12.

3, 6, 12...

You might describe this Game as "Multiply by 2." In this case, we have agreed that what is funny is "Multiplying the last number by 2." (Instead of having a daunting, limitless number of possibilities, we have a clear focused pattern to follow.)

3, 6, 12, 24, 48...

Both patterns are completely valid, and they both started from the same first unusual thing. The same thing will happen with the Game of the scene. Any number of Games can come from the same starting place. However, once the pattern has been locked, there is no need to stray from it. There is no need to find more interesting or unusual things. Think of it this way: If each number in the pattern gets a laugh and you have to choose another number to contribute, why wouldn't you choose what has already worked?

In case the number example confused you, here is another quick example. In this example, let's say the first unusual thing is "orange." The following are three different patterns that you could create from the same starting place:

- orange, blue, yellow (colors)
- orange, pineapple, apple (fruits)
- orange, baseball, globe (round objects)

GAME MAKES YOUR LIFE EASIER

In both of the abstract number examples in the previous section, each new number represents another funny moment in a scene. In order to continue to make each scene funny, you will still have to come up with new numbers. However, thanks to the Game, your thought process isn't all over the place. You'll be thinking of certain numbers instead of all numbers. A major benefit of Game is that you know what works, so you don't need to be wildly creative. The narrowing down of limitless possibilities in this way makes the task of being funny infinitely easier. With a Game, you put boundaries on what choices you could be making and, in doing so, lighten your cognitive load.

The Game makes being funny in a Long Form scene easier by forcing you to focus on a single comic idea. Its nature is to take away options so that you and your scene partner don't have to keep searching for new unusual, funny things. Having a Game in your scene is the closest thing in improvisation to having a script. You don't have to wrack your brain for funny things to say. You now have a method that provides you with funny things to say. The method is asking the question "If this unusual thing is true, then what else is true?" to build your scene off of your initial funny discovery.

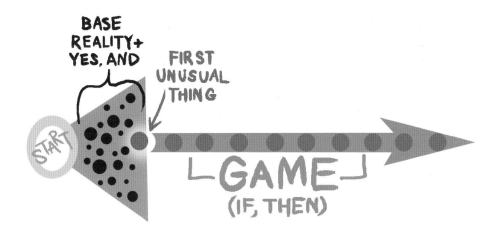

Sports can serve as a great analogy for the Game. Think of Game as the sport you choose to play. If you agree to play basketball with other people, you all know that there are certain rules that will be followed and certain things you can expect to happen (e.g., you must dribble the ball if you want to move with it). If anyone were to deviate from these rules or constantly make up new rules (the equivalent of throwing random unusual things into the scene), the Game would no longer be fun to play or watch. The Game would fall apart.

You may be thinking that following rules in improv will be constraining. However, following the rules of a Game in an improv scene is no more constraining than following the rules in a game of basketball. As is the case with basketball, there is an inexhaustible amount of variation within the rules. Even though there are rules, the specific way you play while adhering to those rules is never predetermined. Larry Bird, Michael Jordan, and Shaquille O'Neal all played the same game with the same rules, yet they all had completely different styles. Similarly, there is plenty of room for individual expression within the constraints of the Game of the scene. The Game is just giving you a structure within which you can be creative.

You could also think of performing a successful Long Form scene as trying to get from one side of a forest to the other. Without a clear-cut path, you and your scene partner could encounter heavy brush, mud, or any number of things that would make getting to the other side very difficult. You might disagree about the best way to get to the other side, and this could keep you from working together. A path would make the task of getting from one side of the forest to the other much easier to accomplish. Game is the path leading you and your scene partner through the forest of a Long Form scene. The path provided by the Game makes performing a Long Form scene with someone else effortless and enjoyable.

Now that we have defined what Game is and why it is important, it is time to move on to how to find it.

CHAPTER 4:

Finding Game

There are two ways that improvisers can go about finding the Game: by performing **Organic Scenes** or **Premise Scenes**. In an Organic Scene, the first unusual or interesting thing will be found *during* the course of the scene. In a Premise Scene, the first unusual or interesting thing is found in information generated *before* the scene begins in a Long Form "opening" (this concept will be discussed in detail later). Premise Scenes begin with an initiation that implies a base reality and a first unusual thing.

In both Organic and Premise scenes, the pattern or Game will be found during the course of the scene. Let's go back to our number examples. We saw two different patterns spring from the same first unusual thing (the number 3). A Game couldn't be fully described until a few Game moves built a pattern off of the number 3. This holds true for all scenes, no matter how detailed an initiation may be. This is because you can never know exactly how your scene partner will react to a first unusual thing. In all two-person scenes (whether they are Organic or Premise), both improvisers will need to work together to determine what pattern a first unusual thing is part of.

The UCB believes that there is no intrinsic value in how you get to the first unusual thing in your scene. Organic and Premise scenes are both equally valid. Compare it to conducting an interview. You can sit down and start talking until you find something interesting to talk about, or you can have a preinterview and determine what you want to talk about ahead of time. Both approaches could yield equally successful final results.

There is nothing wrong with starting with something as simple as a Who, What, or Where and building a great scene from there. There is also nothing wrong with an initiation that clearly establishes a reality and a first unusual thing, as long as this first unusual thing is derived from an opening. The comedy of the scene will come from what follows these initial choices. Once again, no matter how intricate of a premise the first line of the scene may contain, the Game that follows will always be different from what either improviser could have predicted or expected.

Finding the Game Organically

THE FIRST UNUSUAL THING

Since the Game is what is funny about a scene, finding the Game is your primary goal as an improviser. Finding the Game organically begins with identifying the "first unusual thing" in an Organic Scene. Organic Scenes will begin with one of the two improvisers establishing something about the relationship, activity, or location in order to begin building the base reality of a scene. In order to get to a first unusual thing, both improvisers will need to use Yes And to get a full sense of the base reality. Once the base reality is established, both improvisers should be listening for anything that would be unusual, interesting, or out of the ordinary given this context. The first unusual thing should always stand out in contrast to the base reality.

Don't put pressure on yourself to be funny in the very first line of an Organic Scene. In other words, don't force the first unusual thing. You and your scene partner will need to take a few lines to Yes And each other until the first unusual thing is found.

Once the first unusual thing has been discovered, the improvisers will shift away from Yes And and move onto asking the question "If this unusual thing is true, then what else is true?" Once we have used this question to create a pattern from the first unusual thing, we have found our Game.

FRAMING

Framing means letting your scene partner know that you feel that they have said or done something unusual within the context of the base reality. When you frame, you highlight or underline the unusual so that it stands out to your scene partner.

One of the simplest ways to frame the unusual is to simply react with an exclamation as soon as you hear the first unusual thing. We do this all the time in real life when presented with something unusual (e.g., "What?," "What are you doing?," "Excuse me?," etc.).

EXAMPLE 1

PLAYER 1:   "I think Timmy is making strides in art class, but he is still having difficulty with social interactions."

PLAYER 2:   "I think like many *great* artists, he finds mundane, everyday interactions difficult."

PLAYER 1:   "What?"

Another way to frame the unusual is to react honestly to what has happened.

EXAMPLE 2

PLAYER 1:   "I think Timmy is making strides in art class, but he is still having difficulty with social interactions."

PLAYER 2:   "I think like many *great* artists, he finds mundane, everyday interactions difficult."

PLAYER 1:   "I think he's a little young to be labeled a 'great artist.'"

A father that considers his young son to be a great artist stood out as unusual to Player 1. By simply reacting as he or she would in reality upon hearing this information, Player 1 framed the unusual for Player 2.

Another possibility is to have your character agree and add specifics that make what you've found to be unusual clear.

EXAMPLE 3

PLAYER 1:   "I think Timmy is making strides in art class, but he is still having difficulty with social interactions."

PLAYER 2:   "I think like many great artists, he finds mundane, everyday interactions difficult."

PLAYER 1:	"I agree that his stick figures are striking examples of minimalism, but he does need to get along with the other children."

By adding a specific that made it clear that the child's artistic ability is merely age-appropriate (drawing stick figures), while still agreeing that the child is exceptional, Player 1 showed Player 2 that he felt the unusual thing was considering a young child to be a great artist.

At the start of an Organic Scene, both improvisers are unsure of when they will reach their first unusual thing. Be sure to use framing as a way to ensure that you and your scene partner are ready to shift from Yes And to If Then at the same time.

EXAMPLES OF GAME IN ORGANIC SCENES

Let's look at an example of finding the Game in an Organic Scene.

EXAMPLE 1

Two improvisers are given the suggestion "bedroom."

[PLAYER 1 pulls out two chairs and places them close together. He gestures for PLAYER 2 to join him in the chairs. He leans back to give the appearance of lying up in a bed, so his scene partner matches this posture.]

PLAYER 1:	"Man, I'm exhausted."
PLAYER 2:	"Yeah. It's already 3 a.m."
PLAYER 1:	"This one-night stand is lasting longer than I thought it would."

The players have established a reality and found the first unusual thing in three lines. The characters in this scene just finished having sex. They are in a bedroom late at night.

Player 1 provided the first unusual thing in his second line. This line is unusual because it is not something you would actually say out loud to someone you are having a one-night stand with. Player 1's second line is the starting point for the rest of the comedy in this scene. Now the pattern of the rest of the scene will be determined by how Player 2 chooses to respond or react to this unusual thing. In other words, this is where we will find the Game of this scene.

PLAYER 1:   **"Man, I'm exhausted."**

PLAYER 2:   **"Yeah. It's already 3 a.m."**

PLAYER 1:   **"This one-night stand is lasting longer than I thought it would."**

PLAYER 2:   **"What are you talking about? We just finished having sex."**

With the above line, Player 2 has given a clear indication to Player 1 of the Game she would like to play. By providing specifics indicating that they have made love recently, Player 2 has suggested a Game in which Player 1 has an unusual fear of intimacy. We can assume from this line that Player 2 has more reasonable or conventional expectations for what a one-night stand should be.

PLAYER 1:   **"Man, I'm exhausted."**

PLAYER 2:   **"Yeah. It's already 3 a.m."**

PLAYER 1:   **"This one-night stand is lasting longer than I thought it would."**

PLAYER 2:   **"What are you talking about? We just finished having sex."**

PLAYER 1:   **"It's getting weird. We're getting too close. You're already hanging around my apartment naked, your clothes are all over the place..."**

PLAYER 2:   **"*You* just took those clothes off of me before we had sex!"**

Player 1 made a Game move in his third line by answering, "If this unusual thing is true, then what else is true?" More specifically, Player 1 asked himself, "If my character has an unusual fear of intimacy, then what else can I interpret as a sign that things are moving too fast?"

Walking around nude and leaving your clothes all over the place are things that one could imagine happening during a typical one-night stand. These specifics are turned into a Game move when Player 1 interprets them as signs that things are getting serious.

Player 1's reaction was "**on Game**" because he made a pattern out of his funny behavior with new specifics. This line let Player 2 know that Player 1 understood the Game.

Player 2 played the Game in her third line by continuing to remind us of the expected norm against which this unusual pattern of behavior is funny. While Player 1 has an irrational fear of commitment, Player 2 just expects common civility from Player 1. Her third line pointed out why Player 1's remarks about her nudity and her clothes being all over the place were unreasonable.

At this point, both improvisers are playing the Game of their scene. We can describe it as "irrational fear of commitment." They can now adhere to this pattern of behavior to play this Game for the rest of their scene.

As we stated before, the first unusual thing does not dictate the entire Game of the scene. Let's go back to the start of our example scene and find a different Game by responding differently to the first unusual thing.

EXAMPLE 2

Two improvisers are given the suggestion "bedroom."

[PLAYER 1 pulls out two chairs and places them close together. He gestures for PLAYER 2 to join him in the chairs. He leans back to give the appearance of lying up in a bed, so his scene partner matches this posture.]

PLAYER 1:   "Man, I'm exhausted."

PLAYER 2:   "Yeah. It's already 3 a.m."

PLAYER 1:   "This one-night stand is lasting longer than I thought it would."

PLAYER 2:   "I've only been here 24 hours."

In this scenario, Player 2 reacted to the same first unusual thing. This time, Player 2 established a different Game by adding information that makes their character have the unusual behavior. In this scenario, Player 2 answers the question, "*If* someone says, 'This one-night stand is lasting longer than I thought it would,' *then* maybe my character has overstayed her welcome." A one-night stand lasting more than 24 hours *is* unusual. If a one-night stand did last this long, it is plausible that someone would make a remark about it.

PLAYER 1: **"Man, I'm exhausted."**

PLAYER 2: **"Yeah. It's already 3 a.m."**

PLAYER 1: **"This one-night stand is lasting longer than I thought it would."**

PLAYER 2: **"I've only been here 24 hours."**

PLAYER 1: **"I know. So that's *more* than a one-night stand. Technically, the one-night stand is supposed to be over when the sun rises."**

PLAYER 2: **"I didn't think about it that way. You're right... we're dating!"**

Player 1 responded to Player 2's "Game move" by grounding the scene with logic. In his eyes, the one-night stand should be over by now.

Player 2 took this opportunity to make her unusual behavior more specific. Player 2 responded by revealing that her character has interpreted the length of this one-night stand to mean that she and Player 1 are dating. It is clear now that she is trying to accelerate the progression of their relationship.

The improvisers have once again found the Game of their scene. We could describe this Game as "accelerating a relationship." They will continue to play this Game by following the patterns of behavior that have been established. Player 2 will continue to make Game moves that attempt to accelerate this relationship by assuming a serious commitment from a casual encounter. Player 1 will continue to be reasonable and grounded.

Yes And is considered to be one of the most fundamental precepts of Long Form improvisation. However, many new improvisers are confused by this concept and erroneously bring it into the Game section of the scene. While Yes And is extremely important at the start of Organic Scenes, overly focusing on Yes And once you have reached the Game section of your scene can cause things to get unnecessarily complicated. In the base reality section of the scene, improvisers must Yes And each other until they find their Game. In the Game section of the scene, improvisers switch from Yes And to If Then.

Also note that there is no abstract value to a "fuller" or "larger" base reality. There is no merit in Yes And-ing taking too long to establish the base reality of the scene. The purpose of Yes And is not to establish the most complex, in-depth base reality possible. You want to use Yes And to establish a base reality and find the first unusual thing as efficiently as possible. You will find the first unusual thing efficiently if you remember to Yes And in a specific and personal way. Drawing upon your own unique opinions and life experiences when Yes And–ing will help you get to a satisfying Game quickly.

REVISITING AGREEMENT

Yes And isn't the only source of confusion when it comes to playing Game. New improvisers also get very confused about the concept of agreement when it comes to finding and playing Game in Organic Scenes. This is because they have trouble understanding the idea that there are always two levels of communication going on during an improv scene. One level is between the two improvisers performing the scene; the other is between the two fictional characters being portrayed by the improvisers.

The improvisers must always come to an agreement about the Game that they are playing in their scene. This does not mean that the two fictional characters must agree on everything said in their dialogue.

The improvisers will come to agreement about their reality, what they have found to be unusual, and how they are going to heighten and explore this unusual thing. The characters are simply going to behave in a way that will support and sustain this pattern of unusual behavior, even if that means the characters disagree with each other. Improvisers are always agreeing; characters are not.

Let's return to some examples from earlier to highlight how agreement serves the scene:

EXAMPLE 1 (Finding the Game Organically)

PLAYER 1: **"Man, I'm exhausted."**

PLAYER 2: **"Yeah. It's already 3 a.m."**

PLAYER 1: **"This one-night stand is lasting longer than I thought it would."**

PLAYER 2: **"What are you talking about? We just finished having sex."**

The line in red is an example of an improviser agreeing and a character disagreeing. Player 2's *character* clearly does not think that the one-night stand is lasting unusually long, but by reacting to information that stands out as unusual, the *improviser* has come to an agreement with her scene partner.

EXAMPLE 2 (Framing)

PLAYER 1: **"I think I'm going to take my kids to the circus this weekend."**

PLAYER 2: **"My kids loved it. They ended the show by blowing up half of the audience."**

PLAYER 1: **"They blew up half the audience?"**

In this example from our section on framing, the character being portrayed by Player 1 doesn't pretend that blowing up half of an audience is normal. The character reacts to the information by questioning it in the line in red. By reacting at the top of their intelligence, this *improviser* comes to an agreement with Player 2 about what is happening in this scene.

Let's look at one new example to illustrate how agreement between the fictional characters and agreement between the improvisers differ in the service of finding a Game:

EXAMPLE 3

You and your scene partner are given the suggestion "ledge." Your scene partner steps out and initiates physically by pantomiming that he is standing on a ledge. He says, **"Please, push me off the ledge. I have nothing left to live for."**

This improviser doesn't really want you to push him off the ledge. What he wants you to do is talk him out of suicide. If you push him off the ledge, you are saying "yes" to his character's request instead of the improviser's implicit request, which is: "Start talking me off the ledge." You should be thinking, What does this other improviser want? In order to agree with what the other improviser has initiated, you must say "no" to the character's request and instead start talking him down, or whatever you would do in this situation.

Pushing your scene partner off of the ledge would be very unusual. By saying "no" to this request, you have said "yes" to the reality of the scene, making it easier for both of you to recognize the first unusual thing later in this scene.

Once you have found a Game, you are agreeing to play this Game and this Game only in your scene. You must agree with each other in order to play Game together. Both improvisers will do this by asking, "If this unusual thing is true, then what else is true?" Every time you or your scene partner uses this question to play within this pattern, you are agreeing with each other.

REVISITING LISTENING

Listening is also extremely important when finding the Game organically in a scene. Poor listening puts you at risk for missing the first unusual thing in your scene. Failing to identify the first unusual thing will delay you from finding a Game, which, in turn, may cause you to feel the need to force an unusual thing by saying randomly weird or clever things. If you are listening, you will be able to identify the very first unusual thing that occurs. Listening helps you to find and play a Game as soon as possible.

New improvisers often fail to listen because they are searching so desperately for the Game of the scene in their own head. You shouldn't have to search hard for the Game because it lies in your scene partner. Either your scene partner will provide the unusual thing or frame what you have said, thereby identifying it as unusual. You will only be able to find the Game if you truly listen to the specific choices and information being provided to you by your scene partner. Your Game is waiting for you there, not in your own thoughts or clever ideas.

ALWAYS PLAY AT THE TOP OF YOUR INTELLIGENCE

Like listening, playing at the top of your intelligence is a principle of scene work that must be employed for the entirety of a Long Form scene. Playing at the top of your intelligence and addressing the first unusual thing in a scene at the moment it is introduced will start the Game, the pattern that will be made out of this funny behavior or concept. If your scene partner introduces something unusual and you fail to react at the top of your intelligence, you have introduced something else unusual. Now the audience is watching a silly scene with no grounded reality from which to grow. If your scene partner makes a bold move after the Game has been found, they still need you to react. They want you to play at the top of your intelligence so that you can both focus on and extend the comedy being provided by your Game.

Playing at the top of your intelligence is often absent in scenes where improvisers have misunderstood the principles of agreement and Yes And. You are more likely to discover what the other improviser wants in a scene if you simply react at the top of your intelligence to their character's actions or words. Remember, you want to Yes And the scene, not literally everything the improviser says. We want to agree with the improviser, not agree with the character.

FILTERS – ACKNOWLEDGING STATUS AND YOUR ENVIRONMENT

Let's take a closer look at how playing at the top of your intelligence factors into playing the Game of the scene. We have established that playing at the top of your intelligence is about reacting and staying committed to the character you are building through these reactions. But how do you know *how* to react in a scene?

Reacting in an improv scene is often more complicated than simply sharing *your* initial internal response to a stimulus. In improv, you can't just share your gut reaction, because you wouldn't in real life. We don't reveal every impulse and unadulterated reaction to the things happening around us. By taking into account the circumstances of the scene and allowing these circumstances to help you decide how you will react, the base reality of your scene will be more realistic.

In real life, the way you react to a stimulus is tempered by your status in relation to the status of others and your environment. The same is true for reacting as a character in Long Form. You must always consider with whom your character is interacting and where this interaction is taking place. You can think of status as causing you to have a filter through which your initial reaction must pass.

In real life, more often than not, there is almost always a difference in status between two people. You talk differently to your boss than you talk to your wife, son, garbage man, etc. Establishing and respecting status in a scene is important. How someone speaks to you will always cause some sort of specific internal reaction no matter who says it. However, the manner in which you express your reaction after it has passed through your filter depends in part on the status of the person with whom you are dealing.

Let's look at how using this concept of a filter in regard to the character's status could cause you to have wildly different reactions to the same simple line in a scene: "Get me a cup of coffee!" No matter who says it, this line is likely to cause the same initial reaction. It is a blunt command that most people would find to be rude. However, considering your status in relation to the other character should completely change your response.

If the other character is your younger brother, you might respond by barking, "Get yourself a cup of coffee!" Let's say the other character is an old woman. You might not want to get her a cup of coffee, and you may still find her way of asking to be very rude, but you might decide that your character has respect for the elderly. Maybe you use a subtle facial expression to show the audience that you are visibly annoyed or surprised, but you respond by saying, "Okay...how do you take it?" Now let's imagine that the other character is your boss. You may definitely not want to get him a cup of coffee. You might *hate* your boss. However, status is going to temper your gut reaction. Maybe in this scenario, you simply let out a subtle sigh of frustration and pour the cup of coffee. Through a tightly clenched jaw, you respond, "Here you go, boss." You have communicated how you really feel to your audience without neglecting to acknowledge how this scene would play out in reality. Additionally, by choosing to play low status to your scene partner, you are Yes And–ing his high-status initiation.

Environment also tempers your responses and how your character will react in scenes. If you have established that you are in an apartment, the line "Hey, wanna make out?" is going to get a different reaction than it would if you have established that you are in Central Park. Your character's internal reaction may be, "Yes, I want to make out" in both situations, but your character might be more hesitant to act on this impulse in the middle of Central Park. Now let's change the environment to a church. Maybe your character still wants to make out, but you might flirtatiously respond, "Not here." Change the environment again: This time you are in a church at your grandmother's funeral. Even though the immediate, internal reaction may be the same, it is easy to imagine your character offering a response line to show that you are angry or offended. Since real people act differently if they are in an apartment, a park, or a church, this aspect of the scene should be taken into account in a Long Form scene.

Now let's consider another scenario in which both status and environment would be taken into consideration. You initiate by complaining of a terrible toothache. Your character encounters a homeless person out on the street who offers to hit you with a brick to knock you out, giving you a respite from the pain. Your immediate reaction would be to not want to get hit with a brick. This, combined with your environment (a random city street) and your status in relation to the other character (a sense of entitlement), is probably going to cause you to outright refuse this strange offer.

Now let's change the Who and the Where. You are now in a dentist's office. Various degrees and diplomas verifying this dentist's qualifications surround you. The dentist enters and you once again complain about having a terrible toothache. In a calm, authoritative, and professional-sounding voice, the dentist proposes hitting you with a brick in order to knock you out, giving you a temporary respite from the pain. Again, your immediate reaction is probably going to be to not want to get hit with a brick! However, the environment and status tied to this scenario may keep you from outright refusing this still-strange offer. After allowing your initial reaction to pass through *this* filter, your character may even seriously consider getting hit with a brick. You are dealing with someone who has a medical degree. This should certainly be enough to persuade you to hear the anesthesiologist out. Your environment and your partner's status as a medical professional have changed how you would express how you are affected.

Respecting status is ultimately what keeps Long Form improvisers from always telling their scene partners that they are crazy in response to the unusual. Allowing your reactions to pass through filters created by environment and status is what keeps you from walking out of most scenes. Filters give you a reason to be patient and hear the other character's logic.

Status within a scene isn't only dictated by job title, rank, or age. Status within a scene is more importantly dictated by the characters' behavior toward each other. If your scene partner's boss character from our earlier example said, "Um, excuse me, Thompson, but, uh, if it's not too much trouble...do you think you could please grab me a cup of coffee?," they are still playing a boss, but a very different status has been established. This, in turn, will determine how you are affected. Remember that there isn't one "correct" reaction for a given situation. The important thing is that you are affected in some way.

Let's take a line-by-line look at this scene in the dentist's office to illustrate how playing at the top of your intelligence is important to the Game of the scene. Let's pretend that you are Player 2 in the following example:

EXAMPLE 1

Two improvisers are given the suggestion "X-ray."

[PLAYER 1 mimes pulling an X-ray off of a lighted display.]

PLAYER 1:   **"I'm afraid the tooth is going to need to be pulled."**

PLAYER 2:   **"I'll get anesthetic for a procedure like this, right?**

PLAYER 1:	"Yes, I'll be anesthetizing you with brick..."
PLAYER 2:	**"A brick? I don't understand."**
PLAYER 1:	**"I'm going to put you under by hitting you on the head with a brick."**
PLAYER 2:	**"You're going to hit me with a brick?"**

Clearly, Player 1's line in green is the first unusual thing in this scene. We can assume that Player 1 knows that this is an unorthodox (and dangerous) way to anesthetize a patient. Even though the character wants you to let him hit you with a brick, the improviser playing this character wants you to stop him from hitting you with a brick. He wants you to question his unorthodox methods so that he can explore or justify his absurd behavior with logic.

The lines in red are examples of playing at the top of your intelligence. Saying "Hey, hold on a minute," or even "No way!" would be other examples of playing at the top of your intelligence. You have chosen to play the straight man in this scene. A **straight man** is the "everyman" in a scene who must deal with absurdity. A straight man is going to react to the unusual as someone in reality would react. The straight man is often the voice of reason in a scene. By questioning this unorthodox method, you have grounded the scene and supported your scene partner's move by giving it a response that is at the top of your intelligence.

Saying something like, "You're not an anesthesiologist, you're my plumber," would be an example of the improviser saying "no" to the scene. This is an example of denial because saying this would be denying what your scene partner established about the base reality.

If you immediately agree to being hit with a brick, you will have destroyed the reality of the scene. Your character will have become as absurd as the doctor. You have essentially said "no" to your scene partner's idea and suggested your own through your crazy behavior. Now you are going to get hit with a brick, and the scene will be over.

Remember, the Game is not yet "locked" when you find the first unusual thing. By playing at the top of your intelligence, you are framing the unusual and supporting it by making everything else in the scene real. A single improviser can't see the Game alone. When offering a move like Player 1 does in the green line, he needs you to react at the top of your intelligence so his unusual behavior can be justified and explored.

It is important for you to continue to play at the top of your intelligence throughout the rest of the scene to support the Game. Don't say "no" to getting anesthetized with a brick but then "yes" to a noose three lines later. It's like a game of handball. Your scene partner has served the ball to you, hoping that you'll hit it back to him. If you just let the ball go by you, the Game won't get played. After you hit the ball back once, you should be ready to hit it again and again. Let's return to the scene to see how you can continue to be affected as a straight man without just saying "no" to getting hit with a brick over and over.

EXAMPLE 2

Two improvisers are given the suggestion "X-ray."

[PLAYER 1 mimes pulling an X-ray off of a lighted display.]

PLAYER 1: **"I'm afraid the tooth is going to need to be pulled."**

PLAYER 2: **"I'll get anesthetic for a procedure like this, right?**

PLAYER 1: "Yes, I'll be anesthetizing you with brick..."

PLAYER 2: **"A brick? I don't understand."**

PLAYER 1: **"I'm going to put you under by hitting you on the head with a brick."**

PLAYER 2: **"You're going to hit me with a brick? Why aren't you using gas?"**

PLAYER 1: **"It's actually much safer than gas. Almost no one has ever died from a concussion, but a significant percentage of people will have a bad reaction to the gas — memory loss, asphyxiation due to vomiting..."**

"Wait. Is it a medical-grade brick? Like one that is sized and proportionate to my weight?"

First, since you reacted to the first mention of the brick, you have set up Player 1 to justify his unusual behavior. Now that he has supported his unusual behavior with logic, the Game we have found organically has been locked. We can describe the Game as "unorthodox medical procedure."

You are still playing at the top of your intelligence in the orange line, but now you have found a way to move the scene along. You aren't completely convinced by Player 1, but you are willing to hear him out based on the fact that he just gave you a reasonable-sounding logic for using bricks to anesthetize patients. It is important to keep in mind that status implied by title, rank, or age will affect how characters will behave in scenes. The fact that this procedure is being suggested by a dentist may change how you choose to be affected. The important thing is that you continue to play at the top of your intelligence. The specifics you offered in the orange line can fuel the next move in the pattern of "unorthodox medical procedure."

CRAZY TOWN

Failing to be affected can cause you and everything around you in the scene to seem absurd. When this happens, you and your partner have entered what Long Form improvisers call Crazy Town. In a Crazy Town scene, there are so many absurd elements in play that it becomes difficult to distinguish the unusual from the ordinary. If you cannot focus on one funny pattern in a scene, your scene can feel scattered and unsatisfying. Like painting blue paint on a blue canvas, your Game will not stand out against the background of a crazy world. Often, the best way to avoid Crazy Town is to be affected by your scene partner's idea at the top of your intelligence with a grounded reaction.

EXERCISE: RECOGNIZING THE FIRST UNUSUAL THING

INSTRUCTIONS

- Two improvisers take the stage.

- Give them a one-word suggestion.

- The improvisers will begin a scene, looking to clearly establish a reality containing a Who, What, and Where.

- The improvisers should continue to Yes And each other until they discover the first unusual thing.

- The rest of your group should watch the scene carefully for the first unusual thing. Any of the improvisers watching should raise their hand when they think they see the first unusual thing. They should be looking for something that is unusual given the reality that has been established.

- Stop the scene when the first hand is raised. This person should explain what they saw as the first unusual thing. Discuss this first unusual thing as a group.

- It is okay to disagree about what is unusual—some people will see things that others will miss.

- Either have the improvisers resume the scene with the identified first unusual thing in mind or discuss potential Game moves as a group. Throw out different Game moves that could spring off of that first unusual thing.

PURPOSE

- This exercise will help you to develop the skill of recognizing the first unusual thing. New improvisers often have so much to think about during a scene that recognizing the first unusual thing is lost. By watching the scene from the outside, you can focus solely on the first unusual thing. This is an important part of your development as an improviser. It is like a basketball player practicing jump shots outside of game conditions.

- For the improvisers in the scene, the benefit of this exercise is to get practice playing the Game of the scene from the point of the first unusual thing without having to recognize it on their own. This exercise is more akin to T-ball, in which young baseball players are given the experience of hitting a baseball without having to wait for the right pitch.

EXERCISE: REPEAT THE FIRST UNUSUAL THING

INSTRUCTIONS

- Have two improvisers take the stage.

- Give them a one-word suggestion.

- The improvisers will begin a scene, looking to clearly establish a reality containing a Who, What, and Where.

- The improvisers should continue to Yes And each other until they discover the first unusual thing.

- When either improviser feels that their scene partner may have introduced the first unusual thing into their scene, they should repeat the line containing this information back to their scene partner word for word. This is not done in character. This is the improviser repeating, word for word, what the other improviser has said.

- The improviser who said the first unusual thing should repeat the line again. The improviser who identified the first unusual thing will repeat the line for a second time. The improviser who originally said the first unusual thing will repeat the line once more. (The same line should be heard fours times in total.)

- The scene should then continue forward from this point. Now that the first unusual thing has been clearly identified, the improvisers can react to it, establishing a pattern that will set the Game in motion.

- Both improvisers are responsible for making clear choices with regard to how they are reacting or responding to what has been identified as the first unusual thing.

PURPOSE

- The improvisers in the scene are given a chance to practice recognizing the first unusual thing.

- This exercise also provides an opportunity for new improvisers to slow down so that they can process the first unusual thing, giving them a chance to consider why it is unusual.

- The repetition of the first unusual thing also serves as a way to guarantee that both improvisers are recognizing the same first unusual thing. You can think of this as a way of underlining the first unusual thing so that it stands out to your scene partner.

Finding the Game with a Premise

Premise

▸DEFINITION

A Premise Scene starts with an opening line that contains the first unusual thing and an implied base reality. This first unusual thing is discovered in an **opening**. An opening is the beginning of a Long Form performed by the ensemble to generate information after getting a suggestion from the audience. There are many different types of openings. A few of them will be explained in detail in the section on longforms.

The opening line or initiation of a Premise Scene is usually funny. The contrast of the first unusual thing with the base reality laid out in the initiation of a Premise Scene is what makes this initiation funny. The details of the base reality cannot be neglected in a Premise scene. The base reality (Who, What, and Where) is just as essential to a Premise Scene as it is to an Organic Scene.

Premise is the term used to describe a fully formed comedic idea found in an opening that strongly suggests a Game. When starting a Premise scene, an improviser will want to take one of the strongest comedic ideas generated by the group in the opening and initiate a scene with it. An advantage of performing an opening is that it allows the entire group to work together to create comedic ideas. It is always easier to start a scene with a comedic idea that everyone knows than it is to start a scene with a comedic idea that is only from your own head. If you present a premise line based on an opening that your scene partner has participated in, it is going to be easier for them to understand it and come to agreement.

Let's look at some examples of Premise Scene initiations in which the base reality and first unusual thing are both implied in a single line:

EXAMPLE 1

PLAYER 1:   **"Sir, I'm a dog groomer, I cannot cut your hair."**

The base reality of this scene is that we are seeing a dog groomer at his place of business dealing with a customer. The first unusual thing is that the customer doesn't want his dog's hair cut but instead wants his own hair cut.

EXAMPLE 2

PLAYER 1:   **"Hey, I live next door in 4-C...my air conditioner is out. Can I crash at your place tonight?"**

The base reality of this scene is that we are seeing two neighbors in an apartment doorway. Based on how Player 1 introduces himself, we can assume that these characters don't know each other very well. It's possible that they've never met before. The first unusual thing is that Player 1 is asking to stay at his neighbor's apartment in spite of the fact that they don't know each other very well.

As is the case with Organic Scenes, the Game will not be established until the other improviser reacts or responds to this first unusual thing. Since an unusual thing has been introduced in the very first line in a Premise Scene, you will immediately begin asking, "If this unusual thing is true, then what else is true?" in the second line of the scene.

EXAMPLES OF GAME IN PREMISE SCENES

Let's look at how the Games we found in our two versions of the one-night-stand scene could have been found by starting with a premise that was pulled from an opening.

Let's imagine that a longform begins with a monologue as its opening. A monologue opening is a short, true story or anecdote, usually inspired by a suggestion from the audience.

Let's imagine that a group of improvisers were given the suggestion of "bedroom." One of the performers tells the following story:

> "I had a one-night stand that has become legendary among my friends. I met this girl at this bar I used to hang out at near my apartment. We got drunk and around 12:30, I took her back to my place. I actually ended up getting back to my friends at the bar before last call. I know that's kind of sleazy, but in my defense, I was coming off a situation where I had a one-night stand where I basically ended up with a stalker. She ended up staying at my place for like 36 hours as if she was moving in. So I know I'm a scumbag, but I think it's because I was scarred."

You'll notice that this monologue includes two unusual things: an incredibly quick one-night stand with a guy who has an irrational fear of commitment (in red) and a one-night stand with a woman who has overstayed her welcome (in blue). An improviser listening to this story may want to take the irrational fear of commitment described in this story as the comedic idea for a scene.

EXAMPLE 1

[PLAYER 1 pulls out two chairs and places them close together. He gestures for PLAYER 2 to join him in the chairs. He leans back to give the appearance of lying up in a bed, so his scene partner matches this posture.]

PLAYER 1:   "Wow, 3 a.m. already? This one-night stand is lasting a lot longer than I thought it would."

Since both Player 1 and Player 2 have heard the same monologue, the Who, What, and Where of two people in a bedroom in the middle of a one-night stand can be assumed from the content of that monologue.

Player 2, assuming that Player 1 has been inspired by the part of the monologue highlighted in red, might respond this way...

PLAYER 2:   "Are you serious? We just finished having sex."

This response has the effect of making Player 1 seem like someone with an irrational fear of commitment. With this line, Player 2 has established the Game of this scene.

PLAYER 1:   "Wow, 3 a.m. already? This one-night stand is lasting a lot longer than I thought it would."

PLAYER 2:   "Are you serious? We just finished having sex."

PLAYER 1:   "It's getting weird. We're getting too close. You're already walking around nude, you leave your clothes all over the place..."

PLAYER 2:   "You just took those clothes off of me before we had sex!"

Now both players in this Premise Scene are playing the Game of "irrational fear of commitment."

A different premise could be pulled from this same monologue, leading to a completely different Game. In this example, Player 1 is pulling the premise from the section of the monologue in blue.

EXAMPLE 2

[PLAYER 1 pulls out two chairs and places them close together. He gestures for PLAYER 2 to join him in the chairs. He leans back to give the appearance of lying up in a bed, so his scene partner matches this posture.]

PLAYER 1:   "Look, you've really got to go. It's been 24 hours."

Player 2, assuming that Player 1 has been inspired by the part of the monologue highlighted in blue, might respond this way...

PLAYER 2:   "You know, I didn't think about it that way. That means it's not a one-night stand anymore...it's been a whole day! We're dating!"

This response has the effect of making Player 2 seem like she is someone who is artificially accelerating a relationship. With this line, Player 2 has established the Game of this scene.

PLAYER 1:   "Look, you've really got to go. It's been 24 hours."

PLAYER 2:   "You know, I didn't think about it that way. That means it's not a one-night stand anymore...it's been a whole day! We're dating!"

[Player 1 stands up and mimes pulling something off of his bedroom window.]

PLAYER 1:   "Please go and take these curtains that you hung up with you."

PLAYER 2:   "You know what, that's a great idea. I've been thinking of redecorating, too.

Now both players in this Premise Scene are playing the Game of "accelerating the relationship."

TELLING MONOLOGUES

By their very nature, any truthful reminiscences from your life are going to be interesting without being fictional. Any story that you remember when you are called on to deliver a monologue is memorable because something happened that broke the expected pattern of your everyday life. Monologues that are real stories and memorable anecdotes are going to provide you with the type of information that will be useful to improvisers looking for a starting point for scenes. Remember, the audience doesn't know you. You don't want to gloss over any part of the monologue you are telling and assume that the audience will be able to fill in the blanks. Be specific and detailed.

Trust that your true stories will be the best inspiration for scenes. Don't try to perform improvised stand-up. You don't want to riff or go off on tangents inspired by the suggestion. Don't launch into a character. Don't just offer opinions inspired by the suggestion. Most importantly, don't create a fictional story. If you try to be fictional, you will most likely end up being derivative.

Don't put pressure on yourself to be hilarious in a monologue being used as an opening. A great monologue is nothing more than a true reminiscence containing good specifics.

Note: There is nothing that you can't talk about in a monologue. However, in this book we are talking about comedic improvisation, and some subject matter may be so sad or off-putting that you might end up digging yourself a hole that you can't climb out of. If a story is sad or off-putting, you need to have an "angle" on it. Your angle is the ladder that gets you out of the hole.

YES AND, AGREEMENT & LISTENING FOR INTENT IN PREMISE SCENES

When initiating a Premise Scene, you want to clearly and concisely communicate the premise you are pulling from the opening to your scene partner. When responding in a Premise Scene, you will probably be able to immediately start thinking in terms of "If this unusual thing is true, then what else is true?" If your scene partner has done a good job of initiating clearly, you will be able to forgo Yes And as it was employed in Organic Scenes. If the first unusual thing is not clear in an initiation, you might need to use Yes And until a specific first unusual thing is found.

Agreement plays the same role in Premise Scenes as it does in Organic Scenes. The improvisers will come to agreement about the premise being used in an initiation. The improvisers must also come to agreement about how the specific pattern of this Game will be played out over the course of the scene. The characters in a Premise Scene are going to behave in a way that will support and sustain this Game, even if that means the characters disagree with each other. To reiterate a rule from earlier, improvisers are always agreeing; characters are not necessarily.

Finally, you must listen for intent in Premise Scenes. Remember, listening for intent doesn't just mean hearing what your scene partner's character is *saying*, it also means hearing what your scene partner (the improviser) *wants*. This is especially true for Premise Scenes. At the start of a Premise Scene, you must be listening for what your scene partner *wants* from you in their premise-based initiation. Listening to your scene partner for subtext in an initiation will give you direction for most of the choices you will make in the rest of the scene.

YOUR SCENE PARTNER'S PREMISE DOES NOT LIMIT YOUR CONTRIBUTION TO THE SCENE

As a new improviser, you may feel that when your scene partner initiates a premise, they have limited your ability to be creative. Remember, by presenting a premise, they have only offered a base reality and first unusual thing. How you build on this first unusual thing is up to you. Your scene partner initiating with a premise is no more limiting than finding a first unusual thing together in an Organic Scene.

PLAYING AT THE TOP OF YOUR INTELLIGENCE IN PREMISE SCENES

Playing at the top of your intelligence is also important in Premise Scenes. Failing to react to a premise-based initiation will cause your scene to lack reality.

Let's return to the dentist's office from earlier. This time, we'll have Player 1 initiate with a premise:

EXAMPLE 1

[PLAYER 1 mimes pulling an X-ray off of a lighted display.]

PLAYER 1:   **"Your operation has been scheduled for Tuesday. I'll be anesthetizing you with brick."**

This initiation is clearly unusual. If Player 2 doesn't react to this initiation in some way, they will be making their character unusual as well. An absurd premise does not stand out within an absurd context. It is difficult to play the Game of the scene in a focused way if there are multiple absurd things happening in a scene.

A failure to play at the top of your intelligence when presented with a premise-based initiation is a form of denial. More often than not, the improviser initiating a Premise Scene from an opening is expecting their scene partner to play into that premise in a specific way. When the improviser responding to the initiation fails to react, a premise is wasted and a teammate is denied.

EXERCISE: GAME IN SKETCH

INSTRUCTIONS

- View sketch comedy, either alone or with other improvisers. (Some shows you could use for this exercise are *Monty Python*, *Saturday Night Live*, *The Kids in the Hall*, *Mr. Show*, and *Upright Citizens Brigade*.)

- Identify the Game by summing up what is funny about each sketch. Describe the Game in a few sentences or less. Then try to describe it in one sentence. Then distill the Game into five words or less.

- In distilling the Game of each sketch, don't use specifics or create a plot synopsis.

- Examples: The Game of Monty Python's "Cheese Shop" is "specialty shop that does not sell what it claims to specialize in." The Game of Monty Python's "Dead Parrot" is "refusal to acknowledge an irrefutable fact."

- Once you have identified the Game, imagine it existing in another situation with different specifics. (Example: A sketch where a husband refuses to admit he has been cheating as his wife catches him in bed with two women would have the same basic Game as "Dead Parrot." A sketch about a Baskin Robbins ice cream shop that has no ice cream would have the same Game as "Cheese Shop.")

- Another level you could add to this exercise would be to try and write out a new sketch using the Game of a classic sketch. Here is the start of a sketch using the Game from the "Cheese Shop" sketch:

PRIEST: "Welcome, my son. How long has it been since your last confession?"

PARISHIONER: "Six months, Father."

PRIEST:	"Very well."
PARISHIONER:	"I disobeyed my parents."
PRIEST:	"Not a sin."
PARISHIONER:	"Oh...I thought I had failed to honor thy father and mother...I took the Lord's name in vain..."
PRIEST:	"Nope. Not a sin."
PARISHIONER:	"Really? I'm pretty sure that's one of the Ten Commandments."
PRIEST:	"I'm sorry, I don't consider everything a sin."
PARISHIONER:	"But I'm here for confession."
PRIEST:	"Yes, that's right. We're in a confessional, I'm a priest; confess away."
PARISHIONER:	"I thought impure thoughts about a girl in my class."
PRIEST:	"Sorry, can't forgive that one."
PARISHIONER:	"Why not?"
PRIEST:	"No way for me to be sure you did that."

[The parishioner pulls money out of his pocket.]

PARISHIONER:	"Look! This is money I stole from a classmate!"
PRIEST:	"Hmm, did you steal it or did you borrow it?"
PARISHIONER:	"I stole it! I have no intention of returning it!"
PRIEST:	"Sorry, I'm still gonna give you a pass on that one."

PURPOSE

- Identifying the Game of written sketches is a great way to train your mind to recognize Game outside of the classroom or rehearsal studio.

- Getting good at this will help you to identify Games in your improvised scenes that might be strong enough to develop into written sketches. If you find that the specifics of the Long Form scene you are trying to write up into a sketch just aren't translating to the page, you can try to find a new or better situation or scenario to set your Game in, just like the alternate scenarios we were able to generate for the Game of "Dead Parrot."

EXERCISE: INITIATING FROM MONOLOGUES

INSTRUCTIONS

- This exercise requires a group of at least three or more improvisers.

- A suggestion will be thrown out by one of the improvisers. Someone else in the group will be inspired to step out and tell a monologue inspired by this suggestion.

- After the monologue, discuss all of the comedic ideas you heard as a group. One way to recognize interesting or comedic ideas is to listen to what made your group laugh. You should also be listening for what was the essential "point" or "reason" for the story. (This can often be described as the "one-line" version of this monologue.) In addition to this central, core idea, there will often be many great details that are interesting in and of themselves, which will also be great fodder for scenes.

- Next, go through the comedic ideas one by one and take turns offering scene initiations that attempt to frame the idea in the context of a scene. Use this process: Take the comedic idea and imagine a scene that could come from this idea. Then, try to imagine what the first line of this scene would be. Offer this as your initiation.

- As a group, discuss which initiations were most successful in clearly communicating the comedic idea you want to explore and an implied base reality.

- You can add another layer to this exercise by pairing up after discussing the comedic ideas as a group. One improviser will initiate using a comedic idea from the monologue identified by the group. The second improviser will then attempt to respond to this initiation in a way that takes the scene in the direction intended by the initiator.

PURPOSE

- Discussing potential initiations from monologues as a group will help you to get better at identifying the strongest ideas. You want to use the ideas that are going to be funny to most of the people in the audience, not just those ideas that you find to be funny.

- Premises are easiest to identify in monologues. This exercise will let you put your focus on communicating premises clearly in a single line.

HOW FULLY FORMED IS YOUR PREMISE?

Since finding the Game organically and starting with a premise are both equally valid methods, determining which method to use can be a point of confusion for new improvisers.

INITIATING

Remember, when improvising off of a single suggestion without an opening, you should focus your efforts on finding the Game organically. Initiating with a premise in this situation means forcing a premise that you have created alone in your own mind. This is antithetical to the ideas of teamwork and collaboration that are so critical to Long Form. Your best bet when improvising off of nothing more than a single suggestion is to enter and establish something about your relationship, activity, or location (Who, What, and Where) and wait to see how your scene partner chooses to Yes And your choice.

Openings will generally yield three types of information: premises, **half ideas**, and **chaff**. Premises are the most fully formed comedic ideas generated in an opening. A premise will strongly suggest a Game. A half idea is information that has some comedic potential and which establishes some part of the base reality of a scene. Chaff is all the superfluous information generated in an opening that is *not* a half idea or a premise. It is information that, when extracted from an opening, is the equivalent of a one-word suggestion. Starting with chaff does no more than allow you to establish some part of the base reality.

CHAFF   **HALF-IDEA**   **PREMISE**

If you are performing off of an opening, pulling a premise from the opening should be your top priority when initiating a scene. Since one of the main purposes of an opening is to generate funny ideas for scenes, it is only practical to initiate with a premise. You've already done the work of creating funny ideas with your teammates; now you can use them in your scenes.

When you consider all of the premises generated in an opening, some will be more fully formed than others. Fully formed premises are the premises that made the most people in your group and in the audience laugh. Using a fully formed premise generated by the group will get you into playing Game faster since starting with a fully formed premise means starting with a comedic idea that everyone in your group already knows.

When initiating with a fully formed premise from an opening, it is important to make it clear that you are making a choice both physically and verbally. Stepping out with a purpose and confidence after an opening is the simplest way to let your scene partner know that you have a fully formed premise in mind. Don't mince words with your initiation. Try to be as direct as possible in getting to what you found to be funny in the premise you have selected from your opening. Be clear in terms of how you want your scene partner to react. Don't start vaguely with the hope that you will get to what is funny about your premise three to four lines in. Aim to make initiations inspired by fully formed premises as tight as the first line of a great sketch.

In your initial attempts to be clear and direct in your premise-based initiations, you may find that they end up sounding forced or unnatural. This is okay for someone who is new to Long Form. In the early stages of your improv training, conveying an idea clearly is your first priority even if what you say sounds somewhat unrealistic and stilted. As time goes on, you will want to make more of an effort to be as natural as possible in your premise initiations. As you gain confidence in your ability to isolate premises and lay them out clearly in initiations, think about how someone in this situation would convey that information.

Let's say that a monologist told a story about her difficulty with remembering names, so severe that she once forgot her boyfriend's name while introducing him to her parents. Included in the story were details about how she tried using instructional tapes to improve her memory. Here are two premise-based initiations, inspired by the monologue. They are both meant to start a scene about a class filled with students whose memories are so poor that the objective of the class is to simply help them learn their own names by the end of the semester.

GOOD EXAMPLE

"Okay, everybody, welcome to 'Names Class.' Hopefully by the end of the semester you will all be able to remember your own names."

This initiation is including the base reality and a first unusual thing that clearly communicates the intended premise.

BAD EXAMPLE

"Take your seats, class, so that I can call roll."

This initiation is not specific enough. An improviser saying this line is hoping that they will get to the intended premise in a few lines as opposed to one.

Initiating with the most fully formed premises generated by an opening is not cheating. It is not preplanning. It is making your task in scene work infinitely easier. You could compare initiating with a fully formed premise to climbing a mountain with a map and specific path in mind. The opening is where you prepared for your mountain climbing trip. Intentionally starting with a premise that isn't as fully formed is like scrapping all of your preparation and just saying, "Look, there's a mountain. Let's climb it."

While starting with the most fully formed premises should be your goal, don't worry that you must have a fully formed premise to start a scene. Sometimes identifying the most fully formed premises in the moment is difficult. Hopefully, there will be many interesting and funny premises in your opening. Taking one that is less specific may be more work, but you will still make it to the top of the mountain.

Furthermore, if your opening hasn't generated a lot of premises, or if you are simply having trouble identifying premises generated within an opening, initiating with a half idea and finding the Game organically is always a viable option available to you. While it might be slightly less specific or detailed, a half idea at the start of a scene may appear the same as a fully formed premise to the untrained eyes of the audience. Scenes starting with half ideas shouldn't be lacking purpose or confidence.

If you have no other choice, you can initiate a scene using some of the chaff from the opening. This should be considered a last resort and should only happen when you can't identify any premises or half ideas. You are better off using chaff to initiate with purpose and confidence instead of starting your scene awkwardly or tentatively as you search for stronger information. Starting with chaff is going to be very similar to performing a scene off of a single suggestion. If you find yourself in this situation, follow the guidelines laid out for Organic Scenes. (Establish something about your relationship, activity, or location and wait to see how your scene partner chooses to Yes And your choice.)

RESPONDING

When you are the improviser responding to an initiation, your responsibility is to look for cues given to you by your scene partner based on the type of information they are starting with.

When you are working off of an opening, you should work from the assumption that your scene partner has stepped out first because they have some degree of a premise in mind. Try to remember what information they are taking from the opening. By considering their initiation in relation to the opening, you should be able to identify where on the continuum of information their initiation falls and react accordingly. If your scene partner is using a fully formed premise, you should have a more specific idea of how to respond in order to get to the Game suggested by this premise. If you feel that they may be initiating with a half idea or chaff, begin by Yes And–ing their idea and playing the scene at the top of your intelligence. (In other words, react as you would in an Organic Scene.) If you are not entirely sure whether the information being used to start the scene is chaff, a half idea, or a premise, play the scene at the top of your intelligence. This is always the scene work principle that trumps all others.

The most important thing to keep in mind is that you do not want to interrupt your scene partner, period. Don't cut your scene partner off. Let them get their initiation out. Give them the benefit of the doubt for a line or two—whatever they need to clearly communicate the information they have in mind. If you cut them off before they've finished, you may end up denying a fully formed premise by adding something new that is interesting or unusual. Even sound Yes And–ing should wait until after the initiation has been said. When responding to an initiation inspired by an opening, your responsibility will be to start asking, "If this unusual thing is true, then what else is true?" You need to know what version of this question your scene partner is asking in order to answer it.

GIVE IT TIME

Premise improv can be very difficult for beginners. There are a lot of balls to juggle when simultaneously recognizing premises, retaining them while investing in other people's work onstage, and then successfully delivering them in clear initiations. Realize that these are skills that develop with practice. The more you do these things, the easier they will get.

As you get more comfortable playing with people, you will learn what to expect from them when they are initiating scenes. Some people on your team will be extremely direct when getting to fully formed premises. Some people will need to be given space in order to get to the premise or half idea they have in mind. As you get to know each other in this way, you will be able to approach scenes without feeling rushed. In turn, you will have a better chance at building scenes together that resemble written works and real-life experiences. This is the value of ensemble. There is inherent panic in the first few moments of almost every scene when you are starting out. Just as it will take time for the rules in this book to become second nature, realize that becoming a true ensemble will take time as well.

Again, the UCB does not see any intrinsic advantage in either of these methods of finding the Game (Organic or Premise). One isn't better than the other. Just be sure to use rehearsal time to get lots of practice with both.

EXERCISE: IDENTIFYING INFORMATION FROM THE OPENING

INSTRUCTIONS

- This exercise requires at least three improvisers.

- One improviser will tell a monologue inspired by a one-word suggestion.

- A second improviser will then offer a single-line initiation inspired by the monologue.

- The third improviser (or any other improviser in the group) will then guess what part of the monologue the initiation is coming from.

- The improviser initiating will confirm whether or not the correct section of the monologue was identified.

- Switch roles and repeat.

- You can also try a version of this exercise where you guess whether the initiation was using a premise, half idea, or chaff.

PURPOSE

- This exercise will help you get better at initiating. If your teammates had trouble identifying the inspiration for your initiation, maybe you weren't "nailing it over the head" as hard as you thought you were.

- This is a great opportunity to practice initiating with each type of information generated from an opening.

- You will also get better at recognizing the difference between premises, half ideas, and chaff in initiations. Getting better at making this distinction will improve your ability to respond effectively and efficiently in scenes.

CHAPTER 5:

Playing Game

O nce you and your scene partner have *found* the Game, you will spend the rest of the scene *playing* the Game. In order to play the Game that you have found, both improvisers will be asking themselves the question, "If this unusual thing is true, then what else is true?"

Three versions of this question are used to play the Game of a scene:

1. "If this unusual thing is true, then what else is true?" This question helps you to **heighten** the Game. Heightening is the act of making a Game move in a scene that is in keeping with—yet more absurd than—anything that has preceded it.

2. "If this unusual thing is true, then why is it true?" is asked when **exploring** the Game. Exploring is the act of making a Game move in a scene that provides the logic, philosophy, or rationale behind absurd behavior.

3. "If this unusual thing is true, then what is my reaction?" Asking this question will result in **reacting at the top of your intelligence** to play the Game by supporting the reality of the scene. Any line that doesn't heighten or explore the Game should be answering this question.

Once you have found the Game of the scene, playing the Game means working with your scene partner to heighten and explore the Game to its fullest potential while reacting at the top of your intelligence. Playing the Game requires improvisers to make use of all of the key scene work principles involved in the base reality of the scene: agreement, listening, commitment, and playing at the top of your intelligence.

Heightening

▸DEFINITION

Let's think of a Game as a machine that pumps out "funny." Game is the engine of the scene. It is your job to make choices in the scene. Your choices provide the fuel for the engine. If Then just helps narrow down the available choices. **Heightening** narrows down the available choices even further.

Heightening is the act of making a Game move in a scene that is more absurd than anything that has preceded it. Each heightened Game move will deviate even further from the expected pattern of reality. It is important to heighten within the parameters of your Game. Random absurdity will not help heighten your Game. When you are answering, "If this unusual thing is true, then what else is true?" in order to find Game moves that are increasingly absurd, you are heightening your specific Game. Heightening the pattern of behavior is an important part of playing the Game because it keeps your Game funny and interesting to the audience.

Heightening is the responsibility of both improvisers in a scene. The burden of finding new specifics that fit in with the Game shouldn't have to fall on the shoulders of just one improviser. Both improvisers are responsible for moving the scene forward and making new discoveries that will heighten the Game. While it is easier to explore as a straight man, it is still possible for you to play this role and provide heightened Game moves. The straight man in a scene can still actively heighten the Game by mentioning things that have happened in the past, noticing things in the environment, etc.

IF THIS UNUSUAL THING IS TRUE, THEN WHAT ELSE IS TRUE?

Heightening may seem like a difficult task. Asking, "If this unusual thing is true, then what else is true?" is how you find heightened Game moves that are in keeping with the Game of the scene. Heightening with this question helps you to add new Game moves to the pattern that started with the first unusual thing. Game moves come in the form of lines of dialogue and actions. Heightening saves you from having to constantly create new randomly funny things to say to your scene partner out of nowhere.

You don't have to come up with randomly funny lines. You need to come up with answers to a specific question.

Improvisers in a scene should let the pattern sustained by If Then do the hard work of the scene for them. Once you start heightening a Game together, it actually becomes easier to continue doing so. Imagine having to push a car from Point A to Point B. If you had to push the car, wait for it to stop, and then start pushing it from a point of rest again (the equivalent of having to come up with a new stand-alone joke to garner laughs), then that task would be very difficult. It would be much easier to get the car rolling and then just keep it rolling (the equivalent of playing the Game to garner laughs). Instead of starting over, you will be able to build off of the momentum of all of the other heightened moves you have already made.

Here's another analogy to consider: Do you think it would be easier to: (1) write a brand-new sitcom—including an entirely different premise and characters—every week, or: (2) write a new *episode* of an existing sitcom for which the premise and characters are already known? The first option would be far more difficult than the second. Heightening a Game is just using what has already been established in your scene, just as sitcom writers use what has already been established about their show. Kenneth's relentlessly positive attitude in every episode of *30 Rock* is an example of Game. The writers of this show essentially ask themselves, "If Kenneth is relentlessly positive, then what would he say or do in this given situation?"

Heightening by asking, "If this unusual thing is true, then what else is true?" is an efficient method for creating comedy. This method will make performing scenes easier. At the beginning, you will find yourself literally asking this question in your head. Over time, it will become second nature, and you will find yourself automatically answering, "If this unusual thing is true, then what else is true?" in your scene work. You will know that you are truly in the moment when you find yourself automatically asking If Then questions without thinking so hard about it for each and every line.

EXAMPLES OF HEIGHTENING IN SCENE WORK

Let's return once again to our example of the dentist who wants to anesthetize his patients by hitting them with a brick. This time, we will allow the scene to continue in order to get some examples of heightening.

EXAMPLE 1

Two improvisers are given the suggestion "X-ray."

[PLAYER 1 mimes pulling an X-ray off of a lighted display.]

PLAYER 1:   "I'm afraid the tooth is going to need to be pulled."

PLAYER 2:   "I'll get anesthetic for a procedure like this, right?"

PLAYER 1:   "Yes, I'll be anesthetizing you with brick..."

PLAYER 2:   "A brick? I don't understand."

PLAYER 1:   "I'm going to put you under by hitting you on the head with a brick."

PLAYER 2:   "You're going to hit me with a brick? Why aren't you using gas?"

PLAYER 1:   "It's actually much safer than gas. Almost no one has ever died from a concussion, but a significant percentage of people will have a bad reaction to the gas—asphyxiation due to vomiting, memory loss—"

PLAYER 2:   "Hitting me with a brick could also result in memory loss!"

PLAYER 1:   "If you're uncomfortable with getting hit with a brick, I'd be more than happy to fill up a surgical glove with smaller rocks and hit you with that."

PLAYER 2:   "I don't have a problem with what I'm getting hit with, it's that I'm getting hit."

PLAYER 1:   "I would understand your concern if some stranger off the street was going to hit you with a brick, but I'm a trained professional."

PLAYER 2:   "So wait. Is it a medical-grade brick? Like one that is sized and proportionate to my weight?"

[PLAYER 1 mimes pulling a brick out of a cabinet.]

PLAYER 1: "Oh no, it's a standard construction-style brick. But I spent over eight years in medical school learning how to strike you with it *medically.*"

[PLAYER 1 rears back, brick in hand.]

PLAYER 2: "Wait! Wait. I really don't want to get hit in the face with a brick."

PLAYER 1: "Okay. I think I understand what your objection is. There's been some interesting research out of Harvard involving manual asphyxiation, or the 'sleeper hold,' in layman's terms. Let me show you..."

[PLAYER 1 grabs PLAYER 2 by the arms. PLAYER 2 frees himself and steps away from PLAYER 1.]

PLAYER 2: "No! I don't want to get strangled."

PLAYER 1: "Strangulation involves death. This is a controlled procedure that will limit the flow of oxygenated blood to the brain."

Let's read through the scene again. This time, the red lines in parentheses and *italics* will illustrate the improviser's thought process and show you how they used "If this unusual thing is true, then what else is true?" to get to another heightened Game move. Heightened Game moves are colored blue and labeled HGM# (explanations to follow):

EXAMPLE 1

Two improvisers are given the suggestion "X-ray."

[PLAYER 1 mimes pulling an X-ray off of a lighted display.]

PLAYER 1: "I'm afraid the tooth is going to need to be pulled."

PLAYER 2: "I'll get anesthetic for a procedure like this, right?"

PLAYER 1: "Yes, I'll be anesthetizing you with a brick..."

PLAYER 2:   "A brick? I don't understand."

PLAYER 1:   "I'm going to put you under by hitting you on the head with a brick."

PLAYER 2:   "You're going to hit me with a brick? Why aren't you using gas?"

PLAYER 1:   "It's actually much safer than gas. Almost no one has ever died from a concussion, but a significant percentage of people will have a bad reaction to the gas—asphyxiation due to vomiting, memory loss—"

PLAYER 2:   "Hitting me with a brick could also result in memory loss!"

1 THINKS: *(If I'm a dentist who thinks that using a violent method like hitting someone with a brick as an anesthetic is a sound medical procedure, then what else would I consider to be an appropriate way to anesthetize my patients? I can offer to hit my patient with a different type of hard object.)*

PLAYER 1:   "If you're uncomfortable with getting hit with a brick, I'd be more than happy to fill up a surgical glove with smaller rocks and hit you with that." (HGM1)

PLAYER 2:   "I don't have a problem with what I'm getting hit with, it's that I'm getting hit."

PLAYER 1:   "I would understand your concern if some stranger off the street was going to hit you with a brick, but I'm a trained professional."

2 THINKS: *(If my dentist seems serious about using a brick to anesthetize me, then what type of brick is he going to use? I can ask if it is a special "medical" brick.)*

PLAYER 2:   "So wait. Is it a medical-grade brick? Like one that is sized and proportionate to my weight?" (HGM2)

[PLAYER 1 mimes pulling a brick out of a cabinet.]

PLAYER 1:   "Oh no, it's a standard construction-style brick. But I spent over eight years in medical school learning how to strike you with it medically."

[PLAYER 1 rears back, brick in hand.]

PLAYER 2:   "Wait! Wait. I really don't want to get hit in the face with a brick."

1 THINKS: (*If* I'm a dentist who employs violent methods in my treatment of patients, and I am dealing with a patient resistant to my methods, *then* what sort of similarly violent, alternate method can I offer to use? I can offer to put my patient under using a "sleeper hold.")

PLAYER 1:   "Okay. I think I understand what your objection is. There's been some interesting research out of Harvard involving manual asphyxiation, or the "sleeper hold," in layman's terms. Let me show you..." (HGM3)

[PLAYER 1 grabs PLAYER 2 by the arms. PLAYER 2 frees himself and steps away from PLAYER 1.]

PLAYER 2:   "No! I don't want to get strangled."

PLAYER 1:   "Strangulation involves death. This is a controlled procedure that will limit the flow of oxygenated blood to the brain."

This Game can continue as long as both improvisers are able to answer more If Then questions.

The first thing to notice is that it takes a few lines before the first heightened Game move happens. The improvisers used the lines prior to the first heightening to establish a base reality, find and frame a first unusual thing, and clearly establish a Game before any heightening occurred. No matter how long it takes you to do this, all of the aforementioned elements of a scene should come before any heightening.

Also notice that there are technically only *three* heightened Game moves in the first 17 lines of this scene. The rest of the scene is still funny even though heightening doesn't happen in every line.

Heightening isn't the only way to be funny. If you try to force heightening in every line, you are likely to sacrifice the "flow" or believability of the scene. When you force heightening to happen, you and your scene partner will end up with something that feels more like a list than a scene.

Finally, notice that both Player 1 and Player 2 make heightened Game moves, even though this scene follows the "Character, Straight Man" format.

The heightening in this scene is good. They don't repeat the first unusual thing over and over. Instead, they find new specifics that fit their Game by asking, "If this unusual thing is true, then what else is true?" Additionally, each new specific or answer to this question is slightly more absurd than what has come before.

HEIGHTENED GAME MOVE EXPLANATIONS

HGM1: Getting hit with a surgical glove filled with small rocks sounds as unpleasant as getting hit with a brick. In fact, it seems like it wouldn't be effective! Therefore, a surgical glove full of small rocks is more absurd than a brick.

HGM2: The fact that this dentist sees nothing wrong with his proposed method of anesthetization is unusual. When the straight man momentarily humors the dentist, things become more absurd in two ways. First, he asks about "medical-grade bricks." There is no such thing as a "medical-grade brick." We have moved further from the expected pattern of reality. Beyond the new specific, the fact that he is now honestly considering getting hit with a brick is also more absurd. The scene has heightened with his behavior.

HGM3: Using a common wrestling move to anesthetize a patient seems more absurd than striking someone with a hard object while still maintaining the pattern of "violent, unorthodox medical procedures." The fact that it is presented as a reasonable alternative by this dentist contributes to the absurdity.

The absurdity of each subsequent Game move in any scene is always going to be somewhat subjective. Follow your gut in making moves that you feel truly heighten your game. If the next Game move you make doesn't seem heightened to some members of the audience (or even some members of your ensemble!), it will still serve your scene as long as it follows the pattern of your Game by answering, "If this unusual thing is true, then what else is true?"

Now let's return to one of our "One-Night Stand" example scenes for more examples of heightening. Let's look at the version of the scene that played the "accelerating a relationship" Game. Read through the scene once without any analysis. See if you can guess which lines are heightened Game moves:

EXAMPLE 2

Two improvisers are given the suggestion "bedroom."

[PLAYER 1 pulls out two chairs and places them close together. He gestures for PLAYER 2 to join him in the chairs. He leans back to give the appearance of lying up in a bed, so his scene partner matches this posture.]

PLAYER 1: "Man, I'm exhausted."

PLAYER 2: "Yeah. It's already 3 a.m."

PLAYER 1: "This one-night stand is lasting longer than I thought it would."

PLAYER 2: "I've only been here 24 hours."

PLAYER 1: "I know. So that's *more* than a one-night stand. Technically the one-night stand is supposed to be over when the sun rises."

PLAYER 2: "I didn't think about it that way. You're right... we're dating!"

[Player 1 stands up and mimes pulling something off of his bedroom window.]

PLAYER 1: "Please go and take these curtains that you hung up with you."

PLAYER 2:	"You know what? That's a great idea. I've been thinking of redecorating, too."
PLAYER 1:	"*We're* not going to redecorate together."
PLAYER 2:	"I agree...we should get a new place, pumpkin!"
PLAYER 1:	"You don't know me well enough to call me 'pumpkin—'"
PLAYER 2:	"You know, if we don't get a new place we should at least rethink the tile in the bathroom."
PLAYER 1:	"Again, *we* don't have to rethink anything because *you* don't live here."
PLAYER 2:	"Oh my God. Pumpkin! Are you asking me to move in?"
PLAYER 1:	"What? No! I want you to leave."
PLAYER 2:	"Where are we going, our honeymoon?!"

Let's read through the scene again. Once again, the red lines in parentheses and *italics* will illustrate the improviser's thought process, and show you how they used "If this unusual thing is true, then what else is true?" to get to another heightened Game move. Heightened Game moves are colored blue and labeled HGM# (explanations to follow):

EXAMPLE 2

Two improvisers are given the suggestion "bedroom."
[PLAYER 1 pulls out two chairs and places them close together. He gestures for PLAYER 2 to join him in the chairs. He leans back to give the appearance of lying up in a bed, so his scene partner matches this posture.]

PLAYER 1:	"Man, I'm exhausted."
PLAYER 2:	"Yeah. It's already 3 a.m."

PLAYER 1: "This one-night stand is lasting longer than I thought it would."

PLAYER 2: "I've only been here 24 hours."

PLAYER 1: "I know. So that's *more* than a one-night stand. Technically the one-night stand is supposed to be over when the sun rises."

PLAYER 2: "I didn't think about it that way. You're right... we're dating!"

1 THINKS: (*If Player 2 is accelerating our relationship, **then** what else might she have done in my apartment before the scene started? She has already hung up new curtains in my apartment.*)

[**PLAYER 1** stands up and mimes pulling something off of his bedroom window.]

PLAYER 1: "Please go and take these curtains with you." (HGM4)

2 THINKS: (*If I am trying to accelerate our relationship, **then** what else can I suggest, inspired by Player 1's request to take my curtains, to accelerate our relationship? I think he is asking me to take the curtains because he wants to redecorate.*)

PLAYER 2: "You know what, that's a great idea. I've been thinking of redecorating, too." (HGM5)

PLAYER 1: "*We're* not going to redecorate together."

2 THINKS: (*If I am trying to accelerate our relationship, **then** what other subtext can I pull from this statement that suggests things are getting even more serious? I will assume he is suggesting that "we" get a new place. If I am trying to accelerate our relationship, **then** what else can I call my scene partner to show familiarity? I will call him by a pet name.*)

PLAYER 2: "I agree...we should get a new place, pumpkin!" (HGM6)

PLAYER 1:   **"You don't know me well enough to call me 'pumpkin—'"**

2 THINKS: *(**If** Player 1 seems resistant to getting a new place, **then** what else can I suggest that we do in this apartment that would still be a sign of a serious relationship? I can suggest that we retile the bathroom.)*

PLAYER 2:   **"You know, if we don't get a new place we should at least rethink the tile in the bathroom."**

1 THINKS: *(**If** Player 2 is assuming a sense of familiarity that doesn't match the amount of time we've spent together, **then** what else can I point out about our time together so far that illustrates that we are not dating? I will use her line about rethinking the bathroom tile to point out that she hasn't been in the bathroom yet.)*

PLAYER 1:   **"Again, *we* don't have to rethink anything because *you* don't live here."**

2 THINKS: *(**If** I interpret subtext in everything Player 1 says to be the sign of a serious relationship, **then** what else can I assume from his pointing out that I don't live with him? I think he is asking me to move in.)*

PLAYER 2:   **"Oh my God. Pumpkin! Are you asking me to move in?"**

PLAYER 1:   **"What? No! I want you to leave."**

2 THINKS: *(**If** I interpret subtext in everything Player 1 says to be the sign of a serious relationship, **then** what else can I assume from his asking me to leave? I think he is coming with me and that we are going to go on our honeymoon.)*

PLAYER 2:   **"Where are we going, our honeymoon?!"**

A lot of heightening happened in this scene! Again, the improvisers took a few lines to establish a first unusual thing, frame the unusual, and define a Game before any heightening occurred. Both improvisers made heightened Game moves even though this is a "Character, Straight Man" scene.

Let's take a closer look at the heightening to see if it meets the qualifications of answering, "If this unusual thing is true, then what else is true?" and having each additional Game move be more absurd than the last.

MORE HEIGHTENED GAME MOVE EXPLANATIONS

HGM4: Player 1 makes the first heightened Game move, even though he is playing the straight man. Notice that Player 1 has not betrayed this choice. Player 1 *(the character)* remained grounded and committed to his desire for Player 2 to leave. Player 1 *(the improviser)* is thinking, "How can I help Player 2 to stay even longer?" As an improviser, Player 1 offered another specific illustrating Player 2's unusual behavior. Bringing curtains on a one-night stand is more absurd than just assuming a relationship from a one-night stand. It is also worth pointing out that this heightened Game move begins with action and not just with words.

HGM5: Player 2's first heightened Game move fits into the pattern established. People who are dating don't redecorate; couples redecorate. Player 2's acceleration of this relationship has grown more absurd.

HGM6: Player 1 sets up Player 2 for further heightening with the line "*We're* not going to redecorate together." He played the scene at the top of his intelligence. As the straight man, he reacted in a way that helps keep the scene in a grounded reality. In fact, he does this for the rest of the scene. Every time he points out the reality of the situation, he sets up Player 2 to misinterpret his words as an invitation to stay longer and make things more serious. Good heightening doesn't happen in isolation; good heightening is the result of two improvisers working together.

The rest of the scene features heightened Game moves that are very aggressive. The rest of the lines said by Player 2 in this scene are all heightened Game moves. Remember, it isn't necessary for heightening to occur in every line like this. It works here because the improvisers are working together. Player 1 continually sets up Player 2. It also works because every subsequent Game move is more absurd than the last. Player 2 goes from retiling the bathroom to moving in to going on a honeymoon in a short amount of time.

LISTENING HELPS YOU HEIGHTEN

Listening is not only important for finding the Game. Improvisers must listen after the Game has been found as well. Each line in a scene is important. If you stop listening and recede into your own mind for your next line, you could potentially miss extremely important moments in your scene and make your job more difficult.

After the Game of the scene has been found, your mind should begin dissecting each line you hear to see how it fits into the pattern of behavior that has already been established. You should be listening carefully to every line to determine how your scene partner is setting you both up to play the Game again. Have they made a Game move to heighten the Game? Have they set you up to heighten? If you are listening, then you will be able to react accordingly.

The importance of listening has already been emphasized, and it will be emphasized again. It is the most important thing for you to be doing at every moment in a Long Form show.

THE IMPORTANCE OF PLAYING AT THE TOP OF YOUR INTELLIGENCE AS YOU HEIGHTEN

Just as reacting at the top of your intelligence when presented with a first unusual thing in a scene allows you to recognize the starting point of your Game, playing at the top of your intelligence will help you to sustain your Game. The Game should remain the only unusual thing in the scene so that it stands out as you play it. A commitment to the reality of the scene will help the absurdity of each new Game move stand out in contrast.

Remember that reacting at the top of your intelligence is part of playing the Game. In order to maintain the integrity of the scene, it is important that the characters continue to react accordingly as the actions or specifics of the scene get heightened. If there is a straight man in the scene, he can't react to the heightened Game moves that will come two minutes into the scene in the same way that he reacted to the initial Game moves. Think about how your reactions would change in real life after dealing with someone who is acting unusual or unreasonable for two minutes. How you interact with this person would change over time in real life, and this change must also occur in scenes. For example, you may start with polite discomfort, but after two minutes you may exhibit full-on anger. If this doesn't happen, the scene will feel like it is moving laterally, and its humor will be lost.

Continuing to play at the top of your intelligence is also necessary for sustaining the Game of the scene when playing the character with absurd or unusual behavior. Remaining committed to and consistent with your character's point of view and behavior will help you to elicit laughs from the situation rather than relying on clever one-liners.

Also note that it is important for you to stay physically committed to the reality that you created at the start for the entire scene. It is easy to get so focused on the Game that you drop your environment. Staying committed to all of the choices you make, including those about your environment, will help you sustain a reality against which you can play your Game.

EXERCISE: UNDERSTUDIES

INSTRUCTIONS

- Six to eight improvisers take the stage.

- Someone else in the group offers a one-word suggestion to inspire any two improvisers on the stage. The rest of the improvisers will stand against the wall behind these two improvisers. This is referred to as the **back-line**.

- Two improvisers will begin a scene, looking to clearly establish a reality containing a Who, What, and Where.

- The improvisers should continue to Yes And each other and get more specific until they discover the first unusual thing.

- Once the two improvisers performing the scene find the Game, one of the players on the back-line should **tag out** either improviser by tapping them on the shoulder. When an improviser is tagged out, they are taken out of the scene and replaced by the improviser that did the tagging. The person who has been tagged out will then join the back-line.

- Usually, an improviser tagging into a scene will play a new character. For this exercise, the improviser that tags in will take over the character that has already been established. In other words, the scene should continue exactly where it left off, with the same two characters and the same Game.

- Once the first tag-out happens, the rest of the improvisers on the back-line may begin to tag into the scene. Either character can be tagged out and taken over as long as the new improviser enters to play the same Game by asking, "If this unusual thing is true, then what else is true?"

- Afterward, discuss as a group which moves were in keeping with the Game and which moves didn't work.

PURPOSE

- This exercise will help expand your mind in terms of heightening. With multiple people performing the same scene, there should be a lot of creativity and variation with regard to heightening. Hopefully, this will help everyone in your group see the myriad options and possibilities for heightening any Game.

- It will also give your group a chance to practice heightening without having to worry about any of the other responsibilities one must normally consider when performing a scene. Improvisers can watch the scene from the back-line and think of nothing other than heightening.

- This exercise also offers you a chance to examine the subtle differences between those moves that are on Game and those that are not.

Exploring

▸DEFINITION

Heightened Game moves can also be thought of as "funny lines" and "funny behaviors." Clearly, our goal in comedic improvisation is to be funny. However, funny things happening for no reason will rarely result in a satisfying scene. The heart of a great Long Form scene is not just what you are doing, but also why you are doing it. Our term for figuring out why things are happening is "**exploring**."

The exploration of your Game gives you a whole new way to be funny. Exploring is the act of making a Game move in a scene that provides the logic, philosophy, or rationale behind absurd behavior. In addition to asking, "If this unusual thing is true, then what else is true?" in order to find heightened Game moves, you should also be asking yourself, "If this unusual thing is true, then *why* is it true?" in order to explore. Why is the character doing this, or why is this happening? Each exploration Game move is dealing with the details and specifics discovered in the last heightened Game move. When exploration Game moves are made, new absurd elements may be introduced that will also need to be questioned. Think of playing the Game of a scene as a stair step. If heightening is going up, then exploring is going over. Exploring gets you to your next heightening and vice versa.

The diagrams below are visual representations of Games being played with heightening moves alone, and with heightening and exploration.

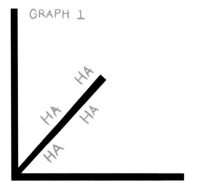

GRAPH 1

HEIGHTENING ALONE

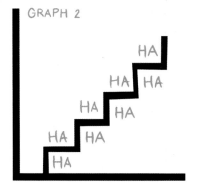

GRAPH 2

HEIGHTENING & EXPLORATION

In these diagrams, the length of the line equals funny. In Graph 1, the Game is being played through heightening alone. In Graph 2, each vertical line segment represents heightening, and each horizontal line segment represents exploration. If you were to measure the length of the line on each of these graphs, the line on the first graph would be much shorter than the length of the line on Graph 2. The Game, as it is played in Graph 2, is going to get a lot more laughs. Strong exploration moves that ground the absurd can be thought of as doubling your comedy.

Exploring can happen in two main forms. The first form is when a straight man attempts to justify the behavior or actions of the absurd character in a scene. When the straight man offers a justification, he is setting up his scene partner for further heightening in the next move. The second form of exploration is when the character or characters with absurd behavior internally ask, "Why do I have this absurd or unusual behavior?" The answer that you come up with is the philosophy or motivation of your character. Once you know this, you can import your character's Game into any situation and know how to act. Your character's absurdity is no longer a result of being crazy or dumb. There is a reason behind it. You have made "the silly" smart.

When making exploration Game moves to answer "why," don't make new absurd choices. Instead, make choices that are plausible and logical in relation to the absurd element you are justifying.

Making a good exploration move is like telling a good lie in real life. The smarter and more logical the lie, the more likely you are able to string someone along. Therefore, the smarter and more logical you are with your exploration moves, the further your Game can go.

Let's imagine a scene in which there is an elephant in your apartment. This needs to be justified. Saying that the zoo you work at has closed down because of low funding justifies the unusual in a smart, plausible way while still being funny. Saying that the elephant was given to you by a magical genie is an exploration move that adds an unnecessary, new absurd element to the scene.

When exploring, you don't have to try to be funny; you should try to be logical. This logical answer, juxtaposed with the absurd behavior, is what will make your scene funnier. When you can form sound and logical explanations for absurd behavior, you are playing your scene at the top of your intelligence. When you are performing, be the character, don't play the character. In other words, you are not playing a "comic character." You are playing a real person. Real people have reasons for their behavior. When you provide real reasons for your character's absurd behavior, delivered in a believable way, you will get laughs. Think of yourself as a lawyer defending your premise.

You don't have to know the logic behind the Game before you find it. Make choices and then create the logic to justify those choices in the moment. It is important to remember that you can be free to make choices in the moment and then discover your point of view later through exploration.

All other lines that play the Game will be reactions at the top of your intelligence. When absurd behavior is questioned or challenged, the straight man has set up the other improviser to either heighten or offer the logic, philosophy, or rationale driving their character.

You do not want to play your Game by heightening only. If you heighten without exploring and reacting at the top of your intelligence, you will run past of a lot of comedy in your scene. There is comedy in the philosophy and logic driving a character's actions. Defending or justifying an absurd behavior with logic is, by its very nature, funny. Sometimes knowing the reason behind an absurd action can be even funnier than the absurd action itself. Additionally, if you are too focused on heightening a pattern and don't think about playing the rest of the scene, you may reach a level of absurdity so quickly that it will become too hard to continue thinking of increasingly absurd moves. Finally, exploring and reacting at the top of your intelligence helps the audience invest in your scene. If your scene only heightens, it will likely become too silly and disposable. Determining why a character has absurd behavior helps your scene mirror the reality of life. Absurd or unusual behavior is questioned, challenged, or justified in real life. No matter how stupid or ridiculous their behavior is, people in real life always have reasons for their actions. When you explore or react, you are providing this realistic behavior in an absurd reality. This makes your scene and your characters more realistic, and, in turn, gives your audience more to relate to.

Just as a scene shouldn't be all heightening, you shouldn't focus solely on the exploration, either. Once you have finished reacting or offering an exploration, you should look for a way to provide the next heightened Game move. Adding another heightened specific will, in turn, inspire the next round of exploration, and so on.

Scenes that incorporate heightening and exploration are going to be more satisfying. A good scene might heighten and still be forgotten. A great scene will go back and forth between heightening and exploration. This will result in smart comedy as opposed to silly comedy.

EXAMPLES OF EXPLORATION

Let's look at an example of using exploration as a way to ground an especially silly premise.

EXAMPLE 1

[PLAYER 1 initiates physically. He mimes sitting at a bar. PLAYER 2 mirrors this choice.]

PLAYER 1:   **"Thanks for meeting up to talk. I ordered you a beer."**

PLAYER 2:   **"Thanks."**

PLAYER 1:   **"So...my big news is...I am in love with a dolphin."**

This is a funny (or at least specifically unusual) premise that will probably get a laugh on its own. However, to sustain the laughs in this scene beyond the "crazy" choice, you will have to support it with reasonable logic. Player 1 might explore his unusual behavior in the following way:

PLAYER 1:   **"Dolphins are smarter than most people and have far superior hearing, which means that not only does she hear what I'm saying, she understands me more than any human being that I've ever dated."**

Player 1 can now heighten by talking about the absurd aspects of his relationship with this dolphin. He can always return to the core logic provided by this exploration Game move to support the increasingly ridiculous specifics that he and his scene partner will come up with (e.g., he has to wear scuba gear to be with the dolphin, she let him hold his fin on the first date, etc.).

Now let's return once again to our example of the dentist that wants to anesthetize his patient by hitting them with a brick. This time, we will analyze all of the examples of exploring and reacting at the top of your intelligence in this scene.

The red sentences in parentheses and italics still illustrate the improviser's thought process, and show you how they used the question

"If this unusual thing is true, then what else is true?" to get to another heightened Game move. **Heightened Game moves are colored blue and labeled HGM# (explanations to follow):**

The purple sentences in parentheses and italics will illustrate the improviser's thought process showing you how they used the question "If this unusual thing is true, then why is it true?" to explore. **Exploration Game moves are colored green and labeled EGM# (explanations to follow):**

The orange lines in parentheses and italics will illustrate the thought process leading to reactions that are at the top of one's intelligence. **These "top of your intelligence" reaction lines are in black and labeled TOIR# (explanations to follow):**

EXAMPLE 2

Two improvisers are given the suggestion "X-ray."

[PLAYER 1 mimes pulling an X-ray off of a lighted display.]

PLAYER 1:   "I'm afraid the tooth is going to need to be pulled."

PLAYER 2:   "I'll get anesthetic for a procedure like this, right?"

PLAYER 1:   "Yes, I'll be anesthetizing you with a brick..."

PLAYER 2:   "A brick? I don't understand."

PLAYER 1:   "I'm going to put you under by hitting you on the head with a brick."

2 THINKS: *(If my dentist is going to anesthetize me with a brick, then what is my reaction? I will react by asking about gas, the more conventional method of anesthesia.)*

PLAYER 2:   **"You're going to hit me with a brick? Why aren't you using gas?" (TOIR1)**

1 THINKS: *(If I'm a qualified, experienced dentist with unconventional methods, then why do I believe that my method is a viable and safe way to anesthetize patients?*

I am going to point out the dangerous health risks related to gas in comparison to my method.)

PLAYER 1: "It's actually much safer than gas. Almost no one has ever died from a concussion, but a significant percentage of people will have a bad reaction to the gas—memory loss, asphyxiation due to vomiting..." (EGM1)

2 THINKS: (If my dentist is rattling off these consequences, then what is my reaction? It would occur to me that memory loss is also a consequence of getting hit with a brick.)

PLAYER 2: **"Hitting me with a brick could also result in memory loss!" (TOIR2)**

1 THINKS: (If I'm a dentist who thinks that using a violent method like hitting someone with a brick as an anesthetic is a sound medical procedure, then what else would I consider to be an appropriate way to anesthetize my patients? I can offer to hit my patient with a different type of hard object.)

PLAYER 1: "If you're uncomfortable with getting hit with a brick, I'd be more than happy to fill up a surgical glove with smaller rocks and hit you with that." (HGM1)

2 THINKS: (If my dentist is moving on from a brick to hitting me with a surgical glove full of rocks due to my objections, then what is my reaction? It might occur to me that he doesn't understand the nature of my objections.)

PLAYER 2: **"I don't have a problem with what I'm getting hit with, it's that I'm getting hit." (TOIR3)**

1 THINKS: (If my patient is concerned about one of my methods, then why isn't he considering my qualifications? I will remind my patient of my status as a trained professional.)

PLAYER 1: "I would understand your concern if some stranger off the street was going to hit you with a brick, but I'm a trained professional." (EGM2)

2 THINKS: (**If** my dentist seems serious about using a brick to anesthetize me, **then** what type of brick is he going to use? I can ask if it is a special "medical" brick.)

PLAYER 2: "So wait. Is it a medical-grade brick? Like one that is sized and proportionate to my weight?" (HGM2)

1 THINKS: (**If** my patient is concerned with the tools I am using, **then** why am I confident in what I have chosen to use for this procedure? I will remind my patient of my status as a trained medical professional once again.)

[**PLAYER 1** mimes pulling a brick out of a cabinet.]

PLAYER 1: "Oh no, it's a standard construction-style brick. But I spent over eight years in medical school learning how to strike you with it medically." (EGM3)

2 THINKS: (**If** my dentist is about to hit me with a brick in spite of my objections, **then** what is my reaction? I will make a direct and passionate plea to reiterate my fear.)

[**PLAYER 1** rears back, brick in hand.]

PLAYER 2: "Wait! Wait. I really don't want to get hit in the face with a brick." (TOIR4)

1 THINKS: (**If** I'm a dentist who employs violent methods in my treatment of patients, and I am dealing with a patient resistant to my methods, **then** what sort of similarly violent, alternate method can I offer to use? I can offer to put my patient under using a "sleeper hold.")

PLAYER 1: "Okay. I think I understand what your objection is. There's been some interesting research out of Harvard involving manual asphyxiation, or the 'sleeper hold,' in layman's terms. Let me show you..." (HGM3)

[PLAYER 1 grabs PLAYER 2 by the arms. PLAYER 2 frees himself and steps away from PLAYER 1.]

2 THINKS: *(If my dentist is moving toward me to strangle me, then what is my reaction? I will make another direct and passionate plea to reiterate my fear.*

PLAYER 2:   **"No! I don't want to get strangled." (TOIR5)**

1 THINKS: *(If my patient is protesting a common practice, then why is he protesting? Maybe he is misinterpreting what I consider to be a very common practice. I will disabuse him of his misinterpretation.)*

PLAYER 1:   "Strangulation involves death. This is a controlled procedure that will limit the flow of oxygenated blood to the brain." (EGM4)

Notice that the first "exploration Game move" in this scene happens before any heightened Game moves. This is because the first unusual thing should be reacted to and/or justified before the behavior can be made into a pattern. By focusing on exploration before heightening, the improvisers performing have made their comedy smart and not just silly.

All of the exploration Game moves and reactions in this scene are also funny. Remember that heightening isn't the only way to be funny. By offering strong reactions and justifications, these improvisers have maximized the comedy in the scene.

It is also worth noting that both characters are asking questions in this scene. New students of improv are often told to avoid questions. Remember, this rule only applies to the beginning of an Organic Scene when you are working to establish a reality and discover the first unusual thing. Asking questions in the Game section of the scene is acceptable, and often necessary to play the Game of the scene. Questions like the ones in this scene, which are helping the improvisers play their scene in a way that mirrors real life, actually serve the scene and are necessary for sound exploration Game moves.

EXPLORATION GAME MOVE EXPLANATIONS

Let's first look more specifically at each exploration Game move in this scene:

EGM1: Player 1 offers a reason for his character's absurd behavior. In his mind, there is risk and danger involved in most medical practices. This is a thought process that medical professionals employ in real life. By using realistic human behavior in the service of the absurd, Player 1 gets a laugh while making this scene smarter. This is the start of a philosophy that he can return to later in the scene.

EGM2: In this line, Player 1 doesn't have to search for a new philosophy. The same philosophy that was driving his character in his earlier exploration Game move is driving his character here. His understanding of risks involved with any available method of anesthesia is due to his standing as a trained medical professional. He is using his expertise to act in the best interests of his patient.

EGM3: Again, Player 1 simply returns to the philosophy already established to account for new absurd specifics. He has remained consistent and committed to his philosophy. This, in turn, makes his behavior a pattern. Each time he hits the pattern, he gets another laugh without having to do much more "work."

EGM4: Player 1 offers a justification of the strangulation heightened Game move that completely fits in his established philosophy. "Medical strangulation" is a method that he, a trained medical professional, is qualified to employ.

TOP OF YOUR INTELLIGENCE REACTION EXPLANATIONS

Now let's look more specifically at each reaction line that also plays the Game of the scene.

TOIR1: The first reaction is an example of strong top-of-intelligence play. The straight man in this scene is simply questioning the unusual and setting his scene partner up to offer a philosophy. It is unglamorous, but it is a necessary part of playing this Game.

TOIR2: The straight man reacts by challenging the philosophy of the absurd character. He points out that getting hit with a brick shares a consequence with gas-based anesthesia (memory loss).

TOIR3: The straight man once again reacts at the top of his intelligence by pointing out the similarity between getting hit with a brick and getting hit with a glove filled with rocks. He challenges the absurd as a person might in our reality. He can't believe this is happening, which is what one normally thinks when the unusual happens in the real world.

TOIR4: Player 2 reacts at the top of his intelligence, setting up Player 1 to heighten.

TOIR5: Player 2 reacts at the top of his intelligence, setting up Player 1 to offer another exploration Game move justifying the new absurd specific of using strangulation.

Now, we are going to look at the version of the one-night-stand scene that played the Game of "irrational fear of commitment."

EXAMPLE 3

[PLAYER 1 pulls out two chairs and places them close together. He gestures for PLAYER 2 to join him in the chairs. He leans back to give the appearance of lying up in a bed, so his scene partner matches this posture.]

PLAYER 1:   "Man, I'm exhausted."

PLAYER 2:   "Yeah. It's already 3 a.m."

PLAYER 1:   "This one-night stand is lasting longer than I thought it would."

PLAYER 2:   "What are you talking about? We just finished having sex."

PLAYER 1:   "It's getting weird. We're getting too close. You're already hanging around my apartment naked, your clothes are all over the place..."

PLAYER 2: "*You* just took those clothes off of me before we had sex!"

PLAYER 1: "See, we're spending too much time together. We are already fighting. Let's move on with our lives!"

PLAYER 2: "I've been in your apartment for 15 minutes."

PLAYER 1: "I'm trying to be a nice guy here. Every minute passed when we had sex is sending you the wrong message. I don't want to lead you on."

PLAYER 2: "It wouldn't be leading me on; letting me stay until the morning is just civil."

PLAYER 1: "No, that's cowardice. That's just some guy risking hurting you because he doesn't want to deal with the awkwardness of doing the right thing and asking you to leave."

PLAYER 2: "Look, we both know what a one-night stand is. We have sex, go to sleep, and maybe have breakfast."

PLAYER 1: "Okay, we have different ideas of what a one-night stand is. I think it ends right after sex and you think it ends at breakfast. So let's have breakfast. But it's just breakfast. I don't want you to show up tomorrow expecting breakfast. I think I have some waffles in the freezer..."

PLAYER 2: "I'm not upset because I might be getting cheated out of breakfast! All I want to do at this point is put on my clothes and get out of here." [Player 2 sits down to put on socks.]

PLAYER 1: "Now you're making me nervous."

PLAYER 2: "Why?"

PLAYER 1: "Sitting implies that you're comfortable enough to lounge around my place. I have given you the wrong idea..."

PLAYER 2:   "I'm getting dressed to leave, you jerk."

PLAYER 1:   "This is what I was afraid of. You stayed too long and now you are mad at me because you have false expectations. In a perfect world, there would be a portal in my bed that you would slip through right after we climax."

PLAYER 2:   "So I would just disappear?"

PLAYER 1:   "No! You keep looking at my intentions as dishonorable. The portal would drop you right into your own bed."

PLAYER 2:   "I should have never come here."

PLAYER 1:   "That's an even better idea! We should have had sex in a neutral place so that none of these kinds of misunderstanding would ever happen."

Let's reread the scene with all heightening, exploration, and reactions labeled.

The red lines in parentheses and italics illustrate the improviser's thought process and show you how they used the question "If this unusual thing is true, then what else is true?" to get to another heightened Game move. **Heightened Game moves are colored blue and labeled HGM# (explanations to follow):**

The purple sentences in parentheses and italics will illustrate the improviser's thought process, showing you how they used the question "If this unusual thing is true, then why is it true?" to explore. **Exploration Game moves are colored green and labeled EGM# (explanations to follow):**

The orange lines in parentheses and italics will illustrate the thought process leading to reactions that are at the top of one's intelligence. **These "top of your intelligence" reaction lines are in black and labeled TOIR# (explanations to follow):**

EXAMPLE 3

[PLAYER 1 pulls out two chairs and places them close together. He gestures for PLAYER 2 to join him in the chairs. He leans back to give the appearance of lying up in a bed, so his scene partner matches this posture.]

PLAYER 1:   "Man, I'm exhausted."

PLAYER 2:   "Yeah. It's already 3 a.m."

PLAYER 1:   "This one-night stand is lasting longer than I thought it would."

PLAYER 2:   "What are you talking about? We just finished having sex."

1 THINKS: (*If I think one-night stands should end immediately after I've finished having sex, **then** what else would fit this point of view? Since my character seems to have an irrational fear of commitment, I will point out other things that normally happen at a one-night stand [e.g., we are nude, her clothes are everywhere, etc.] and interpret them as signs of an intimate relationship.*)

PLAYER 1:   "It's getting weird. We're getting too close. You're already hanging around my apartment naked, your clothes are all over the place..." (HGM7)

2 THINKS: (*If my date is pointing out my clothes being all over the place as a sign of a serious relationship, **then** what is my reaction? I will point out that he took my clothes off before we had sex.*)

PLAYER 2:   "*You* just took those clothes off of me before we had sex!" (TOIR6)

1 THINKS: (*If I interpret everything my date does as a sign that things are moving too fast, **then** what can I interpret from her getting angry and yelling at me? I am going to assume that we are in a fight because we are spending too much time together.*)

PLAYER 1:   "See, we're spending too much time together. We are already fighting. Let's move on with our lives!" (HGM8)

2 THINKS: *(If my date thinks we are fighting because he thinks things are getting too serious too fast, **then** what else can I point out about the amount of time we've spent together to illustrate his absurdity? I will point out how little time we've spent together.)*

PLAYER 2:   "I've been in your apartment for 15 minutes." (HGM9)

1 THINKS: *(If my date thinks I am trying to end our evening prematurely, **then** why is my character trying to do this? I think that every minute we spend together is just leading her on.)*

PLAYER 1:   "I'm trying to be a nice guy here. Every minute passed when we had sex is sending you the wrong message. I don't want to lead you on." (EGM5)

2 THINKS: *(If my date thinks asking me to leave after we've had sex is being "nice," **then** what is my reaction? I will give him my grounded view of staying with a one-night stand until the morning.)*

PLAYER 2:   "It wouldn't be leading me on; letting me stay until the morning is just civil." (TOIR7)

1 THINKS: *(If my character doesn't believe staying with a one-night stand until the morning is civil, **then** why does he believe this? He thinks it is cowardly to lead a person on instead of dealing with them directly.)*

PLAYER 1:   "No, that's cowardice. That's just some guy risking hurting you because he doesn't want to deal with the awkwardness of doing the right thing and asking you to leave." (EGM6)

2 THINKS: *(If my date thinks asking me to leave is normal, **then** what is my reaction? I will react by clarifying what a one-night stand means.)*

PLAYER 2:   "Look, we both know what a one-night stand is. We have sex, go to sleep, and maybe have breakfast." (TOIR8)

1 THINKS: *(If my character thinks a one-night stand should end right after sex, then what is his opinion of having breakfast with a one-night stand? He doesn't have breakfast because he is afraid that one breakfast will lead to many future breakfasts.)*

PLAYER 1:   "Okay, we have different ideas of what a one-night stand is. I think it ends right after sex and you think it ends at breakfast. So let's have breakfast. But it's just breakfast. I don't want you to show up tomorrow expecting breakfast. I think I have some waffles in the freezer..." (HGM10)

2 THINKS: *(If my date thinks I'm going to bother him for breakfast tomorrow, then what is my reaction? I am going to put my clothes on and leave.)*

PLAYER 2:   "I'm not upset because I might be getting cheated out of breakfast! All I want to do at this point is put on my clothes and get out of here." (TOIR9)

[PLAYER 2 sits down to put on socks.]

1 THINKS: *(If I interpret everything my date does as a sign that things are moving too fast, then what can I interpret from her sitting down to get dressed? I am going to take her sitting down to mean that she is overly comfortable in my apartment.)*

PLAYER 1:   "Now you're making me nervous." (HGM11)

PLAYER 2:   "Why?"

PLAYER 1:   "Sitting implies that you're comfortable enough to lounge around my place. I have given you the wrong idea..." (HGM12)

2 THINKS: *(If my date is misinterpreting something as innocuous as sitting down, then what is my reaction? I am going*

PLAYER 2: **"I'm getting dressed to leave, you jerk." (TOIR10)**

1 THINKS: *(**If** my character has an irrational fear of commitment and believes that typical one-night stands lead to confusion and hurt feelings, **then** what does he think one-night stands should be like? He wishes that women would immediately be transported out of his apartment the second after sex is over.)*

PLAYER 1: **"This is what I was afraid of. You stayed too long and now you are mad at me because you have false expectations. In a perfect world, there would be a portal in my bed that you would slip through right after we climax." (HGM13)**

2 THINKS: *(**If** my date wishes that there were a portal in his bed for me to slip through after sex, **then** what is my reaction? I am offended and will assume the worst from his last statement.)*

PLAYER 2: **"So I would just disappear?" (TOIR11)**

1 THINKS: *(**If** my character wants a portal in his bed for transporting women away after sex, **then** why does he want this? By staying in line with the previous exploration, I am going to claim that this portal idea is another example of how I am a gentleman. The portal helps avoid hurt feelings.)*

PLAYER 1: **"No! You keep looking at my intentions as dishonorable. The portal would drop you right into your own bed." (EGM7)**

2 THINKS: *(If this one-night stand has gone this poorly, then what is my reaction? I am going to regret coming here.)*

PLAYER 2: **"I should have never come here." (TOIR12)**

1 THINKS:	(**If** my character has an irrational fear of commitment and believes that typical one-night stands lead to confusion and hurt feelings, **then** what is his ultimate one-night stand scenario? He believes people should avoid using their apartments and have sex in a neutral place.)
1 THINKS:	(**If** my character wants to have sex in a neutral place, **then** why does he want this? In staying in line with the previous exploration, I am going to claim that having sex in a neutral place helps people avoid hurt feelings.)
PLAYER 1:	"That's an even better idea! We should have had sex in a neutral place (HGM14) so that none of these kinds of misunderstanding would ever happen." (EGM8)

Before we discuss the exploration and reactions in this scene, let's point out a few things.

Make note of when Player 2 says, "What are you talking about? We just finished having sex." While this is a reaction at the top of Player 2's intelligence, it is also still establishing the base reality by letting us know the full context of the scene. Reactions at the top of your intelligence that happen early on in a scene will help you to find and solidify your Game before you actually start *playing* it.

Also note that this scene features heightening before exploration. The scene still works in spite of this. It is important to realize that every scene is not going to build in exactly the same way. (If you look back at the earlier "One-Night Stand" example, you will notice that it doesn't really ever explore or develop a strong reason why the character is trying to accelerate the relationship.) Always make choices that feel right for the scene you are performing. As long as you are looking to heighten, explore, and react at the top of your intelligence, your scene will turn out great even if it doesn't do all of those things in the exact order recommended in this chapter.

EXPLORATION GAME MOVE EXPLANATIONS

Let's discuss the exploration in this scene.

EGM5: This first exploration Game move begins to establish a point of view for Player 1's character. From his perspective, he isn't rushing his date out of his apartment because he is rude. He is trying to avoid hurting his date's feelings. He sees his irrational fear of intimacy as being considerate of others.

EGM6: This exploration is consistent with and strengthens Player 1's established logic. He feels as though he is protecting Player 2. He clearly sees himself as noble or altruistic. He isn't acting rude for no reason. There is a motivation for his behavior that makes his character seem more like a real person.

EGM7: Player 1 doesn't need to create new logic. He needs to build on what is already there. The desire for a bed portal is altruistic, suggested as a means to avoid hurt feelings.

EGM8: The idea of meeting to have sex in a neutral place is absurd and heightens the Game of "irrational fear of commitment," but is satisfying because it stays true to his established rationale of looking out for the feelings of his date.

TOP OF INTELLIGENCE REACTION EXPLANATIONS

Now let's look more specifically at each reaction line that also plays the Game of the scene.

TOIR6: In this first reaction line, Player 2 is pointing out the reality of the situation. By acting as a voice of reason, Player 2 makes Player 1's unusual behavior stand out in contrast.

TOIR7: Again, Player 2 reacts by offering the expectations a person might have in this situation. She is also setting up Player 1 to justify his unusual behavior.

TOIR8: In this reaction line, it seems as though Player 2 is trying to reset the conversation. She is taking a step back to make sure that she and Player 1 are operating from the same definition of one-night stand. This is what people often do in real life when they are confused.

TOIR9: Player 2 is reacting in line with the heightening of the scene. By showing her growing frustration with Player 1, she keeps the scene grounded while setting her scene partner up for further heightening.

TOIR10: Player 2's line of "I'm getting dressed to leave, you jerk" clarifies her point of view. She is clarifying her behavior in light of Player 1's interpretation of her decision to sit down and get dressed.

TOIR11: This is a reaction line that challenges the last heightened Game move. Player 2 continues to play the scene at the top of her intelligence.

TOIR12: In this line, Player 2 responds authentically, and she also sets Player 1 up for another heightening. Honest reactions will often serve as fuel for further heightening and exploration.

LISTENING HELPS YOU EXPLORE

If you continue to utilize listening throughout your scene, you will make playing your Game much easier. Listen to your scene partner's reaction to each of your lines. Each reaction will offer new information that informs your own choices and helps you to continue to heighten and explore your Game.

Listening is essential for exploration. Each new line may contain new specifics that will require justification. If you fail to listen and choose to play your Game by spouting off a never-ending rant, you will contribute so much information to the scene that your scene partner will not know which choices to justify or support.

If you don't listen, you will be essentially doing the scene by yourself, and you will inevitably "run dry." The lack of new information generated from working together will ultimately cripple your scene.

A failure to utilize listening when playing Game is referred to as steamrolling. Doing this will make you look bad to the audience and will make other members of your ensemble dislike performing with you. Although you may be getting laughs, acting selfishly and autonomously will make the scene a terrible experience for your scene partner.

WORK TOGETHER TO PLAY THE GAME

Long Form improvisation is not a solitary pursuit. While the stand-up comedian will get laughs from their own cleverness, the Long Form improviser will get laughs from the efforts of a group. It is much easier to listen to your scene partner for ideas than it is to come up with ideas on your own, out of the blue. In Long Form, you don't have the pressure of being hilarious by yourself. You can relieve some of the burden of being funny by working with someone else.

It is also important to note that listening is much more than a tool to make improvising easier. It is absolutely necessary for the success of any scene. No matter how strong you may believe your own idea is, it will be impossible to make your idea a reality on your own. This is because you will never be able to plan out what your scene partner may say or do.

The creation of a Long Form improv scene should come from somewhere to occur between both improvisers. This approach should actually make building scenes easier. It is like having two people work together to lift something heavy instead of one person doing it alone.

The only way you can truly embarrass yourself in Long Form is by NOT listening onstage. If you start plotting out the scene in your own head, you will be denying those ideas that your scene partner is contributing. If you disrespect your scene partner in this way, the scene will suffer, and you will ultimately be making yourself look bad.

THE IMPORTANCE OF PLAYING AT THE TOP OF YOUR INTELLIGENCE AS YOU EXPLORE

When you react at the top of your intelligence, you force yourself to use logic to explore your Game. Once you have found a Game, you want to play it as intelligently as possible. This means making exploration moves that support your Game in the most logical way. Playing at the top of your intelligence also means sustaining the reality of the scene (or everything that is not the Game) after the Game has been found. We want everything else in the scene that is not a Game move to be as close to reality as we know it. Sustaining this reality supports the pattern of absurd behavior. Offering reactions that are at the top of your intelligence will sustain the reality. A failure to react at the top of your intelligence will make the reality of the scene unnecessarily absurd or clever. This will only distract from the humor already being generated by your Game.

Commitment helps you to play at the top of your intelligence for the duration of the scene, whether you are reacting or exploring. Staying committed to your character's logical, realistic, top-of-intelligence point of view will help guarantee that you and your scene partner will be able to fully explore each new heightened Game move.

QUESTIONS IN THE SERVICE OF EXPLORATION

When you are playing the Game of the scene, playing at the top of your intelligence often manifests itself through your character asking questions. Asking a question often happens at the very beginning of your Game in order to frame the first unusual thing in a scene. By asking a question in reference to the absurd, you will ground your scene in reality and allow your scene partner a chance to ground his or her bizarre actions with reasonable logic.

Once you have found your Game, questions give you an opportunity to continue to explore it. We know that it is important to explore the logic behind what is absurd; otherwise, your scene will heighten too quickly, and you will miss nearly half of your opportunities to get laughs. Ultimately, questions will be necessary when you are playing at the top of your intelligence. Your character will ask questions at points during the scene when you would ask questions in real life.

EXERCISE: UNDERSTUDIES - REPRISE

INSTRUCTIONS

- Six to eight improvisers take the stage.

- Someone else in the group offers a one-word suggestion to inspire any two improvisers on the stage. The rest of the improvisers will stand on the back-line.

- Two improvisers will begin a scene, looking to clearly establish a reality containing a Who, What, and Where.

- The improvisers should continue to Yes And each other and get more specific until they discover the first unusual thing.

- Once the two improvisers performing the scene find the Game, one of the players on the back-line should **tag out** either improviser by tapping them on the shoulder. When an improviser is tagged out, they are taken out of the scene and replaced by the improviser that did the tagging. The person who has been tagged out will join the back-line.

- Usually an improviser tagging into a scene will play a new character. For this exercise, the improviser that tags in will take over the character that has already been established. In other words, the scene should continue exactly where it left off, with the same two characters and the same Game.

- Once the first tag-out happens, the rest of the improvisers on the back-line may begin to tag into the scene. **However, in this version of Understudies, you can't tag someone else out until the previous Game move has been explored. You may tag in to explore the last heightening, but you can't tag in to heighten again until exploration happens.** An improviser from outside of the group should be watching and stop the scene if someone tags in to heighten before exploration occurs.

- Either character can be tagged out and replaced as long as the new improviser enters to play the same Game.

- Afterward, discuss as a group which moves were on Game and which moves didn't work.

PURPOSE

- This version of Understudies will force you to focus on exploration by making you do it after every new heightening. This doesn't always have to happen so rigidly in scenes, but it is a great way to strengthen your exploration muscles.

- Multiple people working the same scene should offer a lot of creativity and variation in terms of exploration. Your goal as a group should be to make moves that complement and fall in line with earlier exploration moves.

- It will also give your group a chance to practice exploring without having to worry about any of the other responsibilities one must normally consider when performing a scene. Improvisers can watch the scene from the back-line and focus on exploring.

EXERCISE: PREMISE LAWYER

INSTRUCTIONS

- A group of at least three improvisers takes the stage and form a circle.

- One improviser steps into the circle to play the Premise Lawyer.

- Improvisers standing on the circle will raise their hands when they have a premise in mind.

- The premise lawyer will call on an improviser to hear their premise.

Note: The premise should be absurd so that it challenges the Premise Lawyer to defend it. For example, "I want my employees to double their productivity" isn't a premise, because wanting employees to increase productivity is not an unusual thing. A similar premise that would work might be, "I want my employees to work a 22-hour workday in order to double their productivity."

- The Premise Lawyer will then offer an exploration move that supplies a "why" for the absurd or unusual behavior or idea central to the premise.

EXAMPLES: (1) Premise: "I don't think people should drink water." Possible Exploration Move: "I'm really into conservation, so I think people are just wasting water every time they drink it."; (2) Premise: "Reading should not be taught in schools." Possible Exploration Move: "If we teach the children to read, they will eventually overthrow adults and assume control of the world."; (3) Premise: "I think bald women are more attractive." Possible Exploration Move: "Hair tends to get everywhere. I find bald women to be more hygienic."

VARIATIONS

- There is never only one correct way to justify a premise. To prove this and get more of your group involved, stand in a line. One member of your group will offer a premise. Go down the line until every other member has offered a different exploration move that justifies the premise. This version forces you to think creatively as the more "obvious" justifications are taken.

- The Premise Lawyer can offer his or her exploration move in character through a line of dialogue.

- After the Premise Lawyer has had a chance to defend a premise, the rest of the group can get involved and offer some exploration moves.

MAKE THE ABSURD BELIEVABLE

To play Game, you should always be heightening, exploring, or reacting. The key to making any Game work is making the absurd believable.

If you think about our day-to-day lives, we do ridiculous and completely idiotic things all of the time. When you make a poor choice or say something ridiculous in real life, your intention is not to make yourself look like a fool. It often seems like we are making the right choice in the moment. There is logic to and a reason for our actions.

This is how you want to approach playing characters in scenes. Your goal should be to make the absurd believable at all times, whether you are heightening, exploring, or reacting. Don't take on wacky or silly affectations. When you commit to the scene, you give your characters logic and reasons for their absurdity.

Let's return to the dentist scene once again.

Hitting someone over the head with a brick is the absurd element of the scene. For the sake of the scene, you should protest that. If you blindly agree to this procedure, you are ignoring the reality of a real presurgery patient and doctor interaction. Your character is now suddenly more absurd than the first unusual thing.

There are other options that exist within the extremes described in the above paragraph. If you respond to the brick line by saying, "Hmmm… that seems a little weird," you are resorting to clever commentary. As an improviser, you are acknowledging the funny idea in the scene instead of reacting to it as a character. If you respond to the brick line by exclaiming, "You're crazy! I'm out of here!" you have gone from "zero to sixty." This is a response you have to earn. People don't come to conclusions immediately about things that seem unusual.

When you take the time to react, question, or offer moves that fit your character's logic, you are making the absurd believable. Be as real as you can. Stay true to the moment of the experience every step of the way throughout a Long Form scene.

CHAPTER 6:

Using Character to Play Game

Creating characters in Long Form improvisation is much more than speaking in a funny voice or moving around the stage with a silly walk. The vast majority of the time, you will be able to portray characters that are very different from yourself without ever changing your voice or the way you walk. When you do make specific choices about how your character sounds or moves, it should be to support a Game, not to get a laugh for acting weird.

CHARACTER TYPES

Beyond playing a version of yourself at the top of your intelligence, there are essentially three possibilities for portraying characters in a Long Form scene.

CHARACTERS CLOSE TO SELF

The first possibility is to play an **everyman character**. An everyman walks, talks, and sounds like you do, and he has a rational, grounded point of view that adheres to the expected pattern of reality. The straight man is almost always an everyman character. If the character you are playing could just as easily walk and talk the way that you do, it isn't necessary for you to adopt any sort of affectation.

For example, you might be called on to play a doctor in a scene. Even though you aren't actually a doctor, you can choose to have the doctor you are playing walk and talk exactly as you do. Choosing to play yourself will increase the chances of starting the scene in a grounded reality, making it easier for you to recognize the first unusual thing in your scene.

Once a Game has presented itself, the doctor you are playing may become more of a character because of his ideology or point of view. However, there is no reason to change the way you speak or move. The viewpoint will separate the character from you, the improviser.

CHARACTERS DIFFERENT FROM SELF

The second possibility is to play a support character. A **support character** sounds or moves differently from you in order to serve the reality of the scene. These differences are necessary to play the character in a realistic way. These differences are not there to get laughs. When you are playing a support character, it is important that you do so truthfully, not to a heightened degree in order to get laughs. Your character choice is aiding the reality of the scene.

For example, if you are a twenty-something male improviser and your scene partner labels you as an old woman in their initiation, it will be distracting to the reality of the scene if you have your old woman sound and move like you do. Remember, you don't have a costume or makeup to make this character believable. Changing the way you walk or talk, without being too broad, is going to better serve your reality than being an old woman who walks and talks like a young man. You might want to adopt a feminine pitch to your voice, move slowly, and walk with a stooped posture to portray this old woman.

If you are a female improviser playing an NFL linebacker, you will also need to change the way you sound and move. If you don't, one of two things will happen. Either you will be a distraction from the Game of the scene by drawing attention to yourself as an improviser, or worse, you will unintentionally take over the Game of the scene, because the strange behavior of this NFL football player (i.e., his acting like a woman) will automatically stand out as the most unusual thing. Make a character choice as the NFL football player, play it realistically or at the top of your intelligence, and find a Game organically within this situation.

CHARACTER AS GAME

The third possibility is when the character you are portraying essentially is the Game of the scene. These characters are referred to as **Game characters**. Just as the Game of the scene has a funny, consistent pattern, a Game character that is serving as the Game of the scene will have a funny, consistent pattern of behavior. When a Game character is in a scene, the Game of the scene is played through heightening and exploring the Game character's behavior. "Bigger" or "more extreme" characteristics are justified in these circumstances because they don't distract from the Game; they are an integral part of the Game.

If you are playing a lifeguard who is acting like an intense Vietnam veteran, the absurdity of the lifeguard's behavior will become the Game of the scene. The Game will be played through asking, "If this lifeguard is acting like a Vietnam vet, then what other things might he say or do?" Your behavior as this character will answer this question and become the Game of your scene.

In this example, playing this scene like a "normal" lifeguard won't support your Game. As an improviser, you must be conscious of both content and performance choices. Maybe if you refer to the other summers you have worked as a lifeguard as your previous "tours of duty," you will do so in a grave voice, squinting your eyes and staring off into the distance. Using the term "tours of duty" is a content choice. Saying it in a grave voice and squinting your eyes would be performance choices. Your response to kids running around the perimeter of the pool might be a panicked barking of orders to napalm the entire YMCA, delivered with the urgency you would expect to hear from someone trying to evacuate a base camp under fire. Again, ordering the napalm is a content choice; doing so with urgency is a performance choice.

PORTRAYING CHARACTERS IN LONG FORM

CHARACTERS AT THE TOP OF YOUR INTELLIGENCE

Acting and commitment to character choices are just as important in Long Form improvisation as they are in written materials such as plays, television shows, movies, etc. The fact that you are creating your characters in the moment without rehearsals, costumes, or a script doesn't make you exempt from acting well when portraying them. Whether you have trained as an actor or not, a Long Form scene requires you to do the best acting that you possibly can. Act to the best of your ability. Don't use bad acting as a source of comedy in your scene. Play your character as though you are trying to convince the audience that the character is real. Every time you succeed in doing this, you are playing your character at the top of your intelligence.

The importance of "acting well" in Long Form improv cannot be stressed enough. However, this is not to say that you need to spend two years studying at an acting conservatory in order to perform Long Form improvisation. You will act well if you play at the top of your intelligence, which will have the effect of grounding your characters in reality. Most of the time, simply speaking, moving, and reacting as you do in everyday life will be enough to serve the scene.

A key element to making your character choices work in Long Form is your commitment to the choices you make. Once you have created a specific perspective for your character, it is important that you remain true to it. If you have adopted a different manner of speaking or moving in order to play your character, it is important that you remain consistent and committed to these choices. Commitment to these choices will take the focus away from the fact that "the improviser is playing a character," and put it on what the character is doing and saying. You should never sell your character out for a laugh (e.g., commenting on how poor your accent is or calling out that you are extremely tall for a child).

The characters you play onstage should only differ from yourself as necessitated by the Game. Character eccentricities without justification or relevance to the Game are distracting. This is not to say that there is no room for character work in the Upright Citizens Brigade style of improv, but characters in UCB improv must always support or embody a Game.

Character choices should be inspired by the suggestion or the choices made during the creation of the base reality of your scene. You should not make choices to simply show off your favorite stock characters. In other words, don't rely on your **bag of tricks**. While you may have a great Southern Lawyer or Hyperactive Six-year-old in your back pocket, arbitrarily forcing these characters into a scene will ring false. Honor the process and your scene partner by making choices in the moment that serve your scene. However, if it serves the scene, pulling your Southern Lawyer or Hyperactive Six-year-old out of your bag of tricks is valid and appropriate.

CREATING GAME CHARACTERS

When you create a Game character for yourself in a Long Form scene, you use the same process you use to find a Game in an Organic Scene. Broad choices or preplanning are unnecessary when it comes to creating memorable characters. Let's say you start a scene with this simple initiation:

"Ugh. Birthday cake. How meaningless."

By choosing a specific attitude or point of view that is unusual and breaks the expected pattern of reality, you have already told us a lot about your character with only a few simple words. You have provided a starting point for developing a character. This statement is not really about birthday cake; it's about the type of person who has this response to being thrown a birthday party. From this line, you can develop a character by asking, "If this unusual thing is true, then what else is true?"

By asking this question, you might decide to adopt a specific voice affectation or movement to continue filling out this character. Maybe this person speaks in low tones at a slow tempo. Maybe he shuffles his feet when he walks. You will also want to ask why your character is behaving this way to ensure that you explore as well as heighten this character's Game.

The following are lines of dialogue that would be considered heightening Game moves for this Game character:

"A birthday is just one year closer to death."

"Material possessions mean nothing, for eventually we will all fall into the great abyss of nothingness."

The following are lines of dialogue that would be considered exploration Game moves for this Game character:

"Instead of singing the birthday song, my family would gather around to contemplate the indifference of the universe towards us all."

"My father was an existentialist. My mother was a nihilist."

All of these lines would be supporting the initial choice you made with your first line. When you are playing a Game character, you won't feel desperate about making each line funny. If you make choices that are consistent with your character, you will get laughs. Making choices that support your character will allow you to play the Game of your scene.

Usually, the most inspired and fully realized characters come from a real place in the improviser's life as opposed to being cartoonish archetypes. A family member, coach or good friend can serve as inspiration for those characters you have to play that are especially different from you. You can even draw on characters you have seen in television, films, the news, or documentaries as a reference to play those characters that are outside of your natural type.

PRIMARY   SECONDARY   TERTIARY

The more you actually know about the type of person you are playing, the better you will be able to make your character seem real. When drawing on real people and fictional characters that you are familiar with in order to portray a character, you should always choose the option that you are closest to. **Primary sources** are the real people that you actually know and have interacted with. Whenever you have the opportunity to tap into a primary source when portraying a character, you should. **Secondary sources** are real people that you have seen in media, such as documentaries or news programs. **Tertiary sources** are preexisting fictional characters. For example, if you were playing a mafia boss, you might draw inspiration from Don Corleone in *The Godfather* or Tony Soprano in *The Sopranos*. These will be the least effective since you will be doing an impression of an impression.

No matter what source you draw your inspiration from, don't allow yourself to slip into caricature. Real specifics will make any character choice seem real and your job easier because you won't have to struggle to fabricate these specifics. Portraying characters three-dimensionally and with integrity will help you avoid cheap or easy laughs. Don't make hacky, obvious or cheesy choices in your portrayal. Committing to the reality will increase your odds of being able to find and play a Game. Find the truth in your characters.

Even the most three-dimensional characters can be problematic if you force them into a scene where they do not belong. You may get laughs, but you will do so at the expense of the greater good of the scene.

EXERCISE: CREATING CHARACTERS FROM BELIEFS

INSTRUCTIONS

- Your entire group should take the stage.

- Walk around and take turns speaking. When someone speaks, everyone else should stop walking and listen. When they have finished speaking, everyone can move again.

- Start by stating personal beliefs or opinions. Stay away from jokes and be as honest as possible. These statements should be simple, even mundane personal opinions. Examples: "You should never read the ending of a book first." "You should take a nap every day." "You should turn the lights off when you leave a room." "Always yield to pedestrians in a crosswalk."

- After walking and sharing statements for a few minutes, form a back-line.

- Take turns initiating scenes as characters that embody one of the personal beliefs that was shared. The personal belief shared will serve as the inspiration or starting point for a character. Each improviser must use a belief other than the one he or she shared.

- As the scene progresses, ask yourself, "If this unusual thing is true, then what else is true?" or, "If this unusual thing is true, then why is it true?" Even though you are starting with something simple, you can find ways to heighten and explore this initial belief (e.g., the person who believes that you should turn the lights off when you leave a room might grow into someone who is militant about conservation).

- You don't literally have to repeat the belief as the start of the scene. For example, if you're working off of someone saying, "You should never read the ending of a book first," you might initiate a scene by saying, "I like to see the mystery of life unfold in the moment." You have started your scene with the intent behind this belief but not the exact wording. You should be asking yourself, "If this type of person never reads the ending of a book first, then what else would they do? What type of person is that to me?" Maybe this person has always packed up their things in a truck, driven to a new city, and then looked for an apartment. Maybe this person is really bad at chess, since he or she avoids thinking several moves ahead.

PURPOSE

- This exercise will help you practice making Game character choices.

- This exercise is also an opportunity to practice committing to or remaining consistent with a Game character.

EXERCISE: USING PHYSICAL CHARACTERISTICS TO CREATE CHARACTERS

INSTRUCTIONS

- Your entire group should get onstage except for one person.

- Start walking around the room and acknowledge each other without speaking.

- You should try to notice, as you walk, which part of your body you naturally lead with. People tend to lead with their heads, chest, pelvis, or feet as they walk.

- Once you have all figured out what you lead with, you should exaggerate leading with that body part and play with how it makes you feel—what kinds of characters does it suggest to you?

- The person sitting out will then call out different body parts. The rest of the group will then simultaneously switch to the announced body part (head, chest, pelvis, feet, etc.) as a group.

- Each time a new body part is called out, allow yourself to discover a character based on how your movements make you feel. Then mingle with the other characters onstage, having two- to three-line exchanges with them.

- Now only two improvisers take the stage to use this same process to make character choices for scenes.

- Both improvisers should create characters by changing how they move physically. The improvisers can either choose a body part to lead with on their own, or another member of the group can give them suggestions. The two improvisers should walk around the stage in this new way until they "find" characters.

- The improvisers should once again be thinking, What kind of people walk this way? What do they enjoy? What do they hate? What kinds of things might they say? What is their status (high vs. low)? What is their worldview (optimist vs. pessimist)?

- Once both improvisers seem ready, have someone else from your group give them a one-word suggestion to inspire a short scene.

- The two improvisers should be able to incorporate whatever they have decided about these characters into the scene, no matter what the circumstances of the scene are.

- If your scene partner is the first to speak, and verbally identifies you as a character different than what you have decided upon, you should abandon your character choice and go with theirs while maintaining your physical behavior. Example: Your movement caused you to feel like you were an old person who has difficulty walking. Before you can make this clear with dialogue, your scene partner interprets your movement as the walk of a toddler and labels you as such. While maintaining the same walk, you should play this scene as a toddler.

PURPOSE

- This exercise shows you how you can bolster your character choices through physicality. If you're playing a high-powered CEO who is confident and in charge, you could make the quick choice to lead with the body part that makes you feel this way.

EXERCISE: USING STATUS TO BUILD A CHARACTER

INSTRUCTIONS

- Your entire group should get onstage.

- Start walking around the room and acknowledge each other without speaking.

- As you pass each other, you should try to act as if you are a bit higher in status than everyone else you interact with. Each interaction should also serve to increase your status.

- Try to find different ways to express your status (e.g., not making eye contact, walking with a swagger, walking with good posture, etc.).

- After a few minutes, someone will announce that everyone in the group born in the months of January through June should reverse and become lower in status with each interaction, so that about half the group will be going for high status and half low.

- After a few more minutes, everyone should go for low status, trying to be the lowest status of every interaction.

- When you have finished acting low in status, have everyone take a seat and discuss the exercise. Talk about how people with higher status look and behave compared to someone with low status.

- Now, only two improvisers get up onstage.

- Someone else in the group should assign one improviser to be high-status and the other low-status.

- Someone else in the group should give these two improvisers a one-word suggestion to inspire a scene.

- Tell them that in addition to the Who, What, and Where, they should make their status toward each other clear in their first three lines. These are quick scenes. Someone else watching the scene should stop the scene after about a minute. It is not necessary for the improvisers to find the Game in these quick scenes.

- Next, have the same two improvisers rewind the scene, repeating the same lines again but with the status reversed.

- Replaying the exact same scene with different status helps to highlight that your role in the scene is not the same as your status (e.g., a boss can be high-status one time and low-status the second but still be trying to talk to his employee about doing overtime).

- Notice the distinction between the assumed status in life and status in the scene. You can be a very high-status butler and a low-status president. When we talk about status, we are referring to the behavior of the characters, not their assumed status in life. You should also notice that high status does not necessary equal "mean" or "evil" or "loud." You can be a quiet, serene, magnanimous high-status character.

EXERCISE: USING PEOPLE YOU KNOW TO CREATE CHARACTERS

INSTRUCTIONS

- Two improvisers should take the stage.

- Each improviser should take on the mannerisms of someone they know well. Specifically, they should think about how this person moves, behaves, etc. Focus on using behavior, not biographical history, as the inspiration for each character.

- The improvisers should then say a few lines of dialogue in character to the rest of the group in order to display their character choices.

- Next, the improvisers will get a one-word suggestion from someone else in the group to inspire a scene using these characters.

- Biographical information from the real person's life should not complicate the scene. For example, if the character in the scene is labeled a doctor, it should not be a point of confusion if the person inspiring this character is not a doctor in real life.

- While the improvisers will start the scene with characters, they will still have to define the relationship between the characters to fully establish the Who of the scene.

- Note that one of the two specific characters can still function as a straight man in this scene, even though the improviser may be behaving very differently from his or her true self.

CHARACTER ENDOWMENT

Sometimes you will be called on to create a character when someone
else makes a choice for you. Let's say that you are a 22-year-old
American college student. You may enter into a scene neutrally,
as yourself, but then your scene partner initiates with:

"I asked you to rustle up those steer and put 'em in the corral."

OR

**"Mr. Freemont, if you don't take your medication, you
won't be able to do your water aerobics class."**

OR

"Billy! Get off the jungle gym now, it's nap time."

In order to Yes And your scene partner in any of these situations, you
would have to immediately be the type of person implied or suggested
by their initiation. Since you are not a cowboy, an old man, or a child
on a playground, you will need to make some character choices to make
your acting in this scene believable.

PEAS IN A POD

If your scene partner steps out and makes a strong character choice, you have the option of matching or mirroring this character choice. These scenes are referred to as peas-in-a-pod scenes.

In a peas-in-a-pod scene, neither character questions or challenges what is absurd because they both accept and agree with the absurdity in a scene. In these scenes, it is beneficial for the characters to acknowledge the outside, reasonable world as we know it so that the world around them can act as a straight man and provide the characters with an opportunity to explore and justify their absurd behavior. In movies like *Bill & Ted's Excellent Adventure* and *Dumb & Dumber*, or the TV show *Absolutely Fabulous*, two peas-in-a-pod characters run through a gauntlet of straight men in the world as we know it. In a peas-in-a-pod Long Form improv scene, the absurd characters must imply the world as we know it (unless a third character enters as a straight man). By doing this, they remind the audience of the base reality against which the unusual is funny, and they provide themselves with opportunities to explore their absurd behavior.

Let's say we're watching an Organic Scene in which this initiation has been offered:

PLAYER 1:   "I don't see what the big deal is with oxygen. I haven't used it in months."

Since this initiation is so plainly absurd, Player 2 has the option of responding to it as a straight man. But if Player 2 wants to match characters here, he may say something like:

PLAYER 2:   "Tell me about it. I can't believe how everyone at that party last night just kept breathing it in."

Player 2 has adopted the same point of view as Player 1. He has not challenged or questioned Player 1's initiation because he shares the same belief.

PLAYER 1:   "My roommate is always saying, 'You'd be dead without oxygen because you need it for your muscles and brain to function.'"

PLAYER 2:   "Fish have muscles and brains, and they don't need air."

PLAYER 1:   "Yeah, and humans are superior to fish. I've trained my muscles and brain to survive on energy drinks."

Even though these characters have the same absurd point of view, they have grounded the scene by reminding us of the real world through the roommate's objection to their theory. By defending their point of view against the roommate's objection, they explore their Game.

Matching your scene partner's character will sometimes help you to start off a scene in agreement. Two peppy cheerleaders, two wild and crazy guys, or two backwoods dimwits from the Great White North are going to have a lot in common, which will make for easy Yes And–ing. Matching can help you start your scenes with characters that have an implied relationship and share common experiences, beliefs, backgrounds, etc.

This technique is best suited for Organic Scenes. In a Premise Scene, matching can be a problematic approach. If you are doing premise-based improv and your scene partner comes out with a strong character, it is best to remain neutral until you know what your scene partner wants from you. Matching could undermine the premise they want to play with.

EXERCISE: THE CHAMELEON

INSTRUCTIONS

- Six to eight improvisers get onstage and form a back-line.

- One improviser will step forward and volunteer to be "the chameleon" in three to four quick scenes. The chameleon will remain center stage as three to four improvisers step forward, one after another, to initiate scenes.

- Without getting suggestions, each of these improvisers will step out from the back-line and initiate a scene with a strong character choice. The chameleon should then **match** that character, and they will perform a short scene.

- Matching means that you play the same type of character by taking on the same energy, beliefs, likes, dislikes, physicality, etc. The chameleon shouldn't repeat their scene partner's lines; they just need to match the character choice.

- After the first chameleon has matched three to four characters, they should step to the back-line, allowing another improviser to step forward to become the next chameleon.

- As the improviser coming from the back-line with a character, do not initiate any of these scenes with a line that makes it difficult for the chameleon to match you. (Example: An improviser steps out playing an incredibly old woman and says, "Young man, it is so kind of you to come visit me." It will be difficult for the scene partner to match this choice since they have been set up to portray a young man.)

PURPOSE

- This exercise will allow you to practice playing Game in a peas-in-a-pod scene.

- This exercise is also a great way to expand your range in terms of playing Game characters. You will be forced to match choices that your scene partners make, which may be very different from the sort of characters you tend to play. Taking risks with character choices in this exercise can get you out of your comfort zone more often in scenes.

CHAPTER 7:

Using Support Moves to
Play Game as a Group

Every member of an improv group should share responsibility for the success of each and every scene. When you are not one of the main characters of the scene, you do this through **support work**. Through listening and paying full attention to the scene that is happening, you will know when support is necessary and appropriate.

Through various support techniques, every member of the ensemble can work together to play the Game of a scene. Once a Game has been found, **support moves** are primarily used to clarify, heighten, or explore the Game of the scene. Support techniques allow those improvisers with an outside perspective on the scene to contribute to its success.

Support moves are made during scenes by the rest of the ensemble from the back-line. Support moves are generally only made in the service of a Game. The following section will review a number of different support moves available to you.

WALK-ONS

A **walk-on** is when an improviser from the back-line enters the scene to help find the Game, play the Game, or support the reality of the scene. Walk-ons that happen before a Game is found should be done to clarify or "underline" a Game that two improvisers are close to finding but seem unclear or unsure of in some way. In these instances, a walk-on will help the improvisers in a scene nail down their Game. Walk-ons can also be used to heighten or explore an already established Game. In some walk-ons, you will directly make a Game move. In some walk-ons, you will provide an opportunity for the characters in the scene to make a Game move. In a peas-in-a-pod scene, a walk-on might simply offer a grounded reality against which the strange behavior can stand out in contrast. Sometimes a walk-on will be made to support the reality of the scene by adding a necessary support character (e.g., a waiter in a restaurant scene or a stenographer in a courtroom scene).

Let's first look at an example of an improviser from the back-line underlining a Game for two people performing a scene.

EXAMPLE 1

[You are on the back-line, watching a scene in progress between a pet store owner and a customer in a pet store. It has become clear to you that a pattern of behavior of an absurdly cheap customer has been established, but from the tentative nature of their play onstage, it seems that the improvisers in the scene are unsure of the potential Game. You could walk on to this scene as the customer's son with a line that brings into focus the Game they've already been playing.]

SON: [walking on] **"Hey Dad, look! Alpo! That's what we had for dinner last night."**

CHEAP GUY: **"Last night and last night only. Remember, that was a special birthday dinner treat."**

You have not imposed your own Game; you have underlined their existing Game. The last line from Cheap Guy indicates that he now gets the Game.

Now that all of the improvisers are on the same page, let's look at some examples of additional walk-ons that heighten or explore the Game.

EXAMPLE 2

SON: [walking on] **"Hey Dad, look! Alpo! That's what we had for dinner last night."**

CHEAP GUY: **"Last night and last night only. Remember, that was a special birthday dinner treat."**

DAUGHTER: [walking on] **"Don't forget, Dad. You promised we could go to the supermarket tonight and have 'free sample' dinner."**

This walk-on has heightened the Game of this scene by showing a new way that this character is cheap.

The improviser playing the daughter could have also walked on to explore the Game move made by Cheap Guy.

EXAMPLE 3

SON: [walking on] **"Hey Dad, look! Alpo! That's what we had for dinner last night."**

CHEAP GUY: **"Last night and last night only. Remember, that was a special birthday dinner treat."**

DAUGHTER: **"You know what Dad always says: 'If we ate wet dog food every day then it wouldn't be special on our birthday.'"**

This line has explored the Game by endowing Cheap Guy with a philosophy that explains why he thinks that Alpo is for birthdays only.

If Cheap Guy and his kids proceed to the checkout, you could walk on to this scene by entering as a cashier. This would be an example of a walk-on that supports the reality of the scene. The cashier may or may not make a move that heightens or explores this Game, but it will allow Cheap Guy and his kids to move the scene forward to where it would go next in reality. Continuing to support the reality of the scene is how the back-line can set up the improvisers in the scene for further Game playing.

Whenever you perform a walk-on, you want to choose a character that naturally fits into the scenario already established. The children and the cashier in the examples above are germane to this scenario. It is reasonable to think that this man would bring his kids shopping with him. It is also reasonable to think that a cashier would be working in this pet store. Having the Cheap Guy's boss show up at the pet store would seem coincidental and forced, even if the boss played into the Game of the customer being cheap.

Make sure that your walk-ons are supportive and altruistic, not self-serving. You should only remain in a scene as long as is necessary to support it and then leave. For example, while a stenographer would remain onstage for the entirety of a courtroom scene, a waiter would exit after taking an order. Self-serving walk-ons will derail a Game that is already in progress. For example, you may have an Old Crazy Cat Lady character that you love to do. If you enter the "Cheap Guy" scene as this character to say, "I need 500 pounds of cat food for my thirty cats," you haven't played the "Cheap Guy" Game; you've only taken an opportunity to make the scene about you. This walk-on also fails to support the established base reality. While it is somewhat reasonable to think that a woman like this might be in the pet shop, this character is distracting because it adds a new unusual element to the scene. This would not be a supportive walk-on.

TAG-OUTS

The tag-out is a support technique whereby an improviser from the back-line takes the Game of the scene to a new time (and sometimes a new place) by substituting him or herself for one or more of the characters already in the scene. A tag-out is communicated through a tap on the shoulder or a wave of the hand. Someone from the back-line tapping you on the shoulder is your signal to leave the scene and go to the back-line. The improviser that tagged you out will enter as a brand-new character and essentially start a new scene playing the same Game with the improviser that was not tagged out. The improviser left in the scene continues playing the same character.

You should only tag into a scene with the intention of heightening or exploring the Game. After tagging in, make any changes to the Who, What, and Where very clear with a strong, physical choice and a concise, clear first line. Doing so will ensure that your scene partner understands the new context in which you wish to play the Game.

You can tag out either character in a scene as long as you bring the Game into the next scene. You want to ask yourself, What is another situation that I can place one of these characters in to continue to play the Game of this scene?

It is up to the rest of the back-line to determine the length of a tag-out. Some tag-outs will develop into full scenes, whereas others may be played out after only a few exchanges. It is your job on the back-line to get your teammates out of the scene when their idea has run its course. Once tag-outs start, you should always be thinking, What is another new situation in which to play this Game?

Let's return to the "Cheap Guy" scene for an example of a tag-out:

EXAMPLE 1

[Let's imagine that the Game has been clearly established with only the Pet Store Owner and Cheap Guy onstage. Watching from the back-line, you tag out the improviser playing the Pet Store Owner to play a Doctor.]

DOCTOR: **"We are going to have to operate on your heart. Because of insurance, it will actually only be fifteen dollars."**

CHEAP GUY: **"Fifteen dollars?! I'd rather die tomorrow than be robbed today!"**

The scene can either continue from this point, or another improviser can tag in to put the Cheap Guy into another situation.

SON: **"Dad, look! A wishing well! Can I have a penny to throw in?"**

CHEAP GUY: **"A penny? No, honey. Daddy is not made of money."**

Tag-outs should only be used to play the Game of the scene. Every tag-out that happens in this series of scenes should focus on heightening or exploring how cheap the character is.

Now let's look at some bad examples that do not play the Game.

EXAMPLE 2

[Let's imagine that once again, the Game has been clearly established with only the Pet Store Owner and Cheap Guy onstage. Watching from the back-line, you tag out the improviser playing Cheap Guy to play the Pet Store Owner's wife.]

WIFE:	"How was work today, dear?"
PET STORE OWNER:	"Pretty typical. Although I did have one customer who was incredibly cheap."

This is a bad tag-out because we're not playing the Game, we're merely referencing it. This is a tag-out that is following the plot of the Pet Store Owner, not the Game of being severely cheap.

Let's take a look at another tag-out that doesn't work.

EXAMPLE 3

[Let's imagine that once again, the Game has been clearly established with only the Pet Store Owner and Cheap Guy onstage. Watching from the back-line, you tag out the improviser playing the Pet Store Owner to play the Cheap Guy's wife.]

WIFE:	"Honey, don't forget. Katie's parent-teacher conference is this Friday."
CHEAP GUY:	"Hopefully her teacher will be able to explain why she's having so much trouble with math lately."

Again, this tag-out is following the plot of Cheap Guy's life. We are not interested in the story of his life; we are interested in seeing other situations in which he gets to be ridiculously cheap. Tagging in as his wife could potentially lead to playing the Game, but the improviser playing the wife needs to make choices—about what they are discussing or where the scene is taking place—that will focus on the "cheap" Game.

Let's look at another tag-out featuring Cheap Guy's wife that is on Game.

EXAMPLE 4

[Let's imagine that once again, the Game has been clearly established with only the Pet Store Owner and Cheap Guy onstage. Watching from the back-line, you tag out the improviser playing the Pet Store Owner to play the Cheap Guy's wife.]

WIFE:	"Honey, putting a tent in the yard is not a vacation."

CHEAP GUY: "What if I play this tape of ocean sounds on my old boom box?"

A series of tag-outs in quick succession is referred to as a **tag-out run**. In a good tag-out run, the back-line will be mindful of the length of each new tag-out. In a bad tag-out run, a new tag-out will happen before an idea is given a chance to play out in the previous scene or tag-out. Be sure that you allow the person remaining in the scene to respond to each new tag-out before tagging in again. You don't want to let the ongoing scene get hijacked with tag-outs. Give each new tag-out scene the length of time it needs to be successful before offering another tag-out, whether that ends up being two lines or two minutes.

A good tag-out run will heighten the Game. Let's imagine a scene in a laundromat. A man is late to pick up his shirt. The lady working there explains that since they are busy and have such little space, she destroyed it. Another improviser tags in to play a woman who is late to pick up her wedding dress. Again, it has been destroyed. Another improviser tags in to play a father who says, "Thanks for watching my son. I'm sorry I took longer than five minutes. Where is he?" The woman from the laundromat explains that she killed the son due to being busy and a lack of space. All of these tags follow the same logic while heightening the Game.

SPLIT SCENES

A **split scene** is a technique that allows you to perform two scenes onstage simultaneously. These scenes usually take place in the same time frame but always in separate locations. A split scene happens when two improvisers from the back-line initiate another scene that is somehow relevant to the scene already in progress without ending the original scene. A good time to use split scenes is when someone in the original scene refers to something interesting or important to the Game that is taking place somewhere else, usually at the same time.

When you are initiating a split scene, you can cue another improviser to join you by making eye contact with them. You cue another improviser by grabbing his or her arm, stepping downstage and to the side of the existing scene already in progress without acknowledging it. Stepping downstage is important so that any improvisers already onstage can see you. If you were to start a split scene behind the improvisers onstage, they might assume that you are occupying the same physical space as their characters. A strong initiating line or a physical choice that clearly does not fit the logic of the scene already happening will also serve as a cue to the improvisers onstage that a split scene is starting. As the improvisers performing the split scene begin talking, the other improvisers should fall silent and begin miming as they listen to the new scene. The improvisers in both scenes must give and take focus.

The following is an example of a split scene:

EXAMPLE 1

PLAYER 1: "Mom and Dad said I get to play a game before I go to bed."

PLAYER 2: "Yeah, yeah, they told me when we went over the emergency numbers. You know how to play quarters?"

[From the back-line, Player 3 initiates a split scene. Player 3 makes eye contact with two other improvisers from the back-line. All three improvisers step downstage off of the back-line without acknowledging the improvisers in the scene already in progress. Player 3 mimes holding a drink. Players 4 and 5 mirror this choice.]

PLAYER 3: "You two don't know how lucky you are to have found a responsible babysitter."

PLAYER 4: **"We know. We've been using her for years."**

Both scenes could continue simultaneously, with the improvisers splitting focus between the couple having an evening out and the kids running around wild with an irresponsible babysitter.

Split scenes should be somehow related to the scene that is already happening. They are often used to explore some unusual element that arises in the scene already in progress. You don't want to have two completely random and unrelated scenes happening concurrently.

SWINGING DOORS

A **swinging door** is when an improviser from the back-line momentarily takes one of the two characters in the scene to a different place or time. When one of these moments happens in a scene, an improviser from the back-line will grab an improviser from the scene onstage by the shoulders. The improviser being grabbed is called the "swinging door." The improviser from the back-line will physically turn the swinging door around so that they are face-to-face. (The swinging door's original scene partner should freeze and remain unaffected while this moment happens.) The person from the back-line and the swinging door will then have an exchange. After the moment is over, the person from the back-line will "swing" the swinging door back into the original scene, which will start again exactly where it left off.

This technique is called a swinging door because we are taking one central character and swinging him or her back and forth from scene to scene, like a swinging door between two rooms. Swinging doors can be used to go forward or backward in time, but they should always be inspired by something that has happened in the scene. After a swinging door scene happens, you always return to the original scene.

Swinging doors are used to "show" a moment that was just talked about in the scene without losing the characters and the scene already in progress. If one of the characters mentions something specific, interesting, and/or funny, an improviser might be inspired to use a swinging door to make this moment happen live. It should be one of those moments that you immediately wish that you were seeing onstage, instead of just talking about it.

Let's look at an example:

EXAMPLE 1

[In this scene, the Game that has been established is about a girl that is only attracted to extremely dangerous men. The girl is talking to her mother.]

MOTHER: "Two of your previous boyfriends are death-row inmates. You have a tendency to date dangerous men."

GIRL: "You're totally exaggerating, Mom."

MOTHER: "I am not. I don't want you to be dating this current boyfriend of yours anymore. He's very dangerous."

[An improviser from the back-line can swing the improviser playing the girl out to show her with the boyfriend.]

BOYFRIEND: "I can't believe that your Mom thinks I'm dangerous. I always keep the safety engaged on my Glock."

[The boyfriend can then swing her back into the scene with her mother, in which she can say the following.]

GIRL: **"Mom, you don't know how safe he is!"**

Swinging doors can also be used to explore. A swinging door can help you answer the question, "Why is the character in the scene behaving this way?"

Now let's consider a bad example:

EXAMPLE 2

[In this Organic Scene, the improvisers are still in the base reality section of the scene. No unusual thing has occurred yet in the scene. All the improvisers have established is that they are coworkers in a break room.]

PLAYER 1: **"You look upset this morning, George."**

PLAYER 2: **"I had an argument with my wife before I left for work this morning."**

[An improviser from the back-line swings Player 2 out to show him at home with his wife.]

PLAYER 3: **"Honey! You can't keep an alien in our basement!"**

Player 3 has forced an unusual thing. Players 1 and 2 haven't mentioned anything specific enough to warrant a swinging door. The specific of an alien doesn't feel like it was inspired by anything Player 1 or 2 said. Swinging doors that introduce crazy new ideas to the scene randomly don't support the scene that is happening; they hijack it.

Swinging doors should be used sparingly, at least in comparison to tag-outs and walk-ons. Many new improvisers want to overuse swinging doors because they are relatively "error-free" as far as Long Form goes; if you swing into a scene and it doesn't work, you control your own destiny and can swing yourself back out. Avoid abusing this support technique for that reason.

CUT-TOS

A **cut-to** is an improv technique that allows you to jump time and location to a new scene as you would in a film. A cut-to will also often include a description of what is happening in the new time and location. You will specify exactly where and/or when you are cutting to (e.g., "Cut to the north pole, three years later," or "Cut to graduation day, three weeks earlier"). A cut-to always sets up a new scene that is somehow connected to or inspired by the scene that came before it.

When calling a cut-to from the back-line, it often helps to join the scene you have cut to and initiate the first line to communicate how you think the Game can be played in this new time and location. Let's imagine the Game of the scene involves a woman accusing a middle-aged man of trying to act younger than his age by pointing out his dyed hair, new sports car, skinny jeans, etc. Someone from the back-line says, "We cut to a ball pit at McDonald's," steps into the scene, and says, "Sir, I'm sorry, but you need to be four years or younger to be in the play area."

The new scene that we cut to can involve all of the same characters in a different time or place, one of the characters in a different time or place, or completely new characters in a different time or place. The new scenario that we cut to should always follow the Game of the scene, not the plot or story.

A cut-to can be used when the improvisers in a scene are discussing something specific that has happened in the past or will happen in the future. If it would be more interesting to see this new scenario as opposed to just talking about it, an improviser from the back-line can initiate a cut-to. The new scene we cut to should be playing the Game already established.

For example, if two improvisers in a scene mention going to the prom, and it seems like this new location would help them play their Game, you can shout out, "We cut to the prom!" from the back-line. The two improvisers will be at the prom instantaneously so that they can continue to play their Game in a new location.

The time and location that you cut to don't need to have been mentioned by the improvisers in the scene. If, while on the back-line, you can come up with a time and place that would help the improvisers play their Game, it is valid to cut to this scenario. Let's say you are on the back-line watching a scene in which the Game involves one roommate complaining to another about his decision to decorate their apartment with satanic symbols. Cutting to the future, wherein the complaining kid invites his girlfriend over for a romantic evening, could provide a strong new opportunity to play this Game.

Another benefit of the cut-to is the elimination of moments that would exist in the "reality" of the scene but do not add to the comedy of the scene. For instance, a cut-to can help you skip the anesthesiologist's drive to the hospital where he is going to anesthetize a patient with a brick.

Remember that you can always "cut back" to the scene that you originally cut away from by simply yelling, "We cut back to _____." You would do this if the joke of the cut-to has been exhausted or if there is more to explore in the original scene.

Cut-tos should be used sparingly. You should not use a cut-to before a Game has been found or something unusual has been mentioned. Furthermore, this technique shouldn't be used every time an improviser in a scene has mentioned another location—it should only be used in instances when cutting to that new location will provide an opportunity for the Game of the scene to be played. Do not use a cut-to to advance the plot of the scene; you should only cut to new situations in which the Game can be played.

SCENE PAINTING

Scene painting, like the cut-to, is another support technique borrowed from screenwriting. Scene painting allows you to add the sort of description you would find in a screenplay to an improv scene. Scene painting is editorial narration that allows an improviser from the back-line to add visual details to a scene that enhance the Game. Note: These details must be visual. Let's imagine that you are describing a woman in a scene. You could scene paint and say, "We see that she is dressed in business attire," but you shouldn't say something like, "We see that she is extremely smart," since we can't, in fact, visually "see" this.

In order to scene paint, an improviser from the back-line steps forward and describes these details directly to the audience. To add specificity, an improviser may even walk around and gesture to the details that they are describing in the physical space. An improviser cannot paint the scene when they are in it.

For instance, in the satanic decoration scene hinted at in the previous section, an improviser from the back-line could step forward and say, "On this wall, we see that 666 has been written in dried blood. At the other end of the room, there is a makeshift altar, on top of which there is an inverted crucifix and an animal's skull. The characters are standing on top of a pentagram throw rug." Note that the characters in the scene don't hear these words. The improviser from the back-line has just given the audience rich visuals that relate to the Game of the scene. Scene painting may also provide the improvisers in the scene with new specifics to play their Game. The characters in the scene can now notice these visual details and react to them.

Don't scene paint to add in details that do not relate to the Game of the scene. You wouldn't want to scene paint the satanic decoration scene by saying, "We see a lamp," or, "We see that there are windows in this room," because these details don't directly play the Game.

SOUND EFFECTS

Improvisers can also support a scene by supplying **sound effects** from the back-line. Sound effects should be made to sound as "true to life" as possible. They can be added to the scene by any improviser standing on the back-line.

Sound effects are supportive when they enhance the reality of the scene. For example, if we are watching a scene take place on a battlefield, the sounds of gunfire and explosions could serve to enhance the reality of the scene. If a character in a scene turns on a radio or a television, you can support the reality of that scene by providing music or dialogue from the back-line. Improvisers from the back-line can also provide the dialogue for a movie being watched by two characters in a movie theater.

Sound effects can also directly play into the Game of the scene. If we are seeing a Game about an animal trainer who claims to be good with animals but isn't, it would be on Game for the back-line to provide the sound effect of growling dogs and hissing cats.

You don't want to overuse sound effects or add any to the scene that could potentially distract from the Game of the scene. Never use sound effects to make jokes outside the Game. For example, having a doorbell ring for an unusually long time would be jokey and unsupportive to the improvisers in the scene. Sound effects don't necessarily need to be jokey to be distracting. For example, if a character in the scene opens a cabinet, making a creaking sound would not enhance the scene or help play the Game in any way. Even supportive sound effects that enhance the reality of the scene can possibly take over the scene. You also always have the option to fade out sound effects after a few moments in order to avoid stealing focus.

OFFSTAGE CHARACTERS

Improvisers from the back-line can support the scene by playing offstage characters that we hear but do not see. **Offstage characters** are like walk-ons that never actually walk on.

Offstage characters are often used when a character in the scene receives a telephone call. An improviser can play the other end of the phone conversation by talking from the back-line.

Sometimes, the characters in the scene will mention offstage characters. Let's return to the "Cheap Guy" scene for an example of this.

EXAMPLE 1

[Let's imagine that once again, the Game has been clearly established with only the Pet Store Owner and Cheap Guy onstage. If the Cheap Guy mentions that his mother is waiting for him outside of the pet store, an improviser could play the mother from the back-line.]

MOTHER: [from the back-line] **"Hurry up, son! We want to get home and cook this expired food before it expires any further!"**

In this instance, this improviser was able to contribute to the scene and play the Game without ever actually entering the scene.

As with all support moves, offstage characters should be used sparingly. We don't need to hear from every character referred to by the characters in the scene. Those characters that we do hear from should justify or enhance the Game of the scene in some way. Be sure not to hijack the scene that is happening onstage with offstage characters.

PLAYING ANIMALS & INANIMATE OBJECTS

Improvisers can flesh out the environment in a scene by playing inanimate objects and animals. Adding these elements to a scene can enrich the world in which the scene is taking place and give the other improvisers something real to react to.

It isn't necessary to play animals every time that they are mentioned. If your team were performing a scene about a cat that is unusually strong, seeing this cat knock over furniture and wreak havoc would be playing into the Game of the scene. Playing a cat would be more of a distraction in a scene like our "Cheap Guy" scene, which takes place in a pet store. The cat is not especially relevant to the Game, and seeing someone play this cat would be distracting.

Improvisers should play physical objects only when they contribute to the scene or Game in some significant way. There was an improv group in New York that once did a scene about newlyweds on their honeymoon. After discussing whether or not they should get on the cheap-looking, coin-operated vibrating bed in their motel room, the six improvisers from the back-line entered the scene and physically built a vibrating bed using their bodies. It ended up being an inspired moment of support that made the scene stronger. If your team is performing a scene that takes place in a casino, stepping out from the back-line to play a slot machine is probably only going to distract the improvisers from finding a Game in this scene. Even if a Game has already been found, the slot machine is an incidental object that will not add to the funny ideas being explored onstage.

As with all support techniques, playing any inanimate object, animal, or anything else that doesn't talk should only support the scene in progress. You don't want to distract the improvisers in the scene or steal focus. Be selective in deciding when to portray objects or animals. Don't play incidental objects that have no impact on what the scene is really about. For example, if two people in a scene are eating dinner, we don't need to see another improviser play their table. If an improviser mentions that he or she is wearing a hat, it would be excessive and unnecessary for someone from the back-line to play the hat. Physical support moves should be made to put the focus on what is interesting about the Game of the scene.

MOVING IMPROVISERS THROUGH SPACE

Improvisers from the back-line can physically support their teammates in a scene in order to show things onstage that would otherwise be physically impossible to do alone. Improvisers can work together to allow the performers in a scene to do anything that they can imagine.

For example, if two improvisers were to initiate a scene set on a spaceship, the back-line could help them simulate weightlessness by physically picking the improvisers up and carrying them as the scene continues. Now let's imagine a scene in which two improvisers board an amusement park ride. Instead of letting the improvisers sit in motionless chairs, improvisers from the back-line could lift the chairs into the air and move them in a circular path, simulating the spinning action of an amusement park ride. If we are watching a scene about a superhero, the rest of the ensemble can simulate flight by lifting the improviser playing the superhero into the air and moving him or her through the space.

It is important to be careful when attempting to do any sort of physical support move. You want to be mindful of your own safety, as well as the safety of the members of your group that you will be physically handling. If you are uncomfortable with physical contact due to injuries or any other reason, let your teammates know prior to performance.

SUPPORT MOVES – IN SUMMATION

Supporting your teammates onstage should be your top priority whenever you are performing Long Form. Great improvisers do whatever they can to make everyone else onstage look good. Often, the best way to support a scene from the back-line is to do nothing at all. Keep this in mind whenever you use any of the support techniques mentioned in this section. Only use these techniques to enhance the existing scene. Don't use these techniques to take over someone else's scene and make it about you. Be sure that you are always supporting the Game your scene partners have established.

EDITING

Editing is possibly the most important form of support you can practice in a Long Form show. An **edit** is any technique used to signify the end of a scene. Every improv scene must come to an end at some point, and it is up to the improvisers onstage to determine when that ending will come. A well-timed edit that allows two improvisers to end a scene on a high note can make a great scene seem even more amazing.

One of the greatest compliments that an improviser can get is when they are asked if the scene they just performed was written. If an audience member has asked this, it is probably because the scene was funny, smart, and economical. An edit that ends a scene on a big laugh will make the scene feel like a well-written sketch.

Some beginning improvisers will be hesitant to edit because they are afraid to stop a scene that seems to be going really well. However, the improvisers performing the scene want you to edit at a heightened point, not after it has petered out. Don't think of editing a scene while it was going well as truncating a good scene; think of it as taking the scene out on a high note. You have left the audience with a picture of two improvisers succeeding, as opposed to two improvisers struggling.

The goal of every improviser should always be to make others look good and to make every scene in the show as strong as possible. A well-timed edit is a way for improvisers on the back-line to do both of these things.

WHEN TO EDIT

The success of an edit depends on its timing. You want to edit scenes at a high point, preferably on a big laugh line. A scene shouldn't be edited on the very first big laugh, but after the improvisers in the scene have been allowed to heighten and explore their Game a few times. If the scene has been consistently getting laughs, and a Game move gets a great reaction from the audience, this is a good time to edit the scene. There will come a point in any scene when the improvisers will run out of options for further heightening. You want to be carefully watching the other members of your group from the back-line. In a perfect scenario, you would edit the scene when they reach a point at which you think, Wow, they just heightened this Game as far as it can go.

Since every scene is different, when to edit must be decided on a case-by-case basis. You should be watching every scene actively. If, while on the back-line, you can easily think of multiple additional Game moves for the scene that is happening, you can assume that the improvisers in the scene feel the same way. In this case, you can afford to give the scene more time before you edit. If you watch a scene and you can't think of how you would further heighten it, you want to again assume that the improvisers in the scene feel the same way, and you would want to provide an edit as soon as possible. Some scenes will "supernova," meaning the improvisers will find a Game quickly, play it aggressively, and the whole thing will be done in a minute. Other scenes will last longer because the players have a lot of ideas to heighten and explore, or they are receiving a lot of support from the back-line. In either case, you want to get a sense for when the improvisers are approaching the limits of heightening their Game when deciding on an edit.

A good rule of thumb: If you're thinking that you should edit, you probably should have edited thirty seconds ago. This will help you avoid the state of panic wherein you watch your fellow performers struggle in a scene with nowhere left to go. In this situation, the improvisers have heightened and explored their Game to the point where the scene has started to plateau. If the improvisers have started to repeat information, the scene may be starting to **flatline**. A flatlining scene is one where the edit has been missed. If you miss an edit, give the scene another thirty seconds. If you get a laugh during the next thirty seconds, edit on the laugh. If at the end of those thirty seconds there hasn't been another laugh, cut your losses and edit anyway.

It is best to follow your instincts when editing. If you have the impulse to edit, follow that impulse. Don't ever start to edit and then hesitate. Improvisers are sometimes hesitant to edit a scene because they are afraid of cutting a scene short. Remember, you are editing to take a scene out on a high note and prevent it from petering out.

Obviously, you want to edit a scene before the improvisers begin spinning their wheels. If you wait too long after a scene has peaked to edit, you could turn a great scene, which could have ended with a bang, into a decent scene that fizzles out. A scene that ends poorly because of a missed edit can have a devastating effect on your entire show.

HOW TO EDIT

Now that you know when to edit, let's discuss how to edit. There are many different styles of editing in the world of Long Form improvisation. Your group should choose the style that fits the aesthetic of your show. To avoid confusion, the style of edit should be agreed upon prior to performance, not found during the course of a show. No matter how you choose to edit, the most important thing is to be clear. Communication of the edit to everyone onstage is important. The other improvisers onstage must know that you are editing.

The improvisers on the back-line should take responsibility for editing the scenes. This allows the improvisers in the scene to be able to focus on and fully commit to their performances. Remember, every member of an improv group shares responsibility for the success of each and every scene. Editing is the one form of support that is always required from the back-line in order for a scene to be successful. By listening and paying full attention to the scene that is happening, you will know when a scene should be edited.

Editing from within the scene is referred to as **self-editing**. Self-editing is necessary when every member of your ensemble is performing in a group scene. (Group scenes will be discussed further in the section on Long Form structures.) It is possible to self-edit in two-person scenes. However, we recommend that you don't, because it will take your focus off of playing the Game, and the audience may perceive the self-edit as you bailing on your scene.

The most common style of edit is the **sweep edit**. An improviser from the back-line will sweep-edit a scene by stepping out from the back-line and moving across the stage in front of the improvisers performing the scene. This improviser has broken through the reality of the scene, effectively "sweeping" the stage clean of the scene that was happening. This is a cue to all improvisers onstage that the scene is over, and that it is time to begin a new scene.

Editing a scene does not necessarily mean that you must initiate the next scene. Sometimes you will edit without having an idea for the next scene. If you know that it is time to edit but you don't have an idea for a scene, you can sweep the scene and move all the way across the stage, returning to the back-line again. You have signaled to your team that the scene is over, and by returning to the back-line, you have let them know that you don't have an idea for another scene. Therefore, two new improvisers should step forward to start the next scene.

If you know that it is time to edit and you do have an idea for a scene, you should sweep the scene, but instead of returning to the back-line, remain onstage and wait for another improviser to join you.

The sweep edit is only one of many styles of editing. Some improvisers edit by breaking directly through the middle of the scene to begin a new one. Some improvisers use stomping, clapping, or saying, "Freeze!" to signal the end of one scene and the start of the next. The editing style you choose will depend on the preference of the group. As long as the edit is agreed upon by all members of the ensemble and clear in its execution, it will be effective.

Take editing seriously. Remember, editing is a form of support, and supporting your teammates should always be your number one priority onstage. Editing is another tool for making the other members of your team look good.

CHAPTER 8:

Helpful Hints & Hazards

There are certain "rules" that a new improviser will constantly hear throughout his or her training in Long Form. Many of these rules come in the form of "don'ts." There are certain choices, scenarios, and situations that can lead to troublesome and unsuccessful scenes for new improvisers. These improv rules exist to steer new improvisers toward making choices that will help them to successfully find a Game in a scene. Listed below are some of these rules and scenic taboos.

Rules of Thumb

IDENTIFY "IT"

Sometimes, you may make the mistake of focusing the scene's attention on an object without having a clear idea of what the object is. The best thing to do in this situation is to identify "it." You don't want to let the scene become about guessing what "it" is.

You can avoid this problem by making strong, clear choices. If you can manage to avoid the words "this," "these," "those," "that," and "it" at the tops of scenes—in favor of more specific choices—you will keep yourself from falling prey to this problem. Using these words only delays the inevitable naming of what they represent and slows the scene down.

The longer you talk about an unidentified "it," the greater the audience's expectations become for "it" to be hilarious. The "it" will become a bigger and bigger mystery, and will become the focus of the scene. You and your scene partner will find yourselves distracted by "it," and you will be kept from finding out what is truly funny about the scene. The sooner you make a choice about "it," the sooner you can move on with the scene to discover what is interesting about your relationship or your character's behavior.

If you never identify "it," you will force yourself into a scene in which the "Game" can only be based on vagueness.

Here are some examples of the sort of vague initiations that could lead you to having the "it" problem in a scene:

"I fixed it."

"Look, I got you one of these!"

"Look at that!"

These sorts of initiations are almost always accompanied with vague object work. Object work can be a great way to start your scene in a grounded reality. Just be sure to be clear with the choices you are making about objects. If you must, say specifically what the object is that you are handling or referring to.

If you find yourself in a scene where your scene partner has used "it" or another equally vague word, take the initiative and identify "it" as quickly as you can. For example, let's say your partner initiates a scene by looking offstage, saying:

"Look at that!"

If you find yourself in a scene like this, where your partner has offered a poor initiation using "it" or another equally vague word, you will need to take the initiative. By doing so, you might respond with:

"Wow. Alan has really let himself go since the divorce."

Now, you and your scene partner can move on with the scene, Yes And–ing off of this information about your friend Alan. If your scene partner wasn't picturing "Alan," he must now. Once something is said onstage, it is a reality. If your scene partner did have something more specific in mind, he must drop his idea and go with yours.

THE PROBLEM WITH GIVING PRESENTS

New improvisers will sometimes give their scene partner a present in a scene without saying what it is. While this more closely mirrors reality (you don't tell someone what their present is before they open it), it ultimately leaves your scene partner in the dark as to how to react. You don't want to end up with a guessing game about what the present is.

The best way to avoid this issue is to blurt out what the present is as it is being opened. This way, you are letting the other improviser know how you expect them to play into your idea. For example, if you intend to play a thoughtless husband, identify your present as being something disappointing so that your scene partner can react accordingly.

Remember, being in agreement is the key to success in Long Form improv. The sooner you can agree with your scene partner about what "it" is, the sooner you will be able to work together to find what is funny about your scene.

THE TRUTH ABOUT QUESTIONS

In the world of improvisation, there is an often-misunderstood dictum: "Don't ask questions." This is often misunderstood to mean that you can never ask a question when improvising. In fact, "Don't ask questions" is a rule that only applies to the start of a Long Form scene. When you initiate a scene with your partner and begin to discover the world of your scene through Yes And, questions will not provide you with more information about this world. As we have already discussed, questions can prevent you from clearly establishing the base reality of your scene (who you are, what you are doing, and where you are). Questions will also most likely stall the discovery of the first unusual thing. Constantly asking questions at the top of a scene will keep you from creating characters with strong viewpoints. Questions at the start of a scene are unfair to your scene partner, as they put the onus of creation on him or her. You force your scene partner to do all of the decision-making for both of you.

For example, let's imagine that you started a scene by saying, **"What do you want to do today?"** This initiation hasn't offered any information to the scene. You are not making any choices; you are forcing your scene partner to do so. Remember, at the start of the scene, neither of you knows who you are, where you are, or what you're doing. If you have the impulse to ask your scene partner a question, force yourself to just make a choice and turn your question into a statement. For instance, instead of **"What do you want to do today?,"** you could say, **"I thought we'd go for a bike ride."** Your scene partner might have the impulse to reply, **"Where do you want to go?,"** but the scene will be better off with a statement like, **"Let's ride down to the art museum."**

It is important to distinguish between questions that delay the discovery of the Game and questions that come from an improviser playing the scene truthfully in service of the Game of the scene. There are good questions and bad questions in Long Form improv. A good question will often come as a reaction to the unusual and provide an opportunity for your scene partner to justify the absurd. These sorts of questions (previously described as "framing" the unusual thing in a scene), will actually often serve as the best way to support the choice your scene partner has just made.

Remember, asking a question is definitely okay once you and your scene partner have found the Game of the scene. Since we ask questions all the time in real life, doing so in a scene may be the best way to play a specific moment at the top of your intelligence.

Questions asked in order to explore the Game don't merely have to "tee up" your scene partner to provide exploration. The questions you ask can themselves help add to the exploration in a scene. Let's look back at our scene in which the dentist uses a brick to anesthetize his patients. One of the questions asked by the straight man in the scene was, **"Is it a medical-grade brick? Like one that is sized and proportionate to my weight?"** In this case, the question explores, "If a patient is told that he is going to be hit by a brick, then why would he choose to stay in this office?" The question shows why a patient might give this dentist the benefit of the doubt. If this scene went further, the straight man might ask, **"Is this why your fee is so low?"** This question brings a new dimension to the Game. If a brick is used to anesthetize, then costs related to traditional anesthesia, assistants, and monitoring machines would have all been eliminated.

PRACTICAL QUESTIONS

On a very practical level, asking a question may be necessary when you have not heard your scene partner's last line, or you honestly do not know what he or she is talking about. If you are completely lost with regard to something referenced in a scene (e.g., a mention of string theory, the name of a celebrity, a historical event, etc.), it is better for your character to ask a question so that you—the improviser—can fully participate in the scene.

Don'ts

The following section will review common scenarios that tend to be troublesome for new improvisers. This section will also review common beginner tendencies that hurt scenes. By making you aware of these "traps," we hope that you will have a better chance of fixing the scene when you do fall into them.

DON'T FOLLOW PLOT

New improvisers will often hear the note, "You ended up following the plot in that scene." We are not interested in the story of a Long Form comedy scene; we are interested in the Game. We are not creating a play with a story arc. We are not interested in finding a strong beginning, middle and end, and we aren't improvising to discover what is going to change about our characters. We are improvising comedy sketches, not stories.

To create something that resembles a comedic sketch, you need to follow the Game of the scene. In order to do this, you need to begin by finding what is unusual in the world we have created. A big trap that many new improvisers fall into is running past the unusual to follow the story of the characters instead. This will lead to an artificial and mostly arbitrary creation of facts and plot points, as opposed to a clear pattern of behavior that can be built and sustained through heightening and exploration (a Game).

Improvisers sometimes inadvertently fall into following plot by endlessly Yes And–ing after blowing past the first unusual thing. When this happens, you are likely to end up following the story of your unnecessarily complicated characters and situation by default. These kinds of scenes will often start out fun, but they will quickly run out of steam because there is no pattern to ease the burden of creativity.

As with most rules in Long Form, there is an exception when it comes to plot. *Following plot in the service of a Game* is acceptable. Let's say that you start with a scene in which you are playing a lawyer preparing a client for trial. The Game of the scene is that this lawyer is uncomfortable speaking in public. In this case, it may be easiest to use plot to play this Game. As always, you should be thinking, Where else could I take this lawyer so that I can continue to play this Game? It so happens that in this case, following the story of a trial would provide new opportunities to play your Game (e.g., selecting a jury, presenting your case in court, or speaking to the news media). These are all plot points, but they are plot points that allow for further Game moves. Plots should not be followed to arbitrarily tell a story. Plots should be followed only if they present further opportunities to play the Game.

The main reason we don't attempt to create improvised stories and plots is that it is simply too difficult. Great stories require a blueprint, as well as intricate planning and forethought. Since you are creating your scenes from moment to moment, you are not able to look at anything as a whole in this way. Put your focus on what is interesting or unusual right now. Once you are able to justify the unusual or absurd, you can make a pattern out of this behavior.

Improvised stories tend to come off as silly, unbelievable, or unoriginal clichés. In Long Form comedic improvisation, what keeps the audience engaged is not *where* the story will go, but rather *how* the funny Game will be heightened and explored. If you find yourself following plot in the moment, try to refocus yourself on creating patterns and following behavior.

DON'T TALK ABOUT THE THING

Scenes that become about "the thing" are difficult to execute, because you and your scene partner will find yourself standing around talking about "the thing" until, by necessity, the fact that you are doing so becomes your Game. You will have spent so much time talking about "pizza" that this behavior has become your unusual thing. Now your Game is "people who obsessively talk about pizza." Instead of giving the audience a character with a specific behavior or point of view, they are stuck watching you and your scene partner talk about a "thing." Ultimately, scenes that revolve around a "thing" will lack any action or heightening.

If you find yourself in a scene where you are talking about a thing, you can salvage the scene by forcing yourself to say some lines that start with the words "I," "you," or "we." This will hopefully move you away from the thing and put the focus on the characters in the scene.

DON'T TALK ABOUT CHARACTERS WHO ARE NOT THERE

Another common mistake that new improvisers will make is talking about characters that are not in the scene. For instance, in the example scene in which characters were talking about their friend Alan, the improvisers may be headed for trouble if they spend the entire scene talking about Alan.

If you spend your scene talking about somebody that is not present, all of your strongest specifics will be tied to a character that is not presently onstage. This character is likely to become more interesting than the two people just talking about him or her. Your audience would probably much rather see a scene featuring this interesting character.

As with scenes about "blank," the way to remedy these scenes is to make strong choices about yourself and/or your scene partner. Remember, you can do this by saying lines that start with the words "I," "you," or "we." This will help the audience to become more actively engaged with the two characters onstage. Another possible fix to a scene that becomes about an offstage character is to support the scene by walking on as the character being talked about, or to cut to a scene featuring that character.

EXERCISE: I, YOU, WE SCENES

INSTRUCTIONS

- Two improvisers take the stage.

- Someone else gives them a one-word suggestion to inspire their scene.

- Each line of the scene must be a statement starting with the word "I," "You," or "We."

- The improvisers should also look to incorporate the word "because" whenever possible in order to offer justifications.

- An outside person watching the scene can suspend the I/You/We rule once he or she feels the improvisers in the scene have discovered a Game.

PURPOSE

- This exercise will force you to keep the focus of the scene on its two characters, and to avoid the trap of talking about people who are not there.

- This exercise will also give you a chance to practice exploring by justifying the choices you make.

DON'T TALK ABOUT THE PAST AND FUTURE

Another scenic trap is talking about things that have happened in the past or things that will happen in the future. When you do this, you often end up with a **talking heads** scene. Nothing really happens in a talking heads scene besides standing around and talking.

When you talk about the past or the future in scenes, you are often making very interesting or specific choices about these periods of time. These interesting moments in the past or future are where your current scene should have started in the first place.

When you have the impulse to start your scene by reminiscing or talking about the future, tailor your initiation to actively show this idea instead of talking about it. For example, if you had the impulse to start a scene by coming out and reminiscing about what an ass you were at a party last night, you could instead start your scene at the party. Remember, if you are talking about the past or future, you can't be active in the present.

If you find yourself watching a scene in which all the improvisers do is talk about the past or future, you can take action from the back-line. You can remedy the problem from the back-line by cutting to the moment being discussed. Brief moments of talking about the past or future are okay since this often happens in real life. What you want to avoid is making your entire scene about talking about the past or future.

DON'T TALK ABOUT WHAT YOU ARE DOING

You don't want to spend an entire scene with the characters just talking about what they are doing. Some new improvisers will spend an entire scene doing nothing but talking about what they and their scene partners are doing. If you are doing a scene where two mechanics are fixing a car, you don't want to spend the whole scene talking about fixing the car. You will want to find out what is interesting about the characters and their relationship.

There are two main reasons why talking about what you are doing is problematic. First, you will get caught up in plot as opposed to finding a Game. You will find that every line will be tied to the various steps of the procedure or activity in which you are engaged, and you will miss the specific or interesting details that could lead you to your Game.

Second, talking about what you are doing keeps you from finding Game because it prevents you from playing things realistically. In real life, people rarely talk about what they are doing as they are doing it. This is especially true for scenes taking place at work or any other situation where an activity is performed routinely. Two characters performing a task that they know very well would almost never spend their time talking about the task at hand. Having realistic and normal conversations is more likely to lead you to interesting choices about behavior or point of view. That, in turn, will lead you to a Game.

This is not to say that giving your characters an activity to engage with during a scene is bad. In fact, starting with an activity can be a great way to ground your scene in a reality while also establishing your Where through showing and not telling. Just let this be a detail in your scene that leads you to a strong Game. We want you to establish a What for your scene, but don't make this activity the sole focus and subject matter of your scene.

To remedy this problem when it happens, stay engaged with the activity while starting to talk about something else. If you find yourself getting caught up in the "what" of the scene, put the focus on the characters in the scene. There are a number of ways that you can do this. Give yourself a point of view and find a way to express it. Make a statement about how the other character seems to be feeling. Confess something important. These are all ways that you can begin to take your scene away from the What to make it about the most important thing in the scene, the two improvisers we can see onstage.

DON'T REACH INTO YOUR BAG OF TRICKS

Bag of tricks refers to things that you have done in the past that you know will get a positive response from your audience, whether it's a character, a premise, or a joke. Forcing something from your bag of tricks into a scene when it is not organically called for will always undermine the integrity of the scene and also foster distrust in your ensemble. For example, you wouldn't want to force singing into a scene just because you know you have a great singing voice.

Scenes to Avoid

When performing organic improv, there are some types of scenes that are problematic for beginning improvisers. While it is not impossible to find a Game in these scenarios, new students of Long Form are usually better off avoiding these "black hole" scenes.

TEACHING SCENES

In a **teaching scene**, one improviser lacks the knowledge necessary to participate in an activity. The scene ends up being dominated by one character who dispenses commands and instructions to the ignorant character. It is very difficult for the improviser "being taught" to Yes And or generate new information in such scenes because they are stuck waiting for their "teacher" to provide instruction.

These scenes are sometimes referred to as **puppet master scenes**, since one improviser ends up essentially dictating the actions of the other. These scenes are hard to build because they are lopsided. One improviser is responsible for the majority of the choices being made while the other improviser is forced to just do what he or she is told. In these scenes, since only one person is creating information, you are losing 50% of your opportunities for finding the first unusual thing. Instead of finding a Game, the scene will be bogged down by endless questions, corrections, and instructions.

Teaching scenes can be black holes for new improvisers, as they necessitate your doing many of the things we have already told you to avoid. In teaching scenes, you will end up talking about what you are doing, talking about the thing, asking lots of questions, etc.

A subset of the teaching scene is the you-gotta-do-it scene. These are scenes where one character is constantly doing something wrong, and the other character does nothing but "fix" the problem. No matter what their scene partner does, the "teacher" ends up saying things like, "No! You gotta do it like this." In these scenes, one person is bulldozing while the other person is passive. (An improviser is bulldozing when he or she prevents a scene partner from contributing by making all of the choices in a scene.) It is very difficult to make new discoveries in you-gotta-do-it scenes. The lack of new information will make it impossible for you to find a Game.

It is important to note that avoiding teaching scenes does not mean that we need to avoid playing a teacher in a scene. You can play teachers and set scenes in classrooms. You just want to avoid making the entire scene about teaching something to someone else. Make specific choices about the character that will lead to a Game beyond his or her profession, which should only be a detail in your scene.

Choose to know how to do things in scenes even if you don't know how to do them in real life. Don't make it your first day on the job. Don't say that you've "never done this before." Choose to know. By using what little you know about an endeavor, you will be able to fake it well enough to convince the audience.

Sometimes you will feel like you know absolutely nothing about a profession you are called upon to play in a scene. In these situations, try to draw on knowledge that you've gained from fictional sources like books, plays, television, or movies. If you still feel at a loss for specifics or details related to this profession, you can usually come up with at least a basic term or an action to start with. For example, even though you may know nothing about being a mechanic, you could still use the word "muffler," open the hood of the car, etc.

When you and your scene partner can contribute to the scene equally, you will be in a better position to find a Game.

SIMPLE TRANSACTION SCENES

Organic Scenes starting with simple transactions can also end up being black holes for beginning improvisers. Simple transactions are problematic because in real life they are usually very brief. The improvisers are forced to invent in order to prolong the scene. Inventing is forcing new, unnecessary, and potentially complicated information into a scene in the absence of a Game.

For example, if you choose to start a scene as someone buying a cup of coffee in a deli, you will probably find that you have nowhere else to take the scene. Think of this same situation in real life. The scene should be over as soon as the transaction has ended. To prolong these situations in order to find a scene, new improvisers are often forced to make something "weird" or "crazy" happen. In other cases, these scenes devolve into a negotiation over the price of the goods or services being exchanged, which is uninteresting.

Again, this doesn't mean that you cannot do scenes where a transaction is taking place. The key is to avoid making the entire scene revolve around the transaction, or the What. If you do find yourself in this situation, there are two ways to avoid a bad scene. First, you can choose to know the character you are having the interaction with (maybe you buy coffee in this deli every day, and you know the deli worker well enough to talk about something else with him). A second option is to draw on something from your own life. Think of a time when you were in this situation and you found something interesting about it. Introduce the specifics of this real-life experience into your scene. Don't just invent something crazy; introduce something real from your own experience.

Ultimately, beginning improvisers will be far better off avoiding transactions altogether in Organic Scenes. Long Form scene work is about choices. Choosing to start with a simple transaction puts your scene at risk of being over before anything interesting happens.

DON'T BE OVERWHELMED

Eventually, with practice, you will be able to internalize these rules. You will find yourself following them almost automatically. Beginning improvisers should focus on one or two rules for each practice or performance in order to avoid becoming overwhelmed. You will not be able to work on every rule at once at the beginning of your Long Form education.

CAN RULES BE BROKEN?

The simple answer is yes, but be careful. Remember that these guidelines exist to help you succeed, especially if you are new to Long Form. However, there are instances in which successful scenes can occur in spite of the rules being broken.

Seasoned, experienced, and extremely talented improvisers will break improv rules all the time. Sometimes, experienced improvisers will have a reason for breaking a specific rule that will not be readily apparent to the novice improviser. Don't take this to mean that you should also throw the rules out the window. Sometimes, the rules are being broken for no good reason, but the performers are getting away with it because they are just funny people.

Watch as much improv as you can when you are starting out. You will see rules being broken. Notice when this does work and when it doesn't work. In both instances, you want to ask yourself, Why? There are often explanations for what you may perceive as a rule being broken. For instance, you may see a scene that starts with a simple transaction. If this scene is a Premise Scene inspired by a monologue involving a simple transaction, starting the scene in this way is completely valid. You will also see plenty of scenes where a character is asking questions or saying no. Remember, these behaviors are okay if they are tied to the Game of the scene.

Every rule can be broken. If it serves the Game of the scene to break one of the rules, then you should break the rule and serve the Game of the scene. In the meantime, following the rules will give you the greatest chance at success.

HAVE FAITH IN THE GAME

You may find yourself questioning the merits of Game at this point. It may seem creatively "limiting" when you hear it broken down into "rules." Wouldn't the scene be less predictable and more fun if you could follow any funny whim you have in the moment, even if it is not in keeping with the Game?

The answer is no. Following your whims in an attempt to go from individually funny moment to individually funny moment is, for one thing, very difficult to do. Game gives you a clear structure in which your comedy can exist. Your ultimate responsibility should be to give your audience comedy on par with any written work that they see. The fact that your scene follows a clear pattern (from what you have established at the start) gives it the same structure as a written scene. If you start the scene as Cheap Guy, the audience will expect to see you continue to explore this character. A series of random and unexplained choices will be much less satisfying and much more confusing. The satisfaction of having pleased the audience with a focused Game will far outweigh the satisfaction of following your whims in the moment.

It should also be noted that the Game is nothing more than a pattern for you to follow. The choices about what you include in this pattern are completely and uniquely yours, both in terms of heightening and exploration. No other improviser will play a Game in exactly the same way that you do. Allow your specific choices and details to make the Game your own.

It is sometimes hard for beginning improvisers to embrace the idea of serving the Game. They feel that it is limiting their own individual sense of humor. In fact, the opposite is true. If you serve the Game, the Game will serve you. Once you have found the Game, you will no longer have to worry about where the scene is going or what action you have to take next. You can instead focus on coming up with funny specifics that fit your Game. This is where your comic voice can be heard. Remember, complaining about this would be like a basketball player complaining that the rules of basketball are limiting. While all basketball players play by the rules, there is tremendous variation in their individual styles.

The Game also makes it possible for you to work with an ensemble. Game serves as a common language that all Long Form improvisers speak. Working with an ensemble will allow you to take your comedy to places you wouldn't have been able to take it by yourself.

Improvisers who don't have faith in the Game tend to make jokes for quick laughs. Making jokes that fall outside the pattern of the Game at the expense of the scene undercuts the work you and your scene partner are trying to do. Making a joke that deviates from the pattern may give you the instant gratification of an audience's approval, but if it goes against the logic of your scene and the pattern of your Game, you may find that you have driven your scene into a brick wall.

If you play the pattern of the Game, you will not only get a laugh in the moment, but you will have the opportunity for more laughs in the future. Have faith in the Game and your ability to bring something unique and exciting to it.

SECTION III:
LONGFORM STRUCTURES

Long Form improv scenes are not performed in isolation. Improv shows generally involve performing a series of scenes together as part of a specific structure. Each individual structure is referred to as a **longform.**

A longform is any improv structure that incorporates two or more scenes into a whole piece. A longform is a way to present your improvisation to an audience within a cohesive framework. These structures exist in order to help your work add up to something more than just a random collection of scenes. Tying various scenes and Games together into a single longform will make the performance more impressive to an audience.

Performing scenes within a longform will not only provide a better theatergoing experience for the audience, but it also makes performing each individual scene easier. Some aspects of longforms exist to make finding the Game easier. Furthermore, using a structure allows you to build off of what has already been created as opposed to starting from scratch every time a new scene is initiated.

There are many different longforms out there. We will focus on only a few of them in this text, primarily the **Harold**, the original longform created by Del Close.

We will start our exploration of longform structures by explaining the fundamentals of how an improv group can turn a single suggestion into ideas for many scenes.

CHAPTER 9:

Starting from an
Audience Suggestion

Most longforms begin with a single suggestion provided by a member of the audience. The suggestion can be anything: a single word, a phrase, an object, a text message, a lyric from a song, a line from a movie—anything. The suggestion serves as the inspiration for the entire piece.

The suggestion serves three main functions within a longform. First, the suggestion proves to the audience that what they are watching is truly improvised. Since the suggestion is coming from the audience, it proves that the show is not preplanned. The suggestion also gives you a starting point for inspiration, as opposed to leaving you to choose from an infinite number of possibilities. Finally, the suggestion gives a team a common focus. Having a common focus will help ensure that you and your teammates are on the same page throughout the entire show. A common focus also allows your group to present a performance that feels connected by a theme.

No suggestion is a bad suggestion.

It is up to the improvisers to effectively use whatever suggestion they receive as a vehicle for creating their own ideas, themes, and points of view as a group. At the same time, the more clearly you can show the audience that you have arrived at these ideas, themes, and points of view from their suggestion, the more impressed your audience will likely be. A longform that is funny and clearly incorporates or deconstructs a suggestion will be more satisfying to an audience than a show that is merely funny.

CHAPTER 10:

Openings

Some Long Form shows will jump directly from an audience suggestion into scene work. However, most longforms will start with some sort of group process used to generate information from the suggestion before launching into scenes. This information-generating process is called an **opening**.

During an opening, an improv group takes the suggestion and explores it through the exchange of ideas. How these ideas are shared depends on the structure of the opening being performed.

An opening serves three purposes in a longform:

First and foremost, an opening should generate interesting and funny information that can be used to inspire scenes.

Additionally, the opening is an opportunity for a team to utilize their **group mind**. Group mind is how a team incorporates multiple, individual voices into one single voice. A team with strong group mind will not generate information in isolation. A team with a strong group mind will be working together to generate information as a unit. The opening is the opportunity for the team to use their group mind to come to agreement about their collective points of view or "takes" on a suggestion. Generating information in your opening is like pitching ideas in the writers' room of a sketch show. When scene work begins, each initiation should clearly call back to a piece of information that was generated, collaborated on, and acknowledged by the group. When you start a scene, you should not be drawing an idea from your own head; you should be drawing from the group mind. If you express this initiation clearly and your scene partner was listening during the opening, you should be starting your scene with both players on the same page.

Finally, an opening should be entertaining or engaging in some way. This is the first time that the audience is seeing your group. You don't want to start the show in a low-energy, awkward way. An opening should be dynamic. An opening performed with confidence and a sense of playfulness will "get the audience on your side" right from the start of your show. The opening needs to be more than just bouncing ideas off of each other; it is part of a performance.

PULLING IDEAS FROM THE OPENING

By the end of an opening, your team should have generated a lot of useful information to be used for scenes. It is generally a good idea to use information presented by another player in the opening when you start a scene. This shows that you have been listening to your teammates. Using someone's information helps start your show in the spirit of collaboration.

There is also a practical reason for initiating with information provided by someone else. When you start with someone else's information, you know for a fact that two members of the group remember it. Information that you have provided will of course be memorable to you. However, this information may not have resonated with anyone else in your group. If you start from your own information, your scene partner may not know what direction you intend your scene to go in. If a piece of information that your teammate provided was strong enough for you to focus on, it probably stood out to other members of your group as well. The best information is that which drew everyone's attention. You are likely to get to the Game faster by starting with this sort of information from an opening.

Information from an opening comes in many different forms: words, phrases, stories, sounds, movement, etc. As mentioned in the section on initiating, this information falls into three different categories: premises, half ideas, and chaff. The chaff in an opening is not any more useful for starting scenes than the original suggestion. It doesn't have any inherent comedic potential. Premises and half ideas are useful for starting scenes because they do have inherent comedic potential. Premises will be used to initiate Premise Scenes, where both the base reality and the first unusual thing will be established in a single line. It is as if the opening were the "beginning" or Yes And portion of the scene, and your premise-based initiation is offering the first unusual thing. The improvisers in a Premise Scene are very close to starting with a fully realized Game. Half ideas can be used to initiate Organic Scenes with information that has comic potential, therefore making it easier to find a Game than if you started with the chaff. Half ideas offer something more than a single-word suggestion but less than a fully formed comedic premise.

Let the audience's laughter guide you toward premises and half ideas in the opening. If they are laughing at information in the opening, there must be something funny about it.

To reiterate an earlier point, the UCB sees no intrinsic value in one form of scene over the other (Organic vs. Premise). However, when you are performing scenes from an opening, you should give priority to premises over half ideas. Starting with a premise from an opening will make getting to the Game easier and more efficient, and will increase the likelihood of success. If you can't identify any premises in your opening, or if you have run out of premises to use, you can always fall back on using a half idea to find your Game organically. Since there is a chance that the premise presented by either you or your scene partner will not be recognized, you must always be ready to find the Game organically.

Let's say that these three pieces of information appear in an opening: shopping, shop-a-holic, and return-a-holic. Shopping would be an example of chaff. It is no more than a one-word suggestion. "Shop-a-holic" is a half idea, since it implies a pathology that most people do not have. Since it is somewhat unusual, it possesses comedic potential. "Return-a-holic" is a premise that implies someone whose only interest in shopping is that it allows the opportunity to return items. Since this is not something that exists in our reality, it has much comic potential. You can form an initiation with this information to establish a first unusual thing that breaks from a base reality.

We do not generate Games in the opening. We can only generate funny premises. The Game will always be more intricate as the scene plays out than it was as information in the opening. How the Game is played will be determined by how we choose to heighten and explore after the initial reaction to the premise. A premise becomes a Game based on how you and your scene partner answer the question, "If this unusual thing is true, then what else is true?"

Improvisers will sometimes change great, funny information from an opening when they initiate a scene just to be original. Some people feel that using a fully formed premise is limiting to their own or their scene partner's creativity. This is not true. As we have already mentioned, a Game is not really locked until both improvisers respond to or contribute to a premise. Others will avoid starting with an obvious premise from the opening because they feel that the audience has already heard it and that the idea has already been exhausted. You need to trust that you and your scene partner will be able to find further exploration of this premise in your scene.

If there is some information that is created in the opening that suggests, for lack of a better term, an obvious Game, use it. There is no reason to change a premise if it is already funny and clearly suggests a Game. You would never do this if you were writing with someone else. When two people are writing a comedy movie together and one person comes up with a funny idea, they use that idea. There is no need to change ideas to make them your own, because Long Form is collaborative.

Have no shame about using the funny information from an opening in your scenes. Remember, one of the main reasons for doing an opening is to generate funny information. If your team is successful in doing that, use this information for your scenes. Otherwise, you did a lot of work for nothing.

Set Openings

A **set opening** is any opening with a predetermined structure decided upon by the performers prior to a performance. An improv team can rehearse the structure of a set opening in preparation for use in shows. The same structure can be used to generate completely different ideas for each new performance.

THE PATTERN GAME

The **Pattern Game** is a set opening that all Long Form improvisers should be familiar with. The basic structure of the Pattern Game, and the skills required to perform it, are found in many other set openings. No other set opening better trains an improviser to listen to and create with others. The Pattern Game is perhaps the most difficult and most impressive set opening. A group performing the Pattern Game uses nothing more than simple words to create funny, fully formed premises. A group that can conquer a successful Pattern Game can do any other set opening.

In a Pattern Game, a group of improvisers explores their suggestion and creates information for scenes one word at a time. Inspired by the suggestion, one member of the ensemble will say a word. The group continues to generate new words, each inspired by the previous word. It is important to note that this is more than mere *word association*. Avoid knee-jerk, obvious responses to the previous word. For example, responding to "peanut butter" with "jelly" is bad, but responding to "peanut butter" with "allergy" is good. When performing a Pattern Game, you should think of your thought process as *idea association*. Each idea should inspire another new, specific idea. Let's imagine one of your teammates just said "dog." Word association may result in the response of "cat." However, if you are thinking of "dog" as an idea, you will come up with new specific ideas related to "dog," such as "loyal" or "rabies" or "leash."

The basic structure of the Pattern Game involves continually creating new information in this way by moving away from and then returning to the original suggestion three times.

Like all openings, the purpose of the Pattern Game is to help a group build toward funny half ideas and premises. In order to do this, the improvisers need to listen carefully to the words that have already been said, recognize patterns that are forming, and then add new words in keeping with those patterns.

PHYSICAL PERFORMANCE

As with all Long Form set openings, the Pattern Game begins by getting a suggestion from the audience. Most groups perform the Pattern Game off of the suggestion of a single word. While standing together in a semicircle or U-shape, the improvisers will, in no set order, take turns saying words, with each new word coming in response to the last one.

Teammates should be making eye contact with each other while performing the Pattern Game in order to get "connected." Maintaining eye contact will also cut down on instances of you and your teammates speaking over one another.

Confidence and projection are important to the performance of the Pattern Game. All members of a group should stand up straight and speak loudly and clearly so that the other members of the group—and the audience—can hear each new idea.

A TO C

Here are two patterns off of the same word:

PATTERN 1:   **island, sand, hourglass, grim reaper, *A Christmas Carol*, shopping mall...**

PATTERN 2:   **island, sand, rock, palm trees, coconuts, bananas...**

Pattern 1 has generated lots of different ideas off of a single word. Pattern 2 has only created an obvious list of words associated with an island.

Pattern 1 has generated many ideas from a single suggestion, making it a successful start of a Pattern Game. It was successful because the group made what are called A to C moves. When you "go A to C," you have moved beyond saying the obvious or the expected.

Let's go back and show how making A to C moves would "fix" Pattern 2 at any point in the pattern.

PATTERN 2:   **island, sand, rock...**

Going from "sand" to "rock" was bad because, while this improviser went off of the last word said, they did so laterally. "Rock" is the very first thing the improviser probably thought of off of "sand." If "sand" is the A, the improviser went right to their B, or first thought. When you go from A to B, you often end up just listing synonyms for the suggestion or a subset of elements that belong in the category represented by the suggestion. An example of a subset of elements in a pattern would be: Beatles, John, Paul, George, Ringo. We haven't gotten any new ideas since we already know the Beatles. Saying: John, Paul, George, Ringo, and *then* Beatles would be bad for the same reason.

You might find yourself making moves in a Pattern Game that are obvious or expected when you first learn the Pattern Game. Making these A to B moves is natural. The way you can learn to make less obvious moves is to manually go through the process of "going A to C." You could also think of this process as "going to your next thought."

PATTERN 2a: **island, sand, Rolling Stones**

In this example, hearing "sand" might first make you think of "rock." "Rock" feels obvious and expected coming off of "sand" and "island." Forcing yourself to go from A to C means not saying "rock," but instead going to your next thought. Let's say your next thought off of "rock" was "Rolling Stones." So, "sand" was A, "rock" was B, and "Rolling Stones" was C. When you manually go A to C, you keep your B in your head and say your C out loud. By saying the C, you have started to generate ideas that take your group beyond the initial idea of "island."

Let's look at another example:

PATTERN 2b: **island, sand, broken window**

In this example, instead of saying "rock," which was your B, you went to another possible next thought off of "rock," or your C, which was "broken window."

Both of these new patterns are valid examples of A to C. You could argue that the thought process to "broken window" is clearer than the thought process that got us to "Rolling Stones." Your A to C connection may not always be clear and apparent to everyone else. However, it doesn't matter if your teammates know your exact A to C connection, as long as they make their own interpretation and therefore generate new information for scenes. The important thing is that you use A to C to keep yourself from saying the obvious or repeating ideas, until avoiding that becomes second nature.

Let's return to Pattern 2, extending one move later than we stopped last time.

PATTERN 2:   **island, sand, rock, palm trees...**

Going from "rock" to "palm trees" is a bad move for a different reason. In this case, you haven't gone off of the previous word; you've gone off of the initial word, "island." It seems like you haven't even been listening to your teammates. It is as if you have just been thinking about things to say off of the suggestion.

Let's return to Pattern 2 one move past "palm trees":

PATTERN 2:   island, sand, rock, palm trees, coconuts...

Like going from "sand" to "rock," going from "palm trees" to "coconuts" is a bad example of responding off of the last thing said, but doing so laterally. This move prevents us from getting away from the initial idea of "island."

Let's look at an example of a corrective move coming in Pattern 2 off of "palm trees":

PATTERN 2c: island, sand, rock, palm trees, pie...

Even though your group has essentially wasted the first three moves saying obvious things about islands, it is still not too late for you to fix this Pattern Game. In your head, you might think of "coconuts" off of "palm trees." However, if you push yourself to go A to C and say "pie," you've gotten your group off of "island" and onto the path of creating new ideas.

Let's now continue Pattern 2c with A to C moves that continue to bring the group to new ideas:

PATTERN 2c: island, sand, rock, palm trees, pie, calculus, Einstein...

Making A to C moves will help you to generate more specific and interesting information for scenes so that your entire show isn't comprised of scenes about islands. When you make A to C moves, you will make unique, personal, or unexpected connections. In doing so, you are ensuring that your own voice and perspective on things will be added in as part of the group mind.

Don't get caught up about making "perfect" A to C moves in the moment. If it seems like your Pattern Game is grinding to a halt and everyone is stymied, you are better off saying an A to B move than nothing at all.

AVOID OVERLY PERSONAL PROPER NOUNS

When making A to C connections, you want to avoid using overly personal proper nouns (e.g., Uncle Ted, the name of the street you grew up on, the name of your childhood babysitter, etc.). It will be impossible for your teammates to decode the connection you've made and add on appropriately, because they will have no knowledge about what you've added to the Pattern Game. Note: Proper nouns with which everyone is familiar are fine to use (e.g., Washington, D.C. or McDonald's).

LOOPING BACK TO THE SUGGESTION

A to C helps you to move away from the suggestion. You and your teammates will continue to add new information, each move building off of the last, until you can find an organic connection back to the suggestion. In order to do this, you should keep the suggestion in the back of your mind during the entire Pattern Game. Returning to the suggestion is how you complete a **loop of information** for the Pattern Game. Each Pattern Game should be comprised of at least three loops of information.

Let's return to our Pattern Game inspired by the suggestion of "island" to see a complete loop of information:

EXAMPLE 1

Suggestion: **island**

island, sand, hourglass, grim reaper, A Christmas Carol, shopping mall, Shop 'til you drop, Shop 'til you kill, We're murdering prices, discount vacation, island...

Now let's take a look at another complete Pattern Game loop of information off of the suggestion of "knives":

EXAMPLE 2

Suggestion: **knives**

knives, salesman, walking, sweaty, desperation, video, slick, graphics, gigabytes, latchkey kid, loneliness, dating, suicide, knives...

You want to try to return to the suggestion in between thirteen and twenty moves. Once you have returned to the suggestion, you will begin a second loop by moving away from the suggestion and once again going A to C. The Pattern Game can wrap up once you have organically returned to the suggestion at least three times. By doing this, you will have created at least three loops of information, all inspired by the same suggestion. You can think of the structure of a completed Pattern Game as a "cloverleaf." Each leaf represents a completed loop of information.

Returning to the suggestion is important. While we want to move away from the suggestion in order to generate lots of disparate information to inspire our scenes, it is important that we maintain some connection to the suggestion for our audience's benefit. Coming back to the suggestion lets the audience know that you are generating ideas that truly use and explore the original suggestion. Returning to the suggestion also enhances the performance aspect of the Pattern Game by providing a clear point on which to end the opening.

Remember, Pattern Game is one of the most difficult and challenging set openings to master. It is worth mastering since it exercises key improv muscles in your mind related to listening and memory. Keeping old ideas in mind, and looking for ways to connect back to them, is a skill that is very useful throughout an entire longform. If your group can successfully execute the Pattern Game, you have achieved group mind, which, in turn, will have a positive effect on your entire performance.

Now let's look at how we can add to this structure to develop premises.

ENERGY

The Pattern Game can be difficult, but don't perform it like you are solving a math problem. Don't just say each word or phrase in a neutral way. Add nuance to each word or phrase by allowing opinions or emotions to show through in the way you say them. Think of it as "performing the word," rather than simply saying it.

If your suggestion is "fork," and it leads you to think of a specific cafeteria lady that you encountered as a kid in school, you don't want to just say "cafeteria lady" in a flat, emotionless way. You could say "cafeteria lady" in the voice or tone of this cafeteria lady. Or if you didn't like the "cafeteria lady," you might say "cafeteria lady" with disdain or disgust. Whenever you infuse a word or phrase with specificity, you are offering a richer idea off of which your teammates can build.

If someone on your team makes the choice to bring some sort of energy to your Pattern Game, the next person in the group to respond should not "take a step backward" by saying the next word neutrally. Each new word or phrase should be looking to build upon the energy of the last thing said. This is not to say that every other idea in the "fork" Pattern Game needs to be said in a "cafeteria lady" voice or with disdain. A shift in tone or energy is acceptable as long as the energy doesn't drop completely.

There are multiple benefits to bringing energy to your opening. You will inspire more half ideas and premises in the Pattern Game if you bring your specific take to each new piece of information. Performing each word will offer your teammates more than its dictionary definition, and from this a premise can be built. Becoming more efficient at generating premises with the Pattern Game as a group is further evidence of a strong group mind.

A playful, energetic Pattern Game will also help your group get comfortable onstage, ready to have fun, and "out of your heads." A relaxed, confident, and fun opening will get you into the right mind-set for performing scene work as a group.

By performing each word in your Pattern Game, you will energize your opening and make it more engaging for your audience. Performing the Pattern Game with confidence, energy, and poise is important because the opening is the first time that the audience is seeing your group. If you start out the show timidly or awkwardly, it will be difficult to get the audience on your side and ready to laugh. If you are willing to make yourself look like a jackass here, you won't be in your head about looking like a jackass in your scenes.

DEVELOPING PREMISES

Remember, when performing the Pattern Game, new words are not generated through random word association. Improvisers are also not trying to say words that may be funny in a superficial way, whether due to rhyming or clever wordplay. Words are being said in the Pattern Game in order to develop premises.

Once you have moved away from the suggestion, everyone in your group should be looking to develop premises. You do this by building off of words or phrases that have comedic potential. Once you've found a word or phrase that has comedic potential in a Pattern Game, you no longer need to make A to C moves. This is similar to switching over from Yes And to If Then once you've found the first unusual thing in a scene. You now want to think of how you can build off of funny, interesting, or unusual specific information, either by making them more specific or by adding to what is funny about them. This process is referred to as **riffing**. You riff by asking, "If this, then what?" just as you do when you are playing Game.

Here is an example taken from an actual UCB workshop:

EXAMPLE 3

Suggestion: **pencil**

pencil, school supplies, shopping with Mom, embarrassment, no brand names, *making your own clothes...*

This group started from the suggestion of "pencil" and eventually arrived at the specific phrase "making your own clothes," which elicited a laugh from the rest of the workshop participants. Laughter can be used as a cue for focusing in on specific words or phrases. If the audience has laughed at a word or phrase, you want to ask yourself, "Why did they laugh at that? What is funny about that word or phrase?" The group used the laughter elicited from "making your own clothes" as their cue to build off of this phrase, using the If Then process to create a premise. They continued on:

...making your own clothes, homemade notebook, cardboard lunchbox...

By making these two additional moves, the group has solidified what they found to be funny about "making your own clothes." To this group, "making your own clothes" made them think of being embarrassed as a kid when they didn't have brand-name items. The next two moves solidify this viewpoint.

Using If Then to riff off of something that you find interesting or unusual in the opening is called **making threes**. Making threes means adding at least two If Then moves off of a piece of interesting or unusual information. When someone begins to If Then, they are signaling to the rest of the group that there is something worth exploring. Having at least three moves ensures that you and your group have really taken the time to build an idea together. Once you have given three examples of a funny idea, you probably have said enough to ensure that everyone in your group will recognize and remember this premise. Limiting yourself to about three moves ensures that you don't dwell on any one idea for too long, past the point of usefulness. Generating more than three ideas will often be overkill and diminish the impact of the premise when it is used in a scene. You run the risk of this premise feeling played out to the audience.

Once your group has found a premise through making threes, anyone in the group can easily offer an initiation containing this premise with confidence that everyone else will recognize it.

When you use laughter to identify premises, you are taking your cue from outside the group. You can also find premises from cues generated within the group.

For instance, someone else in your group may have said something that you think is funny or interesting, even if the audience hasn't laughed at it. You can still use the same process of riffing and making threes off of interesting or unusual information. Starting to riff off of these ideas is like saying to your group, "This is funny to me, and here is why."

Another way to find premises using cues from within the group is to recognize funny ideas born from the juxtaposition of words or phrases in the Pattern Game. Let's look at an example of a group building a premise in this way, taken from an actual UCB workshop:

EXAMPLE 4

Suggestion: **whiskey**

whiskey, happy hour, 2 a.m., halter top, vulnerability, saggy boobs, breast-feeding, breast-feeding at happy hour...

In this example, the group started from the suggestion of "whiskey" and generated words that started to build a picture of a depressing bar. They arrived organically at the idea of "breast-feeding" by making A to C moves. Someone in this group found the juxtaposition of "breast-feeding" with the bar setting to be funny. These juxtaposed ideas were then synthesized with the phrase "breast-feeding at happy hour." They continued on by making threes off of "breast-feeding at happy hour":

...breast-feeding at happy hour, doing shots and changing diapers, give me a beer and a Pedialyte on the rocks...

Other members of the group made If Then moves off of the synthesized idea of "breast-feeding at happy hour." This group successfully generated a clear premise for a scene that should be recognized by every member of the group.

Here's another good example of using listening, specificity, juxtaposition, and incorporating what has come before to arrive at a premise:

EXAMPLE 5

Suggestion: **horticulture**

horticulture, bonsai, catch a fly, Zen garden, the sounds of whales, buffet, the sounds of eating buffet...

This group started to create a clear theme of spiritual, Zen ideas off of their suggestion. All of the words were said in a soothing, calm voice. "Buffet" was an organic A to C move inspired by whales. The improviser who said "buffet" heard "whales" and thought of the negative slang term for a fat person. To this improviser, "buffet" relates to whales while also introducing a new, mundane idea that stands out from the pattern of spiritual ideas. The next improviser to speak arrives at a funny idea by synthesizing this new idea with everything that came before. This improviser said "sounds of eating buffet" in the same soothing, calm voice that the original ideas were said in. This presentation of something mundane and unappealing as something soothing and spiritual can now be riffed on and eventually explored further in a scene.

There is a fine distinction between synthesizing ideas organically and randomly connecting words from a Pattern Game. Random connections will feel forced and keep you from finding strong premises. Let's look at an example of a Pattern Game that includes a forced or random connection:

EXAMPLE 5a

Suggestion: **horticulture**

horticulture, bonsai, catch a fly, Zen garden, the sounds of whales, buffet, bonsai buffet...

In this example, you have wasted much of the information your group has created. The improviser who said, "bonsai buffet" does not build off of the bigger theme of spirituality created by the group. Randomly combining two ideas to come to a premise usually feels unearned and not organic. Even if an idea is funny, combining words randomly will be less impressive to the audience than organically synthesizing ideas. Randomly connecting ideas also betrays the momentum of the group mind and is therefore not supportive of your teammates.

Let's look at another example of developing a premise:

EXAMPLE 6

Suggestion: **NASCAR**

NASCAR, Tide, sponsor, AA meetings, cold coffee, phone calls, menthols, patches, Patch Adams, *Patch Jackson* (said in an "action movie" voice)...

"Patch Jackson" received a laugh. This is your team's cue to riff:

Patch Jackson, sad action heroes...
Now you've made the idea more specific and have clearly labeled what is funny about it. You can now build on this idea by making threes. After making threes, A to C will be used to move onto something new.

sad action heroes, good cop/tearjerker cop, Freeze or I'll cry, *tissues*, thermometer, flu shot

After making threes off of a piece of interesting or unusual information to turn words into a premise, you have two options: You can make A to C moves until you find another interesting or unusual piece of information to riff off of, or you can make A to C moves to organically return to the suggestion and complete a loop of information.

"Tissues" was the A to C move that got us away from the "Patch Jackson" riff. Now we are either heading toward another riff or we will complete the loop of information by returning to the suggestion of "NASCAR."

It is important that you find ways to move on within the Pattern Game. Once you've reached your goal of building a funny premise, push yourself to move onto new riffs or complete the loop of information.

You want to be as efficient as possible when developing premises in the Pattern Game. Developing a premise on your feet will not always be as succinct and efficient as the examples in this book.

Let's take a look at a real-life example in which a group eventually finds a premise inefficiently:

EXAMPLE 7

Suggestion: **coupon**

coupon, register, exact change, public bus, school bus, yellow bus, short bus, *bully bus*...

This group started off with some solid A to C moves ("coupon" was A, "cashier" was B, "register" was C; "register" was A, "change" was B, "exact change" was C, etc.). A somewhat strict but very clear pattern was started when the group went from "public bus" to "school bus." Even though this move is neither an A to C move nor the start of a riff, the rest of the team chose to support this choice by continuing the simple "_____ bus" pattern. "Yellow bus" and "short bus" are actual types of buses. Instead of slowing things down by thinking of another real bus, the next improviser to speak said the first thing that came into his mind: "bully bus."

Everyone laughed at "bully bus." Even though they didn't riff at this point to make threes, it still ended up inspiring a great scene involving an extremely short and wide school bus comprised of one giant back row. This bus was dedicated solely to the purpose of taking all of the bullies to school.

The improvisers in this group found this premise through luck, not skill. The improviser that said "bully bus" wasn't even intending to say something "funny," he was merely building onto the pattern created by his teammates. The lesson to take away from this example is that Pattern Games do not have to be performed "perfectly" in order to yield premises. The improvisers in this group made choices in the moment as opposed to getting in their heads about doing things in exactly the "right" way. Eventually reaching strong ideas in your Pattern Game (even if you do so inefficiently) is better than getting in your head and doing nothing at all.

PATTERN GAME CHALLENGE

One way to approach developing premises in the Pattern Game is to put this challenge before your group: Imagine that you were told that you'd be paid a million dollars for three comedy sketches, but you only had one Pattern Game to generate the ideas for these sketches. Broad, generic, or obvious words aren't going to help you find these sketch ideas. In order to be able to come up with these sketch ideas this successfully, you would need to be as specific as possible.

Let's look at both general and specific versions of the same idea. Which of the following suggests a more specific idea for a sketch: "alcoholism" or "breast-feeding at a bar"? How about "recession" or "homemade notebook"? Which sounds funnier: "patriotism" or "red, white, and blue suit"? The more specific you can be, the more likely you are to quickly find solid premises for your scenes.

MORE EXAMPLES

Here are some more examples of successful partial and complete Pattern Games. Remember, while it is helpful to look at these examples for structure, to actually learn the Pattern Game you will need to work with it on your feet.

The following example is only part of the first loop of information in a Pattern Game:

EXAMPLE 8

Suggestion: **coffee bean**

coffee bean, tea leaf, sunset, romantic getaways, romantic honeymoon, romantic songs, CDs you get at Starbucks (this got a laugh), the music of our memories, celebrating your anniversary at the Starbucks where you met...

This team was able to successfully generate a premise. After they ended their Pattern Game, one member of the team initiated with this premise:

PLAYER 1: **"Keep your eyes closed, honey. Do you smell coffee? Happy anniversary!"**

This initiation clearly and efficiently makes use of the premise generated within the Pattern Game. The improvisers don't need to search for a Game through Yes And–ing. Player 2 should know what Player 1 is implying from the very start of this scene.

Now let's look at a full Pattern Game and some sample initiations that could come from it. Please note that this is a real Pattern Game performed by improvisers in a UCB improv class. Since it is real, it is somewhat imperfect:

EXAMPLE 9

Suggestion: **scuff marks**

1st LOOP	2ND LOOP	3RD LOOP
Rollerblades	Parquet floors	Bowling shoes
Croissant	Imitation butter	Nachos
Disco lights	Imitation crabmeat	Beer by the pitcher
Studio 54	Imitation milk	Nacho cheese by the pitcher
Coke parties	Imitation breast milk	6 gallons of ketchup
Velvet rope	Imitation breasts	Extra grease, please
Velvet bedsheets	Imitation body	Side of cholesterol
Heart-shaped bed	Imitation boyfriend	Heart attack combo
Leopard-print underwear	Drifting apart	Defibrillator
Gold lamé	You've changed	Medic alert bracelet
Gold condom	Spare change	Old person on the floor
Gold lube	Sacajawea	Tiled floor
Diamond handcuffs	Two dudes and a chick on a long trip	Scuff marks
Live leopard	E-Z Pass	
Leopard covered in gold	Driving to Arizona	
Safari	Sage	
Quicksand	Cleansing auras	
Mud on my boots	Cleansing your colon	
Scuff marks	Cleansing your shoes	
	Scuff marks	

* Each "riff" is colored in red.

Each loop of this Pattern Game takes the suggestion in a new direction using A to C.

In this Pattern Game, "coke parties" and "velvet rope" evoked the idea of a sleazy lothario character to someone in this group, which inspired them to say "velvet bedsheets." The improvisers in this group continued to build this character until they eventually came to "gold condom." The group started a riff in order to make threes off of "gold condom" with "gold lube," "diamond handcuffs," "live leopard," and "leopard covered in gold." In this case, the group offered more than three moves to support this premise. Giving more than three moves is okay as long as a group remains focused on the same premise.

When it came time for scenes, someone stepped forward with the following initiation based on this premise:

PLAYER 1:   **"I appreciate you practicing safe sex, but I wasn't expecting you to be so extravagant."**

Player 1 has taken this premise into a scene by clearly setting up her scene partner to play the sleazy, extravagant lothario character suggested by the riff. She and her scene partner don't know exactly how this Game will play out yet, but they will be able to start their scene in agreement about which first unusual thing they are starting with.

Let's go back to our example Pattern Game. By going from "leopard covered in gold" to "safari," the group used an A to C move to take them out of a riff. A new theme began to develop with "safari," "quicksand," and "mud on my boots," but instead of pursuing this further until another premise was found, the group found an organic connection back to "scuff marks." Since we want to make these connections back to the suggestion in somewhere from thirteen to twenty moves, it was probably the right time to move on.

These final moves back to the suggestion are just as important as the riff. Making these moves gets you back to the suggestion and allows you to start generating a new loop of information that will provide a fresh take on your suggestion. Another possible benefit of making moves back to the suggestion is that this information will be available to initiate Organic Scenes. You still want to give priority to using premises, but if you can't identify or remember the premises found in a Pattern Game, you can initiate an Organic Scene with the half ideas or chaff that got you back to the suggestion.

The second loop begins with an A to C off of "scuff marks" to "parquet floors." The connection from "parquet floors" to "imitation butter" comes from an A to C between parquet wood flooring and Parquet-brand butter substitute.

At the start of this second loop, it seems like the group is riffing, but they are not. The "imitation ____" pattern contains many obvious or redundant moves. "Imitation crabmeat" and "imitation milk" coming off of "imitation butter" are both just other examples of imitation foods. Going from "imitation breast milk" to "imitation breasts" is a poor move because the group went from something slightly interesting (calling formula "imitation breast milk") to something real. They eventually salvage this pattern by getting laughs off of "imitation body" and "imitation boyfriend." They then neglect to finish making threes. It would have been better if they had offered more specific examples off of the premise of imitation boyfriend (e.g., imitation boyfriend, lies about spooning, synthetic compliments, etc.).

Take note. Although this group eventually found a usable premise, they got to it very inefficiently. In spite of all of its flaws, this loop was part of a Pattern Game that was still considered to be successful in terms of yielding premises for Long Form scenes. To reiterate an earlier point, Pattern Games do not have to be perfect in order to be usable.

Here is an initiation inspired by the premise of imitation boyfriend:

PLAYER 1: **"I'm afraid your parents are going to figure out that you bought me, Kate."**

This improviser has made it clear through his initiation that he is playing the "imitation boyfriend" mentioned in the Pattern Game. Again, neither improviser knows the Game or exactly how this scene will play out, but both are successfully starting the scene in agreement about a funny idea.

The rest of this loop doesn't contain any other clear or specific premises, but there is plenty of information there to inspire Organic Scenes. We could see scenes that start with a homeless man asking for change, Lewis & Clark–style explorers, two friends taking a road trip, someone undergoing acupuncture treatment, or two people in a New Age bookstore. The Pattern Game will have inspired the start of these scenes. The Game will be found through Yes And.

At the start of the third loop of information, the group found a funny idea almost immediately with the "nacho cheese by the pitcher" move. By getting more specific after that move, they eventually get to "heart attack combo," which inspires the following initiation:

PLAYER 1:　　**"I don't care how well it is selling. We need to take the Cardiac Arrest Chicken Wings off of the menu!"**

For initiations, presenting premises clearly is as important as recognizing premises from the opening. In the example above, this improviser has taken the funny premise of "heart attack combo" from the Pattern Game and then given his and his scene partner's characters an opinion about it. He also allows himself to "hit the ground running" by starting this scene in the middle. His initiation implies that they are in the middle of a conversation, in which Player 1 is opposed to the "heart attack combo" and Player 2 is in favor of it. Starting midconversation is a more active way to begin scenes. Player 2 has been set up to play someone who is in favor of the "heart attack combo." Player 2 can now develop a point of view and a pattern of behavior based on the gift given to him by his scene partner.

The third loop ends relatively abruptly. They generate some ideas about old people before connecting back to "scuff marks" in exactly thirteen moves.

All of your initial attempts at the Pattern Game will probably end with some room for improvement, just as this example does. It is important to realize that doing successful Pattern Games will take time and practice, just like any other aspect of Long Form. While you should always shoot for perfection, you can't expect to achieve it every time. However, adhering to the rules will bring you much closer to doing "perfect" Pattern Games.

Our section on examples wouldn't be complete without some bad examples to show you what you shouldn't be doing.

EXAMPLE 10

Suggestion: **rainbow**

rainbow, colors, yellow, red, green, blue

Why this is a bad start to a Pattern Game should be obvious. We don't find any new ideas here, and we are already six moves into the Pattern Game. We have made obvious moves that haven't told us anything we didn't already know after hearing the word "rainbow."

This is definitely a pattern of words (in that they are all words that clearly follow from one another), but these words are not going to be helpful to a group of improvisers. We want more than words in a Pattern Game; we want ideas. You don't want to take a word from the audience and generate another fifty words.

Now let's start over with the same suggestion:

Suggestion: **rainbow**

rainbow, leprechaun, wish, curse, cursing *leprechaun...*

By focusing on ideas and not just words, we have found the start of a funny idea in only five moves.

LENGTH

You don't want to let your Pattern Game (or any opening, for that matter) go on too long. A reasonable length for an efficient and productive Pattern Game is five minutes.

While the opening is important, recognize that scene work is going to be the most enjoyable part of your show. Funny scenes are what your audience is expecting. The opening is primarily a way to get ideas for those funny scenes. Only spend as much time on it as you need to generate scene ideas. If you spend too much time performing your opening, you run the risk of losing your audience.

Audience expectations aside, recognize that an overly long opening is also simply impractical. The average longform is going to feature somewhere between five and ten scenes. Therefore, you need ten ideas at most. If you allow your opening to go on forever and you generate thirty ideas, you have wasted your time. Your team will never need that many ideas in a single longform.

IN YOUR HEAD

Listening is of the utmost importance in the Pattern Game. As an improviser, you must be listening for many different reasons: to capitalize on opportunities to return to the suggestion, to retain those ideas that stand out to you for use in scene initiations, and to recognize new ideas that could take your group in a new direction.

All of these different reasons for listening can put you "in your head" as you attempt to learn the Pattern Game. Being in your head means that you are overwhelmed or lost in your own analysis of the improv you are performing. Your thinking is getting in the way of your doing. It is important to realize that it is completely normal for your openings to be stilted or clunky while you are still learning. This is not a bad thing. In fact, if your group is in their heads to some degree while learning, it probably means that they are being thoughtful about how the piece is evolving. Extensive practice is the only thing that will make this process second nature and allow you to get out of your head.

There are some situations in which being in your head is bad. It is bad to be in your head because you are clinging to ideas that apply to something that was said eight or nine moves ago. You also don't want to be in your head because you are thinking of jokes or clever things to say that are unrelated to what the rest of your group is creating. Finally, you don't want to be in your head because you are spending the Pattern Game judging yourself and fretting over your own performance.

Be patient with yourself when you are learning how to do the Pattern Game. With time and practice, performing the Pattern Game will eventually become second nature, and you will be able to get out of your head. For now, being in your head is normal and acceptable when you are looking for a way back to the suggestion, thinking of how to build off of someone else's idea, or making a mental note of an idea for a scene.

PRACTICE THE PATTERN GAME PIECE BY PIECE

As you dive into the Pattern Game, do NOT attempt to do everything described in this section all at once. Your ensemble should attack the Pattern Game one piece at a time.

For example, you may initially spend a rehearsal working on nothing but your ability to build off of each other's ideas through idea association. In the next rehearsal, you could work on making a closed loop of information by coming back around to the original suggestion. Once you feel comfortable with each of these processes separately, you could move on to combining them.

The first few times you run a Pattern Game, it will simplify the process if you stand in a circle and add new ideas by going "in order." This will ensure that everyone participates, and it will save you from thinking about when you should speak. After this, you can move on to performing a Pattern Game in which anyone can add the next idea.

When working on the Pattern Game, it is suggested that you focus on each of the component concepts in the following order:

1. Idea Association
2. Saying Ideas with Energy
3. Looping Back to the Suggestion
4. Going A to C with Each New Idea
5. Creating Three Loops of Information from One Suggestion
6. Focusing on a Funny Idea
7. Riffing on the Idea You Focused On
8. Making Threes

Mastering Pattern Game will not happen in a single rehearsal. Your group should plan to dedicate lots of time to getting comfortable with this opening.

WHY BOTHER WITH THE PATTERN GAME?

Some improvisers love the Pattern Game. Others can't wait to move on to a different type of opening. It must seem complex to you from reading this description. The fact is that the Pattern Game is fairly complex. However, it is important for new Long Form improvisers to practice the Pattern Game. This is because the Pattern Game works all of the muscles in your brain that will make you a better improviser.

Out of all the possible set openings at your disposal, you should spend the most time working on the Pattern Game. It is an opening in which all of the ideas come from the group mind. It helps you get better at creating, recognizing, and continuing patterns, which are at the heart of all comedy. Pattern Game also strengthens your listening skills.

Finally, when it is performed successfully, it is truly impressive to an audience.

Pattern Game may be difficult, but it is an essential "drill" for our art form. Piano players must initially spend hours playing scales to learn the difficult fingering that they will put to use later on as they tackle increasingly difficult compositions. Someone learning to paint must begin with still life and line drawings of the human form for years before they can move on to discovering their own style. Think of the Pattern Game in the same way. The skills you will take away from your time working with the Pattern Game will be invaluable to you later in your improv career.

EXERCISE: PRACTICING A TO C

INSTRUCTIONS

- A group of improvisers stands in a circle.

- One improviser begins the exercise by saying an idea followed by the letter "A."

- The improviser to their right goes through the process of A to C in their head. This improviser then says their C idea aloud, followed by the letter "C."

- The person to their right provides the new A word by guessing what the previous person's B idea might have been. Once they have a guess, this improviser says it aloud, followed by the letter "A."

- The person to their right uses the A to C process and says their C word idea aloud, followed by the letter "C."

- The exercise continues around the circle in this manner.

EXAMPLE:

> Improviser 1 says, **"Dresser, A."**
>
> Improviser 2 says, **"Soccer, C."**
>
> Improviser 3 guesses that Improviser 2's B was "shorts" and says, **"Shorts, A."**
>
> Improviser 4 says, **"Beach, C."**
>
> Improviser 5 guesses that the B was "summer" and says, **"Summer, A."**

Note: It doesn't matter if you correctly guess what the improviser's B is. For example, Improviser 2 may have thought, Dresser, A, Socks, B, Soccer, C. It is fine for Improviser 3 to come up with "shorts."

PURPOSE

- To practice going A to C in order to get to multiple interesting ideas from a single idea.

- To force you to break down the process of going A to C.

- To get a better sense of how your teammates think and play by looking at how they go from A to C.

The Invocation

The **Invocation** is a set opening developed by Del Close. The suggestion for an Invocation is always an object. Instead of just generating ideas inspired by the suggestion, a team performing this opening explores the suggestion by using their words to "summon" the suggested object via a specifically structured incantation.

IT IS

In the first section of the Invocation, the object is treated as a "thing." The group states facts or truths about the suggestion. Make these facts or truths as specific as possible. These ideas should be stated in phrases all starting with the words "It is." It is important that these facts and truths are not just physical descriptions of the suggestion. By making unique associations to the suggestion, improvisers go A to C within the structure of the Invocation.

EXAMPLE 1

Suggestion: **cell phone**

It is sleek and white.
It is free for me to use on nights and weekends.
It is in my pocket.
It is what brings me bad news via voice mails.
It is not allowed in my lecture hall.
It is the tool I use to make deals for my clients.
It is going off in the movie theater right now.
It is all I want for my birthday, Dad!

The "It is" section will continue with the improvisers generating even more information about the suggestion of "cell phone." In the above example, some of the moves are descriptive, factual truths about cell phones. Some are true statements about cell phones that also suggest specific characters or situations. For instance, "It is what brings me bad news via voice mails" suggests a character that is pessimistic about everything. The move "It is going off in the movie theater right now" suggests a situation in which cell phone use is annoying. At this point in the opening, we have only planted the seeds of possible characters and premises. We will expand upon these ideas in the following sections.

YOU ARE

Once you have generated somewhere from thirteen to twenty "It is" statements about the suggestion, you will move on to the next section, in which each new statement will begin with the words "You are." (Thirteen to twenty moves will allow each member of a group to contribute two or three ideas.) In the "You are" section of the Invocation, the object is treated like a person. In the "You are" section, you move beyond the factual to the analytical. You will do this by "talking to" the suggested object, attributing a personal nature or human characteristics to the suggestion. You can either return to ideas from "It is" or create brand-new ones.

EXAMPLE 1a

You are what I waited in line eight hours for.
You are what I will scream into until my client gets a big enough dressing room!
You are the latest model that every other kid in school has!
You are usually in my hands as I obsessively check for voice mail.
You are ruining the wedding with an obnoxious ringtone.
You are free text messaging. Seriously, what's the catch here?
You are what my students would rather be looking at instead of the collected works of some of the greatest French poets.
You are the vehicle through which he broke up with me!

The improvisers have returned to ideas from the "It is" section and expanded upon them. When you move on to the "You are" section, you do not need to return to every idea in the order that they were originally said. You also don't need to return to every single idea. The ideas that stood out the most will be the ones to resurface in later rounds. The move "You are what I will scream into until my client gets a big enough dressing room!" is expanding upon the agent character implied by the "It is" move, "It is the tool I use to make deals for my clients."

You want to add onto someone else's idea in this round, as opposed to returning to your own. This ensures that you are listening, and it helps you to develop group ownership over the ideas generated. As is the case with the Pattern Game, focusing in on someone else's idea will help ensure that more people in your group are aware of what is funny about this idea. (There will now be at least two people aware of the idea you have expanded upon.) This will increase the chances of both improvisers being on the same page when a scene is initiated using this idea.

THOU ART

After another thirteen to twenty statements in the "You are" round, you will move on to the next section, "Thou art." In the "Thou art" section of the Invocation, the object is treated like a god. Each statement in this section will begin with the words "Thou art." You will return to ideas from the previous two sections, abstracting or distilling them for use in the scenes of the show. To help endow the object with godlike status, you want to deliver each statement with commitment and in a heightened way of speaking. Deliver your "Thou art" statements like a Shakespearean actor performing on Broadway, trying to reach those audience members sitting in the back of the house. You are now dealing with the suggestion on a "grand" level. It should almost feel as though the team is collectively worshipping the suggestion.

New ideas and perspectives on the suggestion are also welcome in this section of the Invocation.

EXAMPLE 1b

Thou art the connection to the outside world that I
gaze at affectionately and crave constantly!
Thou art the wicked messenger of all news that is terrible!
Thou art but a symbol of this generation's simplicity and laziness!
Thou art an amazing deal no mortal man would be able to refuse!
Thou art the weapon I will use to conquer all of Hollywood!
Thou art pissing off the man giving the eulogy!
Thou art a Steve Jobs masterpiece!
Thou art the only thing that would make my 13-year-old life worth living!

In this section, each point of view is specified and exaggerated so that it is memorable to all members of the group. Again, it is best to make "Thou art" statements that expand on other people's ideas from the previous sections of the Invocation. This will let your teammates know what ideas you find interesting while also allowing you to add something of your own to an idea.

Again, new ideas are welcome in "Thou art," and it isn't necessary to come back to every single idea. You also don't have to return to ideas in the order in which they were originally presented.

I AM

After another thirteen to twenty statements in the "Thou art" round, you will move on to the next section, "I am." In the "I am" section of the Invocation, you "become" the object. The Invocation ends with the group summarizing the strongest ideas. Each member of the group will sum up one of the idea threads that have been expanded upon in the Invocation (e.g., the character of the agent, "inappropriate situations to use cell phones," etc.). This is done using a single word, preceded by the words "I am." While you should aim for one, saying two or three words is acceptable. These "I am" statements should also be delivered with a sense of finality.

Each member of the group should speak only once in this section of the opening. No new ideas should be incorporated. Look at this section of the opening as your chance to create an easy-to-remember list of your strongest ideas. Don't go back to obvious or surface-level descriptions of the object in this section. Try, in a single word, to pinpoint the unique perspectives your group developed about the suggestion.

Once every member of the team has spoken, bring the opening to a close by saying, "I...AM...[the suggestion]!" in unison.

EXAMPLE 1c

I AM RULE-BREAKER!	**I AM OBSESSION!**
I AM GIFT!	**I AM INVENTION!**
I AM INTERRUPTION!	**I AM STAR-MAKER!**
I AM DISAPPOINTMENT!	**I AM BARGAIN!**

I...AM...CELL PHONE!

Now all of the words in this "I am" section have a clear connection to "cell phone," even though on a surface level, words like "rule-breaker" or "disappointment" may not be the first things that come into your mind when you think "cell phone."

The Invocation opening, like the Pattern Game, will present both premises and half ideas with which to start scenes.

For instance, the idea thread about the agent suggests a specific character or point of view that can be brought into a scene. Starting a scene with the agent character would be starting with a half idea. The Game of this scene will be found through listening and making strong Yes And moves. On the other hand, the "interruption" idea thread suggests a premise that an improviser could initiate a scene with.

Let's look at examples of each type of initiation from this Invocation.

EXAMPLE 1 – Half-Idea Initiation

[**PLAYER 1** sets out two chairs across from each other.]

PLAYER 1: **"Look, kid, you know I love you. You're my number one client. I'm gonna make a call for you right now."**

EXAMPLE 2 – Premise Initiation

PLAYER 1: **"When Jim was alive he was always there for his friends and family—oh, excuse me."**

[**PLAYER 1** pulls a cell phone out of his pocket.]

PLAYER 1: **"Hey. Yeah, get two tickets. Yeah, center court sounds great."**

INVOCATION OF DEL CLOSE

The following is an example of Del Close performing an Invocation of himself, by himself, for his students. Note that because Del is using himself instead of an object, his first section becomes "He is/ was" instead of "It is."

Invocation of Del Close

He was a young comedian.
He didn't know what he was doing and got into show
business for all the wrong reasons: ego satisfaction,
the fact that is was too easy, very easy, very easy to
impress, very easy to generate a little easy charisma.
But then he began to learn.

You! You! You asshole, you began to learn.
You stayed in your work too long, until it
was too late, and then you began to realize
what you had gotten yourself into.
You surprised him!
You took a step he didn't expect, and you committed
to something that frightened him to death.

Thou art my higher nature, and I have become thee.
Much to my surprise.
I know who thou art.
Thou comest and takest my body and my mind and use
it for thy purpose with my wholehearted permission.
I am the messenger.
I am not what he expected to become.
There is no enlightenment or reward in this life for me.

I am the messenger.
I am the channel.
I am his final doom.
I am the door through which you
will pass, but he may not.
But he understands.
I am the messenger.
Nothing less.
But nothing more.

The specific structure of the Invocation makes it appealing to newer improvisers. The structure guarantees that everyone on your team will know both what to do next and when the opening will be finished. The structure's theatricality also generally makes this opening engaging, satisfying, and entertaining to audiences.

The Invocation also allows a group of improvisers to work together to gather different perspectives on a single suggestion. It generates information for scene work while entertaining the audience. It also emphasizes listening and building on each other's ideas, behaviors essential to the success of any longform.

The Invocation is a good opening for beginning improvisers. The Invocation offers new improvisers a structured way to honor and explore the suggestion given to them by the audience. Whenever you are performing a longform, you should try to imagine a question mark after your suggestion. If you are really honoring the suggestion, the Long Form show you perform should answer this implied question posed to you by the audience. The structure of the Invocation, which forces you to return specific ideas connected to the suggestion, will help you to do this.

Monologues

We mentioned monologue openings briefly in the section on finding the Game with premise. We will now take a more in-depth look at how to perform this opening.

The **Monologue Opening** is a set opening that is usually performed by a single person. The monologist can be a member of the ensemble or a guest performer. The monologist will tell a true story that has been inspired by an audience suggestion. The rest of the ensemble will pay close attention to the monologue, listening for premises and half ideas to inspire their scene work.

HOW TO TELL MONOLOGUES

Any true anecdote or story that a suggestion conjures up in your mind is good enough to be a monologue. The very fact that you have remembered this story means that something happens during it that is a break from the commonplace. This break from the expected, the element that makes this story "a story," is what the improvisers in your group will use as premises for their scenes.

Note that your anecdote or story *must be true*. There are a few reasons for this. First and foremost, fabricating an interesting story that is not true is going to be very difficult for you to do as a monologist. Secondly, an overly absurd fictional story is going to be filled with ideas that have already been exaggerated and heightened, leaving nowhere for the improvisers to go in scenes.

Specifics and details are extremely valuable to the improvisers listening to your monologue. Sometimes a detail will inspire an entirely different premise. In other instances, a detail will provide a half idea that can be used to initiate an Organic Scene. Specifics and details can help inspire strong characters or locations for two improvisers to start a scene.

The monologue doesn't need to be a piece of stand-up comedy. It doesn't need to be "hilarious" on its own. All an improviser needs from a monologue is a true story filled with specifics and details. The monologue is not the time to tell jokes. Like any other opening, the monologue must generate information for scenes. The scenes are what we want to focus on making funny.

HOW TO USE MONOLOGUES

As with any opening, listening is the key to success with monologues. The rest of the ensemble must be listening intently to both the monologue and the audience's reactions to this monologue. The improvisers should be asking themselves things like, Where did the audience laugh?, Why did they laugh at that detail or moment?, and, What is funny about this story?

Improvisers need to go beyond identifying the funny specifics and details present in this story. You want to attempt to isolate potential premises by asking yourself, What is funny about this monologue on a conceptual level? Sum up the essence of the story's humor without using any specifics. Boiling down a monologue to what is fundamentally funny about it will help you find premises. These premises can then be easily inserted into different situations with different specifics.

Another source of premises in a monologue are the funny behaviors and points of view of the people described in the monologue. These behaviors and points of view can be embodied and exaggerated for characters in your scenes.

You may also find inspiration for a character based on how the monologist tells a story. In these instances, you are drawing on the real-time behavior, mannerisms, and opinions of your monologist. For example, if a monologist referred to something very tragic as a "bummer," you might initiate a scene as a character that is cavalier about tragedy.

You must also pay attention to specifics and details in monologues. Although they may not provide fully formed premises for scenes, they are often interesting or unusual enough to provide half ideas to start scenes with.

You want to avoid simply reenacting the story from the monologue that was told with all of the same specifics. The audience has already heard this story. We don't want to give them what they already know. In fact, you never want to use more than one premise or half idea from the monologue per scene that you perform. There are two reasons for this. First, if you use multiple scene ideas in one scene, you will burn through your stock of ideas too quickly. Remember that the entire ensemble is depending on using information from the monologue to inspire scenes. Additionally, including more than one premise or half idea in the same scene will muddy the Game of your scene. Including more than one premise or half idea in the same scene will weaken the base reality, and it will steer you toward Crazy Town.

There are three ways to start a scene using a premise from a monologue. The first way is called **nail on the head**, in which you use an event or line from a monologue almost exactly as it was presented in the monologue. The event or line you take should be funny or have inherent comic potential. In a nail-on-the-head scene, you will want to heighten from this starting point. The second way is called **one step beyond**, in which you start with the same specifics (the

Who, What, and Where) from the monologue, but not an exact line or event. "One step beyond" refers to the fact that you are starting with something that is heightened, or one step beyond what happened in the monologue. In these scenes, you can avoid reenactment by exaggerating the circumstances or character behavior. The third way is to perform an **analogous** scene, in which you change the specifics from the monologue but retain the fundamental premise.

Below are examples of nail on the head, one step beyond, and analogous scene initiations, all based on the same premise pulled from an actual monologue, told by Andy Richter at the Upright Citizens Brigade Theatre:

Suggestion: **dunk**

"That makes me think of basketball, and now I'll sit down. No, um, I was a fairly sporty youth. I played in a number of different sports, but the ADD always got in the way. It really did. I dabbled in a bunch of different sports. The only thing that stuck it out was speech team. I played tennis on the tennis team and I was awful. And I played baseball and I was not so good.

"But football was the one, because of my size and just because of the whiteness of where I was from, football was the thing and you've got to play football. And I played football up until my junior year. I never really had the killer instinct and I would see this *Lord of the Flies* transformation of all my friends. There was this one kid who was just an asshole. It was when we were sophomores and we were scrimmaging the freshman, and he took out a freshman's knee, gave him a compound fracture, and then high-fived everybody because there was a bone sticking out of the kid's leg. And that's where I'd kind of stand there just feeling like, I'm in the wrong place."

NAIL ON THE HEAD

Example 1:   **"Now that's a tackle! You broke that kid's arm! Way to go!"**

Example 2:   **"Listen up, team. We're gonna work all summer. Five days a week. Weight training and wind sprints. However, I am obliged to tell you these**

practices are 'voluntary.' And I think you all
know what voluntary means." [*Laughs*]

Example 3:   **"Listen to me kid, don't get into the grocery business."**

All of these lines are funny or have inherent comic potential. As the scene progresses, do not follow the story of the monologue. Instead, create a pattern of behavior from the event or line of dialogue that you started the scene with in order to find a Game. For instance, in Example 1, we could create a pattern of behavior if the coach says, "Coach, I'm on fire today. I feel like I could break a leg or even a spine." This creates the Game of "football team celebrating violence."

In Example 2, you could create a pattern of behavior if the coach goes on to say, "I don't want you going to see movies this summer, I want you watching last season's game films. But that is just a 'suggestion.'" This line sets up the Game of "mandatory, extreme personal sacrifice being disingenuously presented as voluntary."

Example 3 could progress with the following line: "At the beginning, when you do a cleanup in an aisle, you think you're making a difference. You feel like a hero. But then you realize there's no parade and there's another spill two aisles over." This initiation has been built upon to create the Game of "a grocery store clerk talking about his job like a grizzled war veteran."

ONE STEP BEYOND

Let's say a monologue includes the following sentence: "They'd be talking about, you know, competing grocery stores, how that one has a shitty meat department and, you know, all this stuff..." You might initiate by saying, "Yo, man, you're one of the new guys. We're going over to Whole Foods right now. You have a chain or bat or something?" This would establish the premise of "ganglike rivalries between supermarket chains."

Let's say a monologue includes the following structure instead: "At practice, when we were sophomores scrimmaging against the freshman, one of the guys kind of chop-blocked one of the freshman and gave him a compound fracture, and then got up and high-fived the other guys about, like, breaking a kid's leg so the bone was sticking out. Whoo!

Yeah! We did it! We fucking injured a 14-year-old..." You might then initiate by saying, "Listen up guys, this is Henderson. He's our 14-year-old to hurt today. I'd like to see a broken leg out of him by the end of practice." This establishes the premise of "treating the injury of younger students as a regular part of practice."

Off of this section of the monologue: "Hey coach, I just wanted to say I do know what voluntary means... Thanks a lot for letting us blow off practices this summer." This establishes the premise of "missing the subtext of what someone is saying and taking them literally."

ANALOGOUS

INITIATION:	"Hi, welcome to the Public Museum of Art. Admission is free, but we recommend a donation. [threateningly] And I think you know what I mean by recommend. And I think you know what I mean by donation."
GAME DESCRIPTION:	Something mandatory being presented as voluntary with an implied threat.

INITIATION:	"Look, you're my little brother so I'm gonna be straight with you. This recession has killed the lemonade stand business. I'm gonna have to let you go."
GAME DESCRIPTION:	Overly weary businessman at a small-time, mundane job.
ANALOGOUS GAME DESCRIPTION:	Little kid at a lemonade stand acting like the owner of a small business.

INITIATION:	"We did it! Two heart attacks in our haunted house last night! And it's only October 2nd!"
GAME DESCRIPTION:	Celebrating an unfortunate outcome of doing your job well.

ANALOGOUS GAME DESCRIPTION: **Workers at an amusement park celebrating scaring people to death with their haunted house.**

WHY USE MONOLOGUES?

It is easier to identify and use what is funny in a monologue than it is for other openings. First, the point of telling a monologue is to clearly present something you found to be unusual or funny to an audience. Additionally, listening to funny stories and understanding what is funny about them is something that everyone has done their entire lives. It isn't a skill you have to learn, such as generating and identifying funny ideas in more abstract openings like the Pattern Game or the Invocation. Due to this greater ease in recognizing premises in a monologue, it is more likely that you and your fellow performers will be on the same page.

By pulling the funny premises from a monologue and using them to start scenes, you avoid the work of establishing a base reality and a first unusual thing. Remember, a premise presents a base reality and first unusual thing simultaneously. Starting with a premise will allow you and your scene partner to find your Game much faster than if you were starting from scratch.

Audiences enjoy monologues because it is easy for them to see their suggestion at work. If the monologist has done their job, the connection between the suggestion and the monologue should be very clear. Since it is easy to identify and pull premises from a monologue, the audience should, in turn, see their suggestion reflected in the scene work.

The major drawback of using monologues is that they aren't as group mind–oriented as other set openings. Instead of working together to generate ideas for scenes, all of the information is coming from one person. Additionally, if you are acting as the monologist for your ensemble, it can be difficult to pull ideas from your own monologue, thereby making it difficult for you to initiate scenes. While monologue openings are easier for a group just starting to perform, they are not the best opening for developing a group mind.

CHARACTER MONOLOGUES

Character monologues are used in a set opening in which improvisers take turns creating characters in the moment. Each improviser delivers a completely fictional monologue in character to the audience. All of the characters are inspired by the same single suggestion from the audience. The improvisers will then use the premises and half ideas from these character monologues to initiate the scenes of the longform.

HOW TO PERFORM CHARACTER MONOLOGUES

When you portray a character in this opening, you must make it specific. For instance, if the suggestion of "heart transplant" made you think of a doctor, you can't just portray a "typical" doctor; you have to play a specific type of doctor. Your first impulse should be to think of a real doctor that you know whom you find to be interesting. For instance, if you knew a doctor who smoked and cursed while he examined you, you could use this, creating a character by extrapolating behaviors consistent with smoking and cursing. Doing this will ultimately create a premise you can use to initiate a scene.

If the connection you make to the suggestion brings to mind an archetypical character as opposed to a real person, you can use this character archetype to create a completely fictional, specific character. A simple way to accomplish this is to put an adjective in front of the character archetype you are playing. This adjective should be inspired by your opinion of or knowledge of this archetype. You will extrapolate behaviors for this character based on the adjective you have selected. Once again, if the connection you make to the suggestion is the archetype of "doctor" and not a specific doctor from your life experiences, begin by thinking of your opinions of or general knowledge about doctors. If the first thing you think of is that doctors make a lot of money, you might choose to add the adjectives "heartless" and "greedy" to doctor and then perform a monologue as this character.

Remember, one of the main purposes of an opening is to generate many different premises and half ideas for scenes from a single suggestion. In order to do this, you'll want to have variety in the characters you create as an ensemble. For example, the suggestion of "guitar" could inspire individual members of an ensemble to perform character monologues as an arrogant rock star, a depressed music teacher, an overly aggressive street musician, a pretentious college radio DJ, an evangelical Christian who thinks rock music is evil, a self-important open mic organizer, and a mother who is tormented by her son's loud music. You wouldn't want to take the suggestion of "guitar" and perform monologues as eight different arrogant rock stars.

Each monologue is performed until another member of the ensemble edits it. You edit someone by stepping forward to deliver your own monologue. Once everyone has established a character, the ensemble will begin revisiting the characters they've already created. By returning to these character monologues, the ensemble has a chance to get more specific with the ideas and points of view they've created. Since these character monologues will be revisited two to three times over the course of the opening, each monologue should be short and therefore edited aggressively. When revisiting your character, try to incorporate themes and details from the other character monologues into your own. Do not try to establish relationships between the different characters. Remember, we aren't creating a story with this opening; we are creating information to inspire scenes. Characters don't need to be revisited in the same order. Any member of the ensemble can end the opening with a sweep edit. This will generally happen on a laugh line, when the ensemble feels that enough information has been generated to inspire their scenes.

Variations on the Character Monologue Opening Structure

There are other variations on this opening. After each member of the ensemble establishes a character, you could take over each other's characters when they are revisited. Doing so will make each character more of a product of the group mind than a product of an individual. Taking over another performer's character again requires careful listening so that you can build on what they have already created. You could also perform a version of this opening in which improvisers play new characters that are interacting with the characters created in the first round. Yet another variation would be to create characters that all exist in a single location (e.g., a circus, a rock concert, a courtroom, etc.).

EXAMPLES

Let's look at an example:

EXAMPLE 1

Suggestion: **fire**

PLAYER 1 / LOTHARIO FIREMAN: "I became a fireman because you get a lot of tail. Women are really turned on by lifesaving."

PLAYER 2 / CAVEMAN: "Fire is passing fad. Caveman no believe fire good for human race in long run."

PLAYER 3 / MIDDLE-AGED WOMAN: "This is so depressing. Did we really have to emphasize how old I am by putting forty-eight individual candles on the cake?"

PLAYER 4 / MOOCHER: "Hey man, can I bum a smoke from you? Come on, man, I'll buy you a pack, I swear."

PLAYER 5 / INTENSE SCOUTMASTER: "Don't sign up to be an Eagle Scout unless you're serious about scouting, okay? Eagle Scouts aren't just Eagle Scouts on the weekend. You've got to be scouting 24/7."

In these five monologues, we have five very different takes on the suggestion that could inspire a number of different scenes. In an actual, full character monologue opening, we would hear a few more characters (depending on the number of people in the ensemble) and then we'd return to each character.

HOW TO USE CHARACTER MONOLOGUES

As you stand on the back-line, it is important for you to listen carefully to the character monologue being performed. Listening carefully will help you to incorporate themes and details from other character monologues into your own. Listening also makes you better prepared to explore any premise or half idea presented to you in a scene initiation.

As with any opening, you have the option of taking either a premise or a half idea inspired by something that one of the characters said to initiate a scene.

Once again, there are three ways to initiate a scene using a premise from a monologue. You can initiate a nail-on-the-head scene, in which you play the character you created, using an exact line of dialogue from your monologue. You will then continue to develop the character off of this first line. In a one-step-beyond initiation from a character monologue opening, you play the character you created but do not initiate with an exact line from your monologue. You begin with a line that is heightened one step beyond what happened in the monologue. It is also possible for you to initiate a one-step-beyond scene by offering an initiation that sets up one of your teammates to play the character that they created in the opening. The final possibility would be to initiate with a premise that is analogous to the central premise from a character monologue. In this case, you are not limited to using your own character monologue. You can pull a premise from any character monologue in the opening.

WHY USE CHARACTER MONOLOGUES?

Character monologues are a great way to force your ensemble to make strong character choices. Also, like regular monologues, they are often more immediately satisfying and entertaining for an audience unaccustomed to Long Form.

The one drawback of the character monologue opening is that, since it is less dependent on the group mind, it puts more of a burden on each individual to generate funny ideas by themselves.

EXERCISE: ADJECTIVE, ADJECTIVE, NAME

INSTRUCTIONS

- A group of improvisers creates a back-line.

- One improviser steps off of the back-line to be the character monologist.

- On the back-line, assign two improvisers to provide adjectives, and one improviser to provide a name.

- On the count of three, the assigned improvisers on the back-line yell out the adjectives and name.

- The character monologist immediately takes on these adjectives and introduces themselves in character.

- Example: 1...2...3! "Smelly!" "Creepy!" "Carl!"

  Smelly Creepy Carl: [sniff] "Hi girls. I'm Carl. Sorry about the smell. That's why I came into the ladies' room..."

- After they have performed a one-minute monologue as this character, start over with a new volunteer from the back-line.

PURPOSE

- This exercise allows you to practice performing character monologues without the burden of coming up with characteristics yourself.

FINAL WORD ON SET OPENINGS

The set openings described here are only a small sampling of the many set openings in existence. Ensembles around the country are constantly creating new set openings. Now that you have a sense of a set opening's purpose and the structure of some of the most important ones, you and your group can create a set opening of your own design. Any agreed-upon structure that generates ideas, develops group mind, and entertains the audience will work as a set opening. The most important thing that an opening must do is generate ideas. No matter what kind of opening you create, make sure that it first and foremost provides ideas for scenes.

As a beginning improviser, be careful that your group doesn't spend too much time creating a novel, signature opening. Your primary focus should be on making your scene work well.

ORGANIC OPENING

The **Organic Opening** (also known as "the Organic") is an unstructured opening that can include elements of other set openings without adhering to the overall form of these openings. The form of the Organic is discovered in the process of performing it. In addition to elements of set openings, the Organic often will include simple sounds and movements as a means of creating information. *(Please see the exercise "Follow the Follower" for an explanation of sound and movement.)*

The Organic Opening starts with an audience suggestion and goes wherever the group performing it wants it to go. In a true Organic Opening, even though you have the option to use elements of set openings, absolutely nothing is planned, and anything goes. Whereas all of the previous set openings we have described have a structure and very specific rules, the Organic Opening essentially has only two rules: listen to each other and create patterns.

An Organic Opening should still fulfill all of the objectives of any Long Form opening. It should generate ideas for scenes, help develop group mind, and entertain the audience.

PERFORMANCE

The performance of the Organic Opening is similar to the performance of Organic Scenes. You will get into agreement with your fellow performers at the start and work together to recognize and then develop comic patterns.

Commitment is paramount to the performance of the Organic Opening. Because you will feel less certain when performing the Organic due to the lack of form, there is a tendency to get in your head and hold back until you are sure of what is going on. If you do this, the opening will stall out. Go forward in spite of your fear. If you commit, you will continue to contribute information that can be turned into premises. Since everyone else on your team will be committing, you can trust that the group mind will figure out how the opening will proceed.

While the Organic Opening can take any form, the following criteria are essential to any opening:

- Listening

- Following the lead of the first person who responds to the suggestion

- Creating loops of information *(see page 228)*

- Having each new section of the opening be inspired by the suggestion or something from the previous pool of information

- Continuing your opening until you have sufficient information to perform scene work

- Ending your opening by returning to something dynamic from the beginning

The following exercise can be used to practice the sound and movement element of an Organic Opening.

EXERCISE: FOLLOW THE FOLLOWER

INSTRUCTIONS

- A group of improvisers forms a circle.

- The improvisers will adopt a neutral position (e.g., head facing forward, feet shoulder-width apart, arms hanging by their sides, etc.).

- The objective is to remain neutral, but not frozen. In other words, no one consciously initiates any movements or "leads."

- The improvisers will scan the circle and should look to mirror any slight movements or facial expressions that they see. This could be something as simple as the twitching of an arm or the subtle shift in weight from one foot to another.

- Once two or more people are mirroring each other, the rest of the group must join in.

- At this point, a small sound that complements the movement will be added by someone in the group. The entire group must then mirror this sound.

- From this point on, every repetition of movement and vocalization must be heightened from the last.

- Continue this heightening process until you can't possibly go any further, and the sound and movement necessarily transforms into something else. It's important to note that again, there is no leader. No one is consciously transforming; that will happen as a product of heightening.

- After about three or more transformations, look to end the exercise at a heightened moment.

ALTERNATE INSTRUCTIONS

- A group of improvisers forms a circle.

- Someone outside of the circle gives them a suggestion.

- This suggestion is used to inspire a specific sound and movement. This means rather than starting from neutral, you are starting with a choice. One person initiates with this choice, which everyone else then mirrors.

- The group then heightens and transforms this sound and movement in the same fashion described above.

PURPOSE

- This is a good way to practice getting in sync with other improvisers when using sound and movement to generate information. Sound and movement will be used in this way to generate information in an Organic Opening.

Note: This exercise can also serve as a good warm-up for improvisation since it allows you to practice, in an abstract sense, what we are trying to do in organic Long Form scenes (start from nothing and find interesting ideas to explore).

EXAMPLE

The following is an Organic Opening performed by a group of improv students at the UCB Training Center in Los Angeles:

Suggestion: **fudge**

Since this suggestion is an object, it makes a member of the ensemble think of the Invocation. They step out and address the audience directly.

"It is poured on top of our most popular dessert."

The rest of the ensemble continues with an Invocation for a few moments.

"It is my cute word for mistakes."
"It is my favorite boardwalk treat."
"It is boiling hot, so be careful."

At this point, the group breaks into sound and movement. One member of the ensemble, inspired by the very last Invocation statement, crosses the stage as a waitress, miming a tray of food and drinks. She says, **"Please be careful...very hot!"**

Once again, the rest of the ensemble follows suit. Everyone moves around the stage as waiters and waitresses, saying things like, **"Right behind you!," "Very hot!,"** and **"Watch your back!"** Through commitment to the physicality of being members of a waitstaff with arms raised, holding trays, the group morphs into being airplanes. Everyone commits to this new choice and adds a layer of airplane-appropriate sound effects to their movement. Some members of the ensemble start playing air traffic controllers, directing the improvisers playing airplanes.

This then inspires a member of the ensemble to step forward and tell a short, true monologue.

"I once went on a trip with some friends to Vegas. We boarded the plane and my friend Bill immediately fell asleep. Bill hates to fly so his strategy is to try and sleep through the flight. He was out for about three or fours hours. He woke up expecting to be in Vegas and was horrified to find out that the flight had been delayed and that we hadn't even taken off yet."

This inspires another round of sound and movement. One improviser begins weeping and moaning. The rest of the group immediately follows suit. Everyone walks around the stage, crying and consoling each other. This turns into a giant group hug.

While they're in the group hug, crying and moaning, someone decides to label their actions by shouting, **"Me sad monster!"** The group starts to move around the stage as one character, playing the "sad monster" together. They say things like, **"Me so fat!,"** **"Me eat too much fudge watching romantic comedies!,"** and **"Me also eat too much human flesh!"**

This inspires a member of the ensemble to step forward and say a few lines of a character monologue directly to the audience.

[Eastern European accent] **"I guess I feel depressed because I don't know where the time has gone. One day you're a young vampire and the next thing you know, you're 300 years old."**

Another student steps out to deliver a character monologue as another depressed monster.

"I need to find a therapist to help me control my rage issues. I don't like the Wolfman I become when there is a full moon."

Yet another student steps out to continue this pattern.

"I guess I need someone to help me get comfortable with the fact that causing a mess is part of my job. I'm a total clean freak, but every time someone disrupts my tomb I cause a horrific sandstorm."

The ensemble returns to the sound and movement for a third time, creating an epic windstorm, physically running around the stage in circles and making the sound of a gale force wind destroying everything in its path. Improvisers label things we see flying through the air: a **cow** flies by, then a **goat**, then an **alpaca**, then some **alpaca breeders**. As the improvisers run past each other to physically create this storm onstage, they make a callback to the waitstaff passing each other, once again saying, **"Excuse me,"** **"Right behind you,"** etc.

An improviser breaks from the windstorm and faces the audience to say:

"I am emotion-eating monster!"

The rest of the ensemble supports this move by calling back memorable ideas from this Organic Opening.

"I am intense waitress!"

"I am delayed takeoff!"

[in unison] **"I...Am....Fudge!"**

This Organic Opening incorporated elements of the Invocation, monologues and character monologues. The ensemble used sound and movement as a bridge from one type of opening to another.

This ensemble listened to each other and committed to each new choice. They took turns making strong choices and following the lead of those improvisers making the strong choices. Each new move was inspired by the last. The opening ended with a strong callback to how it started.

Most importantly, this opening generated comedic ideas. Here are three ideas that could be used for the first beat of a Harold:

1. A Premise Scene about a man explaining that he loves an acclaimed hour-long drama so much that he is going to sleep until the next season begins

2. A Premise Scene about a meteorologist who rates the power of a windstorm by what animals it is capable of picking up

3. A half-idea scene starting with two pilots in the cockpit of a plane that is being delayed. (Eventually they find a Game when they argue over who should have to deliver the bad news to the passengers.)

As for Group Games, we could see the following scenes:

1. A Premise Scene about depressed monsters attending a group therapy session.

2. A half-idea scene about a waitstaff trying to navigate through an increasingly crowded restaurant.

WHY DO THE ORGANIC OPENING?

The fact that the Organic is so challenging is one of the primary reasons why a group should work on it. It is an opening that is *completely* improvised because there is no predetermined structure to fall back on. Since it is one of the most difficult openings, it is also one of the most satisfying to perform successfully. When performed well, an Organic is also very impressive to the audience.

The Organic can also be very liberating. Since you have the freedom to do whatever you want, it is fun to perform.

The Organic is the opening that is most likely to help an ensemble break new ground. Groups who experiment with the Organic Opening often develop vital new set openings.

The Organic Opening is a great way for an ensemble to develop their group mind. If your group can get on the same page and create funny ideas in this very unstructured form, doing so in your scenes should become much easier. There is no better opening for showing off your group mind.

However, the challenging nature of the Organic also accounts for one of its major drawbacks. The Organic is so challenging that it is very difficult for new groups to perform successfully. It takes a long time for most groups to get comfortable with the Organic. To overcome this, an ensemble that wants to perform the Organic Opening should spend a lot of time in rehearsal practicing it.

Another drawback of the Organic is that groups can be easily seduced by its free-form nature and lose sight of generating, identifying, and remembering ideas for scenes (the most important function of the opening).

GENERATING TOO MUCH INFORMATION

The main purpose of an opening is to generate ideas for scenes. You don't need an endless supply of ideas. Once you think you have enough ideas to inspire the number of scenes your form requires, your opening should be over. The more ideas you generate, the harder it will be to remember the best ones. If there are five main ideas in an opening, you are likely to remember them all. If there are ten main ideas in an opening, you will probably forget some of them. If there is an overabundance of ideas to choose from, it becomes more likely that you will start a scene using an idea that your scene partner has forgotten, making it more difficult for you to get on the same page. Finally, if you generate more ideas than you end up needing, you run the risk of your audience feeling disappointed that an idea they liked wasn't used.

NO OPENING

It is not mandatory to begin a longform with an opening. Some groups opt to launch directly into scene work off of a suggestion from the audience. A group that has a strong group mind and has been performing together for a long time will usually pull this off with greater success than a brand-new group.

A drawback of performing without an opening is that almost every scene will be an Organic Scene. As the show goes on, you may find it difficult to continue to come up with more ideas for scenes off of one single suggestion.

We advise that new Long Form ensembles take the time to find an opening that suits them. Working together to create premises will make it easier for you to do successful scene work. Rehearsing and performing an opening is also a great way to develop group mind and establish a group identity. Additionally, the muscles you are forced to exercise when performing an opening are the same muscles you will use to perform the scene work that makes up the majority of any improvised show.

FINAL WORD ON ALL OPENINGS

It is easy to get in your head while trying to harvest ideas from an opening, especially when you first begin performing a new opening. It is important that finding inspiration in your fellow players be your number one priority in the performance of any opening. If you listen to them, you will connect to ideas together as a unit. If one of your teammates makes a move, you should be the one to support it and make them look great. Remember, as long as we are all working together and supporting each other, the chance of success greatly increases.

CHAPTER 11:

The Harold

"The Harold" is the grandfather of all longform structures, and the signature longform performed at the Upright Citizens Brigade Theatres in New York and Los Angeles. Created by Del Close in the 1960s, the Harold is the foundation for all other longforms that have followed since.

The Harold is one of the most challenging longforms. It challenges improvisers to perform at the top of their intelligence. The Harold additionally keeps their focus not only on each individual scene, but also on the form as a whole. The Harold is simultaneously very satisfying and enormously challenging.

The Harold incorporates nearly all of the key elements of Long Form. This makes it a great teaching tool for introducing longform structures in general. This is why the Upright Citizens Brigade has made the Harold the core of our curriculum.

STRUCTURE

The Harold is usually performed by a group of six to nine improvisers. It begins with a single suggestion from the audience. The suggestion will be explored through an opening that is predetermined by the ensemble before the start of the show. Any opening, including the Organic, can be used to generate ideas for scenes in a Harold.

After the opening, a series of three scenes are performed, called the **first beat of the Harold**. These first three scenes are generally two-person scenes. The first beat is followed by a Group Game, which is a scene involving most (or all) members of the ensemble. Three scenes that make up the **second beat of the Harold** will follow. In the second beat, the three Games of the first-beat scenes are explored through further heightening and exploration. The scenes in the second beat are presented in the same order they appeared in the first beat. A second Group Game, unrelated to the first, follows the second beat of the Harold. The show ends with the **third beat of the Harold**. In the third beat, the three Games are revisited once again. Your third-beat scenes should be shorter than your second beat scenes. You should look to hit your Game hard and move on. When performing a scene in this beat, you look to incorporate elements from the other scenes. This is referred to as **making connections**. In a "perfect" Harold, the third beat would be one scene that organically incorporates elements of all three Games.

The Perfect Harold

While the "perfect" Harold (wherein elements and Games from the entire Harold are combined into one final scene) is the ideal, you won't always be able to achieve this. The connections you make must organically present themselves. You do not want to force connections if they don't make logical sense. You don't want to force an elephant from a circus scene into a tea party scene just to make a connection. If you absolutely can't find any organic connections between the Games in your Harold, then you should perform three separate third-beat scenes. If you return to each Game successfully, you will have performed a successful Harold.

Perfect Harolds are rare. You are somewhat at the mercy of the fates. If connections do not present themselves, they can't be created. A no-hitter in baseball is a victory, but so is having more runs than the other team.

THE HAROLD STRUCTURE

- **SUGGESTION**
- **OPENING**
- **SCENE 1A SCENE 1B SCENE 1C**
- **GROUP GAME**

- **SCENE 2A SCENE 2B SCENE 2C**
- **GROUP GAME**
- **SCENE 3A SCENE 3B SCENE 3C (or) SCENE 3ABC**

There are a few different ways that you can think of the structure of the Harold. One way is to think of it as a circle. Picture a circle in your mind. Now imagine scanning down the circle from the top. It starts off narrow, gets wide in the middle, and then gets narrow again at the bottom. Think of the top of the circle as your opening. Think of the middle of the circle as your first and second beats of your scenes and your Group Games. This is the point in the Harold where you have generated the most disparate material. Think of the bottom of the circle as the third beat of the Harold, wherein you can find organic connections that tie everything together. A good Harold should resemble a circle in this way.

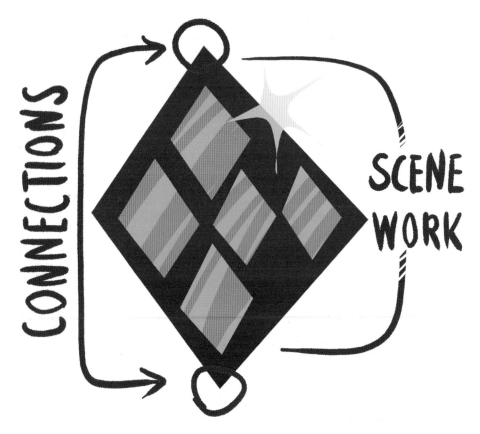

CONNECTIONS

SCENE WORK

Another way to think of the structure is as a diamond. Imagine going down a diamond from the top. It starts at a single point, widens out, and then comes back to a single point. Think of the single point at the top of the diamond as your suggestion. The diamond gets wide as this suggestion is expanded into different ideas. The diamond gets wider still as the ideas are then explored in the scenes and Group Games of the Harold. The end point of a diamond signifies the different Games of the Harold coming together in a single scene.

A FINAL WAY TO THINK ABOUT HAROLD STRUCTURE IS AS

PAINT BEING POURED OVER A SPHERE

IF YOU POURED PAINT ONTO THE TOP OF A SPHERE, IT WOULD FLOW FROM A SINGLE POINT OUT IN ALL DIRECTIONS, EVENTUALLY COMING TOGETHER AT ANOTHER POINT ON THE BOTTOM.

HAROLD

THE PAINT POOLING ON THE TOP OF THE SPHERE IS *THE OPENING.*

THE STREAMS OF PAINT FLOWING TOWARDS THE BOTTOM ARE THE DIFFERENT *SCENES AND GROUP GAMES* OF THE HAROLD.

THE STREAMS OF PAINT CONVERGING ON A SINGLE POINT AT THE BOTTOM OF A SPHERE REPRESENT THE *IDEAL ORGANIC CONNECTION OF EVERY SCENE.*

Once your team has explored the suggestion through an opening, the first beat of the Harold begins. The first beat consists of three different scenes, each one inspired by some information generated in the opening. These scenes are usually two-person scenes. It is possible to do a first-beat scene with more than two improvisers. However, starting scenes with two people usually makes finding the Game of the scene easier.

The first beat is where you will find the Games that will be played throughout the rest of the Harold. It is essential that you establish a Who, What and Where, as well as name the characters in each first-beat scene. Naming your characters will make it easier to revisit them later in the Harold. The Game of the scene will be found by initiating with a premise or a half idea generated in the opening. Once the Game of the scene has been found, the improvisers will heighten and explore it until another improviser from the back-line edits the scene (see pp.192–194 about editing).

Example Harold – First Beat

Let's imagine your Harold starting with Andy Richter's monologue as your opening. The first beat of your Harold might include a nail-on-the-head scene ("football team celebrating violence"), a one-step-beyond scene ("ganglike rivalries between supermarket chains"), and an analogous scene (the art museum scene using the premise of "something mandatory being presented as voluntary with an implied threat"). The above combination is just an example. You can use any combination of "nail on the head," "one step beyond," and analogous scenes in a first beat (e.g., three one-step-beyond scenes, two analogous scenes, and one nail-on-the-head scenes).

EXAMPLE HAROLD

SUGGESTION: **iceberg lettuce**

OPENING: **Andy Richter monologue (see p. 255)**

SCENE 1A: **Football team celebrating violence**

SCENE 1B: **Treating a supermarket like a gang**

SUPPORT IN THE FIRST BEAT

Be judicious about the amount of support work you provide in first-beat scenes. Remember, you cannot support someone else's Game until they have found it. Too much support work early in a first beat can prevent improvisers from finding a Game. You do not want to hijack someone's scene.

The most important job you have in the first beat of someone else's scene is to pay close attention to it. That way, you will be able to support the Game of the scene when necessary. This support may take the form of editing, walk-ons, tag-outs, split scenes, swinging doors, cut-tos, scene painting, sound effects, offstage characters, etc.

Whereas much of the above support is optional, the edit is essential. You must be paying close attention in order to edit the scene on a high note.

PAY ATTENTION

It is important to pay especially close attention to the first-beat scenes of a Harold, in order to ensure that you recognize and remember the Games and specifics of these scenes. Paying attention to the first beat will allow you to support the Games as they are revisited throughout the Harold. This will allow you to use these Games and specifics in the form of callbacks and connections later in the Harold.

In the moment after your first-beat scene is edited, try to distill or sum up the Game in as few words as possible, so you will be able to return to it in the second beat of the Harold. Remember, this is not the Who, What, and Where (or the plot) of the scene; it is the Game, which made your scene funny.

The Games (as well as the many times, characters and locations) established in the first beat will be returned to throughout the rest of the Harold. Each first-beat scene should have its own distinct Game. Starting your Harold with three scenes that are very disparate in terms of content and ideas will cause any connections that you make in the third beat of the Harold that much more impressive and satisfying. If you incorporate specifics from one first-beat scene into another first-beat scene, it is difficult to find your own Game and later make connections in the third beat.

SECOND BEAT

After the first Group Game (explained in further detail later in this chapter), the ensemble will return to each Game from the first three scenes in what is called the second beat of the Harold. Whereas in the first beat you are finding the Game, in the second beat you are finding a new scenario to play the Game you have already found. You can revisit the Game in one of two ways: **time dash** or **analogous**. In a time-dash second beat, you are returning to one or both of the same characters, playing the same Game in a new scene that takes place sometime before or after the first-beat scene. In an analogous second beat, you are playing the same Game in a different context with different characters. Whichever choice you make, you will be making some changes to the Who, What, and Where. You make these changes in order to give yourself new opportunities to play your Game.

Don't feel like you need to make your second beat better than your first beat. Simply return to your Game. Think of sitcoms. They aren't looking to make each episode better than the last; they are just finding new, fresh scenarios for their characters to play their games.

EXAMPLE HAROLD – SECOND BEAT

Continuing on from the first beat of the scenes inspired by the Andy Richter monologue, we might see the following second-beat scenes:

EXAMPLE HAROLD

SUGGESTION: **iceberg lettuce**

OPENING: **Andy Richter monologue (see p. 255)**

SCENE 1A: **Football team celebrating violence**

SCENE 1B: **Treating a supermarket like a gang**

SCENE 1C: **Art museum asking a patron for a donation with implied threat**

GROUP GAME 1

SCENE 2A: **Athletic awards ceremony celebrating violence (time dash, same two characters + additional improvisers)**

SCENE 2B: **Confrontation between rival supermarket gangs (time dash, same two characters + additional improvisers)**

SCENE 2C: **Minister asking a parishioner for a donation with implied threat (analogous)**

(These second-beat choices will be described in greater detail in the upcoming sections "Bringing the Game Back," "Time Dash," and "Analogous.")

WHO'S IN THE SECOND BEAT?

Because it is the simplest choice and causes the least confusion, most second-beat scenes will feature the same two improvisers who performed the first beat of the scene, whether the second beat is a time dash or analogous. The character you portray in the second beat should fulfill the same Game function in the scene as the character you portrayed in the first beat. In other words, do not switch roles. For example, the improvisers who played the art museum guide and the patron in Scene 1C will play the minister and parishioner, respectively, in their analogous second beat. Had they chosen to perform a time-dash second beat, the improvisers playing the art museum guide and the patron would return to those same characters, respectively.

However, this is not the only option. It is also possible for a second- beat scene to include the same two improvisers from the first beat scene, plus additional improvisers from the group. For example, Scene 2B in our example Harold will feature the same two improvisers who played the supermarket employees in Scene 1B, plus additional improvisers from the back-line who will play employees from the rival supermarket. Again, the improvisers from Scene 1B should not switch their roles from the first beat. Adding new improvisers to a second-beat scene is only ever done to serve the Game of the scene.

The second beat usually provides more opportunities for the back-line to make support moves, because the Game has already been established. Depending upon how the Game is being heightened and explored in the second beat, walk-ons, tag-outs, and other support moves are now more likely to be welcome additions to the scene. For example, the back-line might applaud as audience members at the ceremony in the "athletic awards ceremony celebrating violence" scene. Scene 2B ("rival supermarket gangs confrontation") will likely feature other improvisers supporting the scene by playing members of either gang. In Scene 2C ("minister asking parishioner for a donation"), an improviser from the back-line could tag out the priest to play a guardian angel who hints that he "guards better" when donations are made. Notice that all of these support moves are made in the service of the Game. Ideally, good support work will provide opportunities for the improvisers already onstage to play their Game. Good support work should always make the improvisers already onstage look better. Support work is not just an opportunity for you to get more stage time. As in the first beat, the only mandatory form of support in the second-beat scenes are well-timed edits.

It can be deceptively difficult to perform a second-beat scene. You are not just taking the story or the characters from the first beat into the second beat. You are also taking the Game, which can be hard to define even after you have played it successfully in the first beat. The Game is what provided the humor in the first-beat scenes. This is what we want to further explore in the second beat, rather than a plot progression of the first scenes.

In order to bring the Game back in a second-beat scene, you must first be able to identify it. You identify your Game by asking yourself, "What was funny about that scene?" and "Why was it funny?" or, more specifically, "What was the consistent pattern of behavior that was funny?" Try to sum up your Game in the least amount of words possible. Using as few words as possible will help you to boil your Game down to its essence. If you can sum up your Game in about five words or so, it will help you to think of another situation in which to play it.

For example, you might boil down the Game of Scene 1A to "celebrating an unfortunate outcome of doing your job well." This is a good summation because it boils the Game down to the point where you have excluded the specifics of the scene. This puts you in a position to be able to use the Game for either a time dash or an analogous second beat.

A poor attempt at boiling down the Game of Scene 1A would be "rowdy football practice." Football practices are often "rowdy." This description does not include what was unusual or interesting about the scene (celebrating the broken arm).

Another poor attempt at boiling down the Game of this scene would be "a football player who got his arm broken." This example does nothing but describe the plot, and could lead to a plot-focused second-beat scene in which the football player does nothing but ask people to sign the cast on his arm. A problem with both of these examples is that the descriptions are tying the Game to the specific of football. Football is a detail supporting the Game, not an essential element of it.

Once you have identified the Game of the first beat, your main responsibility when performing a second beat is to provide new opportunities to play the Game of the scene. Changing one or more elements of the Who, What, and Where will provide these new opportunities. While it is possible to return to the same Who, What and Where for the second beat of your Game, it stands to reason that you will have used up many of the opportunities for Game moves in the first beat. Therefore, you will have much more available to you if you start with a new Who, What, and Where.

Part of the process when bringing a Game back is to decide whether the Game is served best by a time dash or an analogous second beat. Again, whether you choose time dash or analogous, you will probably be best served by making some specific changes to the Who, What, and Where. Note, these changes to the Who, What and Where are not arbitrary changes into which you then try to fit your Game. Rather, you will choose which elements of the Who, What, and Where to change based on what will provide the most opportunities for playing your Game. The changes you make should prevent you from repeating the same Game moves you made in your first beat.

Let's revisit our example first-beat scene about the art museum employee asking a patron for a donation with implied threats. Now let's imagine that you exhausted the majority of possible Game moves for this particular scenario. It would be a fruitless path to stick with the same Who, What and Where, and stay in the museum for your second beat. When creating a second beat for this scene, you would need to make some changes to the Who, What, and Where in order to provide new opportunities to play your Game. Changing the Who to a minister and parishioner, and the Where to a church, gives you a whole new world of details that you can use to play the same Game.

Now let's look at the problems you could run into if you arbitrarily change the elements of the scene. Imagine that you arbitrarily changed the Who to "gangsters" for the second beat of this scene. This is a change that would not support your Game. Since gangsters do extort people with the threat of implied violence, this change actually neutralizes the humor of the Game. Or, let's imagine that you arbitrarily changed the Where to a "ticket counter at a bus station" for the second beat of this scene. This is a change that does not support your Game since buying bus tickets doesn't involve making a donation.

In your second beat, you should get right to playing your Game. This is possible because you are bringing back the Game you established in the first beat. You don't have to spend any time discovering the Game.

INSTRUCTIONS

- In order to introduce yourself to this process, you should begin by distilling the Game of a successful written comedic sketch that everyone knows.

- The first step is to offer a short comedic synopsis of the sketch.

- Now see if you can still describe what is funny about this sketch after stripping away the specifics. Distill the Game by boiling it down to the funny behavior. You will be best served if you can limit this description to five words or less.

- Once you have distilled the Game, see if you can use this description to come up with ideas for analogous second-beat scenes.

- Once you are comfortable doing this, you are ready to perform this process using a scene that your group has improvised.

EXAMPLE

- *SNL*'s "Coneheads"

- Comedic synopsis: Space aliens with cone-shaped heads poorly attempt to blend into human society.

- Game distillation: poor attempts at blending in

- Analogous second-beat idea: Undercover cops in full uniform with only stereotypical accessories unsuccessfully try to pass themselves off as drug users. They use stilted, dated street slang.

- Analogous second-beat idea: A 40-year-old man trying to pass himself off as a 12-year-old in order to get a low-priced movie ticket. He uses a high-pitched voice and talks about how much he loves Nickelodeon shows.

PURPOSE

- This exercise will help you to more effectively isolate the Game of your scene.

- Doing this exercise often will also make you better at coming up with second beats more efficiently.

Raising the Stakes

When you perform a second-beat scene, do not burden yourself with the goal of being "funnier" or "better" than your first-beat scene. As stated earlier, the goal of a second beat is simply to provide new opportunities to play your Game by changing one or more elements of the Who, What, and Where. This misguided pursuit of being funnier or better in your second beat often manifests itself through improvisers "raising the stakes" of the second beat. Raising the stakes means to arbitrarily choose a high-stakes scenario (e.g., meeting with the President, a deathbed scene, etc.).

Far from guaranteeing a successful second beat, arbitrarily raising the stakes will cause you to perform second beats with Whos, Whats, and Wheres that don't necessarily serve the Game of your scene. Consistently forcing Games into high-stakes scenarios in the second beats of scenes will result in repetitive and clichéd scenes (e.g., Whos such as the President and the Pope, Wheres such as weddings and funerals, and Whats such as surgeries and gunfights).

Let's say you performed a first-beat scene about a 40-year-old businessman who has a terrible problem with authority. Every time he encounters an authority figure of some sort, he starts acting like a rebellious teenage punk. Let's say in the first-beat scene, the businessman had an encounter with his boss about his recent productivity on the job.

Let's say that you approach the second beat of your scene by focusing on "raising the stakes" of the scene. To do so, you put the businessman with the President of the United States. While this setting will technically work, it is no better than, for instance, putting the businessman with the person in charge of restocking a salad bar.

BUSBOY: **"Excuse me, sir...you have to use the tongs."**

BUSINESSMAN: **"Whoa! So you're the big man in charge, huh? Gonna ride me, try to keep me down?**

The "salad bar attendant" scenario works for this Game without raising the stakes. In fact, you could argue that this scenario is better than a scene in the Oval Office because it is more absurd to rebel against a person with very limited authority.

INITIATING YOUR SECOND BEAT

An ideal second-beat initiation will allow the improvisers to hit the ground running by immediately playing the Game from the first beat.

An important part of performing a second-beat scene is to fashion an initiation that clearly and concisely communicates which elements of the Who, What, or Where you are changing, and what response you are looking for from your scene partner. For your second beat of Scene 1C ("art museum guide asking patron for a donation"), your initiation might be, "It's good to see you. You and your family are, of course, always welcome in the house of the Lord, but He does recommend donations, (threateningly) and I think you know what He means by 'recommend.'" This initiation adheres very closely to the structure of the first line of the first beat. While this example makes the second-beat idea very clear, know that a second-beat initiation doesn't always need to parallel the first-beat initiation so specifically. Another possible second-beat initiation for this scene could be, "I couldn't help but notice from up at the altar that you didn't put any money in the donation plate today. For your sake, I hope that Hell isn't as horrible as we imagine it to be."

Furthermore, the person who initiates the first beat doesn't necessarily have to initiate the second beat. For instance, although the museum employee initiated Scene 1C, it is possible for the person who played the patron to initiate the second beat. If you were playing the patron in the first beat, your second-beat initiation might be, "Father, are you suggesting that a failure to contribute to the collection plate might result in eternal damnation?" This line not only makes the changes to the Who, What and Where clear, but it also implies that your scene partner, a priest, has already delivered a veiled threat and should continue to do so throughout the scene.

Beyond formulating a clear and concise opening line for your second beat, how you take the stage in a second beat is important. Be the first to step out onstage, and take your position confidently and purposefully in order to indicate to your scene partner that you have a second beat initiation in mind. When your scene partner from the first-beat scene joins you, deliver your clear and concise opening line. It should let your scene partner know who they should be playing to support your idea. Your initiation should also make it clear whether or not you want additional improvisers from the back-line to join the second beat.

If you are not the first to step out, you should assume that your scene partner has an initiation, and you should remain neutral. Remaining neutral means stepping into the scene without making a choice about the Who, What, or Where before hearing your scene partner's initiation. Once they have offered an initiation, your job will be to find a way to complement their choice. Whether or not you initiate, you should have formulated your own initiation between the first and second beats. You need to be ready to initiate in case your scene partner does not. However, do not try to synthesize or "combine" initiations. If your scene partner initiates before you do, drop your idea and go with theirs.

Now let's look more closely at how to perform time-dash and analogous second beats.

TIME DASH

A time-dash second beat involves either one or both of the characters from the first-beat scene. If you named your characters in the first beat, you should use one or both of those names to make it clear that you are returning to characters that have already been established.

The term "time dash" refers to the fact that, since you are returning with one or more characters from the first beat, you are necessarily going to have to move either forward or backward in time. Otherwise, you'd be simply repeating the original scene. This change in time can be anything from starting exactly where you left off in the first beat, to two years later, to an hour earlier, etc.

You take the second beat to another place in time not to follow plot or story, but instead to take the audience to another point in the character's life that would be a good situation for you to play the same Game. Where you jump to should be entirely dependent on serving the Game. Think of time dash as a device for getting to a new situation with the most opportunities for playing your Game. A time dash allows you to bypass extraneous and uninteresting events that may logically lead up to the point where you want to play your Game, but would not add to the entertainment value of the scene. You don't have to go to "what's next" chronologically. Time dash allows you to jump to the next fun moment for your Game. Don't ask yourself, "What happens next?" Ask yourself, "When and where will our Game happen next?"

For example, Scene 2A ("supermarket gang confrontation") is a time-dash second beat that involves both characters from the first beat later in time. We have placed the store clerks in the middle of a confrontation between rival supermarket gangs. This may appear to be a plot progression since we have followed the character from being initiated into the supermarket gang to fighting a rival supermarket gang. However, this plot progression is an incidental result of playing your Game. This second-beat situation is simply a fruitful new way to play the same Game. (To reiterate an earlier point, following plot is acceptable if you are doing so in service of the Game.) The meeting of two rival gangs provides new opportunities to play the Game of the first beat. Also note that we've passed over the car ride or walk that must have happened to get the characters to this meeting, the discussion of how this fight would be conducted, etc.

Now let's look at some bad examples of time-dash second beats for this Game:

- A second beat in which one of the store clerks is at home telling his mom about gang activity at the supermarket

This second beat does nothing more than report the Game from the first scene to a new character. It does not actively play the Game in a new context.

- A second-beat scene that merely takes place in a supermarket, leaving out the gang-warfare aspect

This scene might be initiated with a line like, "I finished mopping up aisle six. I'm gonna take my break, okay?" This initiation does not include the Game or a new context to play it in. It only uses the Where of the scene. The success of this scene would depend on the other improviser steering it toward the Game by finding ways to incorporate gang warfare. It is unlikely that the other improviser will do this because they will assume that the initiating improviser has an idea for playing the Game since they stepped out first.

- A second-beat scene in which two security guards discuss a recent supermarket gang fight

This is a poor second beat because they are talking about what should have been the second beat, instead of actually performing it. We're missing the gang fight, which provides the greatest potential for playing the Game.

You could look at most comedy movies as a series of time-dash second beats that follow "the Game" of the main character in the movie. For example, once Jim Carrey has the powers of God in *Bruce Almighty*, the movie puts him into a series of different situations that provides further opportunities to play this "Game," an ordinary man with the powers of God. When he is near a body of water, Bruce can simply walk across the water instead of using a bridge. When we see him at his apartment in the morning, Bruce gets coffee by willing Juan Valdez to appear at his window. When we see him outside of his ex-girlfriend's school looking to reconcile with her, Bruce makes clouds form the shape of a heart in order to get her attention. Each new scene that sets up Bruce to make each of these "Game moves" is like a second beat for the "ordinary man with the powers of God" Game.

Don't let the name "time dash" make you think that moving backward or forward in time, or the degree to which you do so, is in and of itself what will make your second beat successful; it is only a by-product of remaining with the same two characters. Sticking with the same characters will necessarily force you to move forward or backward in time.

TIME DASH: MORE IS NOT BETTER

When time-dashing, "more" is not better. A larger leap in time between a first and second beat doesn't necessarily improve the quality of a second-beat scenario. Therefore, jumping far into the future in a time dash is a choice that should only be made if it best serves the Game. A common mistake made by new improvisers is to time-dash ahead to old age. For example, seeing the characters from the supermarket gang scene as old people wouldn't serve the Game of the scene. In fact, doing so would complicate this Game by adding additional unusual things (old people behaving as if they are in a gang, old people working a part-time job usually reserved for teens, etc.).

If one or more of the characters were the fun aspect about a first- beat scene, it is probably a good idea to try and revisit them in a time-dash second beat. Whether you bring one or both of the characters from the first beat into a time-dash second beat will depend on whether that best serves the Game of your scene.

The other way to approach a second beat is to start an analogous scene that plays the same Game, but with two new characters in an analogous situation. Even though the characters and the situation are completely different, the fundamental Game will remain the same.

Let's look at a simple analogy:

A "doctor" is to a "patient" as a "mechanic" is to a "car."

Both examples include a profession and what that profession repairs. Therefore, the two pairs of words are fundamentally the same while being specifically different. Two situations that are fundamentally the same while being specifically different are what we want for analogous first and second beats. The fundamental sameness between the beats will be the Game. The specific differences will be the changes made to the Who, What, and Where.

Let's imagine a first-beat scene in which a high school teacher is teaching a student. A high school teacher and a student have a relationship that is analogous to a drill sergeant and a private (in both cases, one character teaches the other). So, the same Game can likely be played using either set of characters.

Now let's imagine a first-beat scene with the same characters but a different What. Rather than the student being taught by the teacher, the student is serving detention under the teacher. In this case, a more apt analogous second-beat scene might involve a prison guard and prisoner, since it better mirrors the relationship of "person in charge monitoring detainee." The Who, What, and Where for your analogous second beat are chosen depending on what will best allow you to play the same Game from the first beat.

The Game must also be part of your analogy. Let's look at an example in which we include a Game in our first beat. Let's say our first beat was about a firefighter who was scared of fire. In order to understand our Game, we should try to give it a title that doesn't use any specifics. We might call this Game "fear that would preclude a person from doing their job." Once we have boiled our Game down to its essence in this way, we can find potential analogous scenarios. We could, for instance, perform analogous second beats by playing a lifeguard who is scared of water, a podiatrist who has a foot phobia, or a dentist who is afraid of teeth.

Now let's look at a set of example scenes that were performed onstage at the Upright Citizens Brigade Theatre. A first beat was performed that involved a boxer who had a crush on his opponent. The first-beat scene played out this situation as far as it could go. We saw the conflicted boxer asking his corner man how his trunks looked. We saw him try to get himself into a clinch with the other boxer without throwing a punch. We saw him give out his phone number while he hit the other boxer with jabs. By the end of the scene, the team had exhausted the possibilities of the Game of "having a crush on someone with whom you have an adversarial relationship" in the context of two boxers involved in a fight.

The team then made the wise decision to return to this Game in an analogous second beat. Since being in the ring and fighting is the most extreme manifestation of the adversarial relationship of these two characters, it would not serve the Game to time-dash to a different scenario where this adversarial relationship is explored to a lesser degree (for example, the boxers meeting in their twilight years on an ESPN retrospective). The "crush" aspect of this Game is funniest when juxtaposed with the violence of fighting.

To see a rematch also wouldn't work because they exhausted a vast majority of the possible Game moves involving a fight scenario in the first beat. We might see these two boxers go out to eat after the match, but then we are losing a big part of the Game because there would be no reason for the boxers to be aggressive toward each other.

The analogous second beat they performed involved a cop who had a crush on the criminal he was interrogating. The Game was exactly the same, even though both characters were completely different and in an entirely different situation. They didn't need to return to the boxers, because they were only specifics supporting a Game. The first-beat scene was not really about boxers; it was about the Game of having a crush on an adversary.

Here is an example of an analogous second-beat scenario for the boxer scene that would not have worked: An ice cream vendor has a crush on his customer. They could not have played the same Game in this scenario. With this choice, they would have only retained the "crush" element of the first scene. An ice cream vendor and customer don't have the same sort of adversarial relationship that two boxers have. We have lost the humor that was being derived from the crush getting in the way of an adversarial relationship.

An advantage of analogous second beats is that they will create more variables to be used as your group looks for connections toward the end of the show.

To successfully perform an analogous second beat, you must pare down the first beat's Game to its essentials, leaving out the specifics. Doing so should make it easier to find a new Who, What, and Where to play the same Game.

CHOOSING A SECOND BEAT

The main idea to keep in mind when choosing between time dash and analogous for your second beat is "form fits function." One type of second beat is not considered to be superior to the other. You want to make your choice based on what is going to best serve your Game. You want to determine which second-beat option will give you the most opportunities to play your Game without being repetitive.

If you can change the Where and the What, and have the same Who be just as funny, then you will be able to time-dash. If you change the Where and the What, but there are not as many opportunities for the Who to be funny with these new specifics, then you should go analogous and change all three elements of your scene (the Who, What and Where).

Let's say our first beat was about a guy telling dirty jokes at a funeral. You can easily can imagine this same character being just as funny in different situations involving different "Wheres" and "Whats" (a doctor's office, a child's birthday party, a church, etc.). You don't need to change the Who in these new situations.

Now let's return to our boxing example. It is hard to imagine our "Who" from the first beat (the boxers) being as funny in a new "Where" and "What." A boxing ring in the middle of a fight are the "Where" and the "What" offering the most Game moves for this "Who." Since there is not a new "Where" and "What" that will provide as many opportunities to play the Game with this character, you need to find an entirely different Who, What, and Where (i.e., an analogous scene). A cop in a police station interrogating a criminal will provide a whole new world of specifics to be used to play the same Game.

When characters have no relationship outside of the context of the first beat (e.g., customer and convenience store clerk), you should also choose analogous over time dash. If it would be odd or unlikely for these characters to meet again in another context, you should think of an analogous situation for your Game. Let's imagine our boxers meeting up again at a car wash or a restaurant. Putting the characters in one of these situations would feel forced, and would not provide new opportunities to play the Game.

Whether you choose to perform a time-dash or analogous second beat, it is important to remember that the goal of both is to play the same Game that you played in the first beat.

What Do You Do When the Game Isn't Clear?

One of the challenges of the Harold is that you must do a second beat of every first-beat scene, regardless of how the first beat may have gone. So, what do you do when you fail to find a Game in the first beat? The general rule is to start out your second beat with the most specific or unusual thing you remember from the first beat, and Yes And from there. Another way to think about this process is to think of it as "following the fun." Even when a scene goes poorly, there is usually at least one thing that is fun about it. When the scene ends, ask yourself, "What was the most fun part of this scene?" and start your second beat there.

For instance, you may have actually had a Game in your first beat, but are just struggling with how to define it. Your second beat should be fine if you "follow the fun." What you identify as fun will probably be very close to the Game, and will hopefully lead you to playing it again in the second beat.

Or perhaps your first-beat scene was scattered. Instead of focusing on and building off of the first unusual thing, you and your scene partner continued to discover and/or generate multiple unusual things. In this case, pick the unusual thing that was most fun, and try to be more specific by using "If this unusual thing is true, then what else is true?" to find and play a single Game in the second beat.

Sometimes, however, you and your scene partner will have absolutely bombed. In this situation, there was a complete absence of laughter in reaction to your scene. In other words, there is no fun to follow in this scene. In these situations, you can take solace in the fact that you have nowhere else to go but up. Reassess your thought process when starting the first-beat scene. Did you have an idea from the opening? Can you try to be more specific in hitting your idea directly in the second beat? If you were starting organically, the problem may be that you never were specific enough in establishing the Who, What, and Where for your audience. Go into your second beat with the intention of making stronger choices and being clearer and more specific.

THIRD BEAT

After a second Group Game, the ensemble will perform the third beat of the Harold. The same Games will be hit once again. The third beat is where you wrap up your Harold. As such, third-beat scenes will be shorter than the previous scenes. Think of them as a summation of your Games. Imagine a speech. After the speaker says, "In conclusion," you would not expect them to continue speaking for as long as they have up to that point. Since the third beat is the conclusion of your Harold, it should be very short. For instance, sometimes a successful third-beat scene can be as short as three lines.

In each third-beat scene, you will not only be playing your Game again, but you will also be looking to incorporate the Games or elements of the other scenes of your Harold into the scene being performed. As you perform a Harold, you and your teammates will create a number of scenes that, on the surface, will seem to have little in common. However, if you look at them closely, with a little imagination you should be able to find organic connections among the various themes and ideas generated in your Harold. These connections will allow you to end your show in a satisfying way in the third beat. Connecting scenes gives the Harold the feel of a whole theatrical piece, as opposed to a collection of disparate scenes. Furthermore, tying elements together at the end of the show will give it the appearance of being written or planned, which is always a goal of great improv.

Third beats may seem daunting, but in fact, they should be the easiest part of the Harold for you to perform. By the time you have reached the third beat, you have already played the Game of the scene in two other beats. In order to perform a straightforward third-beat scene, you only need to ask yourself, "How could I take my Game to another situation that will provide other opportunities to play it?" If you have already followed your characters from the first beat into a time-dash second beat, you should time-dash them to a third-beat scene. If you took your Game into an analogous situation from first beat to second beat, you should go analogous again.

CONNECTIONS

While your Harold will be technically correct if you simply play each Game again in the third beat, you can achieve a synergistic effect by making connections between your scenes. In a connection, a character, element, or even the entire Game from one scene is transplanted into another scene. There should be some thematic overlap or similarity between the elements of the Games that are coming together in a connection. In other words, connections should be logical and not forced. Connections are a way to remind the audience that the scenes of your Harold exist in the same world. They give your absurd ideas and premises a life beyond the scenes they are in.

Let's look at some connections we could make between the scenes of our example Harold:

PLANNED CONNECTIONS

The football players from Scene 1A ("football team celebrating violence") could appear at someone's door asking for a donation for new uniforms, with an implied threat of violence. This is a logical and unforced connection between the Game of Scenes 1A and 1C. Asking for donations is something that student football teams normally do. Additionally, since the football players in this Harold have been established as violent characters, their threatening behavior in this situation seems logical. You could classify this as a planned connection. In a planned connection, an improviser steps out from the back-line to perform a scene with an idea for a connection already in mind. Planned connections are intentional and premeditated.

DISCOVERED CONNECTIONS

Now let's imagine that one of the improvisers from Scenes 1C and 2C ("asking for donations with an implied threat of violence") steps out to perform an analogous third-beat scene by playing a Salvation Army Santa Claus asking for donations from passersby with an implied threat of violence. The improvisers from Scenes 1B and 2B recognize a potential connection and step off of the back-line as the supermarket gang members. They make it clear that the Santa is standing in front of their supermarket, and they confront him for trying to make money on their turf. This is an example of a discovered connection. The improviser who initiated the third-beat scene did not plan the connection; it was discovered in the moment by another improviser on the back-line.

CALLBACK CONNECTIONS

Now let's imagine a scene in which a college recruiter is at the home of the football player who won the award for outstanding violence in Scene 2A. He is talking to the football player and his parents. The recruiter says, "Alabama is very excited about your son. I've seen how many boys he's put in the hospital. If he comes to our school, he'll not only get a chance to send more kids to the ER; he'll get a degree and we'll keep him out of the supermarket gang culture." A college recruiter scouting this football player on the basis of his violent behavior is simply a continuation of the Game from Scene 2A. The reference to "supermarket gang culture" is an example of a callback connection. A callback connection is a quick reference to something from earlier in the Harold. Again, a callback connection reinforces that everything happening in your Harold exists in the same world. Like discovered connections, callback connections will occur to you in the moment. Callback connections are not confined to the third beat of the Harold; they can technically happen anywhere from the second beat of the Harold on.

A callback connection is a good tool to use if you need an edit point for a scene. An audience will likely laugh at something that is familiar to them when it returns unexpectedly.

FORCED CONNECTIONS

Forced connections come off as illogical and random. There is no value in arbitrarily throwing elements of different scenes together. Having the museum guide from Scene 1C show up as an assistant coach of the football team doesn't serve either Game, and it feels very forced. Forced connections will not be satisfying to the improvisers or the audience.

A WORD ABOUT CONNECTIONS

Connecting the Games or elements of the three separate scenes of the Harold in the third beat is incredibly rewarding to both the audience and the improvisers onstage. Since all of the ideas started from the same single suggestion, everything in your Harold is already connected from the start of your show. The scenes of your third beat allow you to bring out those connections for your audience to see.

By the third beat of your Harold, you will be looking for a high point on which to end your show. Simply continuing to play your Game may not provide this high point. You will want to hit the audience with something they don't expect. A well-executed connection can do just that. A strong organic connection will almost always guarantee you a strong "out" for your Harold. It is the "magic trick" that will leave your audience wondering, How'd they do that?

Some people think that a perfect Harold would end with a connection of all three first-beat scenes in a way that would allow for each of the Games to be played again. Remember, while connections are something to aspire to, a lack of them won't ruin your Harold. A Harold isn't a failure if things don't connect. In fact, a show that simply ends by continuing to play the various Games of the Harold in the third beat will be more successful and enjoyable than a Harold ending with illogical or forced connections. We make connections when they present themselves to us. If a strong connection presents itself, go for it.

THIRD BEATS: KEEP THEM SIMPLE

You should approach your third beat by using what is already "on the table." You don't want to invent new ideas; you want to use what already exists. As with second beats, your first priority when performing a third beat is always to continue playing the Game of your scene. Your secondary priority is to make connections, whether they are planned connections, discovered connections, or callback connections. Make looking for connections the focus of your support from the back-line. Don't let searching for connections distract you from your Game, which is most important for the success of your third-beat scene.

Third beats only succeed when a team is working together. When not performing in your own scene, you should make it your priority to look for connections from the back-line. With many minds working toward the goal of connections, what might at first seem daunting becomes relatively easy, since the entire ensemble shares the burden. Hopefully this will leave the audience thinking not about how funny one person or one line of dialogue was, but how the ensemble came together to create something too cohesive to have been created entirely on the spot.

COMMIT TO YOUR THIRD BEATS

Sometimes, beginning improvisers will fail to commit to their third beats. One of the reasons this happens is that they know that third beats are often very quick, so they look at them as more of an opportunity to tell a "joke" than to do a scene. Another reason for this lack of commitment is a belief that the cleverness of their initiation or callback will carry the scene. You must not sacrifice the basic tenets of scene work, such as behaving realistically and using your environment. Third-beat scenes are still scenes. You must commit to the performance of third-beat scenes just as much as you commit to the performance of any other scene in the Harold.

A Group Game is performed between both the first and second beats and the second and third beats of the Harold. The two Group Games of the Harold are independent of each other. In other words, the second Group Game is not a "second beat" of the first Group Game. The name "Group Game" refers to the fact that most (or all) of the ensemble performs it, and, as is the case with any scene, the focus will be on a single Game. The entire group will work together to heighten and explore this single Game. Group games offer you the possibility to be nontraditional, abstract, and/or presentational in the playing of your Game.

Many of the concepts and principles that make a two-person scene successful also apply to Group Games. The entire ensemble must get on the same page at the start of the Group Game. You must look for and make simple patterns. Give-and-take must be utilized. Once a Game has been found, the ensemble must commit to the pattern of this Game and not complicate the scene through arbitrary invention.

Group Games are an opportunity to use premises generated in your opening that haven't yet been used in the Harold. Group Games can also be a good time to use the audience suggestion in a very direct way. This can benefit your Harold, as sometimes your opening will take you so far away from the suggestion that the audience is left confused as to what your show has to do with their suggestion.

Since you won't be returning to a "second beat" of your Group Games, it is justified and valuable to heighten at a quicker pace than you might in a scene performed in one of the beats. This will give momentum and variety to your Harold. Having the entire ensemble focus in on, play out, and aggressively heighten a Game gives a burst of energy to your show that will carry you into the next beat.

LISTENING IN GROUP GAMES

Since there are so many more improvisers in a Group Game, it becomes even more important to listen. You need to split your attention among more people, which means that you will listen a lot more and talk a lot less than you would in a two-person scene. It is important that you are patient and focused in Group Games, since more players make for more possibilities for subtle shifts in the Game.

HOW TO INITIATE GROUP GAMES

There are two sets of variables at play in any Group Game initiation:

1. How the initiating improviser is communicating their idea

2. How the rest of the ensemble responds

An improviser can initiate a Group Game either **verbally** or **nonverbally**. A verbal Group Game initiation always includes a line of dialogue. A nonverbal Group Game initiation involves one improviser initiating with a sound or a physical action, as opposed to a line of dialogue. In nonverbal initiations, the improviser initiating the scene has only made a choice about the Where or the What but has left other decisions about the scene up to the rest of the ensemble through support.

The rest of the ensemble can respond to a Group Game initiation in one of two ways: **Add On** or **All At Once**.

Add On Group Games always begin with one additional improviser joining the initiator. The rest of the performers in an Add On Group Game will then add to the scene through walk-ons. The improviser initiating the scene does not dictate how the rest of the ensemble will add to the scene. Each improviser joining the scene determines his or her own "Who" and function in the scene, as long as their walk-on is in keeping with the base reality and—if it is already established— the Game of the scene. Once a Game is clearly established, every successive walk-on will ideally offer further heightening or exploration.

It is important to note that in Add On Group Games, you do not have to wait for the initial improvisers to find a Game before contributing to the scene. The improvisers on the back-line in a Group Game can be active in the creation of the Game.

All At Once Group Games begin with most, if not all, of the ensemble joining the scene immediately after the initiation.

You don't necessarily need *every* improviser to step out for an All At Once scene. In fact, it is often a good idea to have one or two improvisers remain on the back-line. This is called **hanging back**.

There are many benefits to hanging back. If an improviser or two hang back, they will be available for support work. An improviser on the back-line can offer support moves that will add variety or heightening to the Game. Furthermore, the "undefined" improviser on the back-line will have the most objective perspective on the scene, and will therefore be in the best situation to give the scene what it needs the most.

The ensemble must always listen carefully to the person initiating a Group Game so that they can support that person appropriately.

When initiating verbally, the improviser initiating the scene will be able to strongly suggest if they want the rest of the ensemble to support by Adding On or joining in All At Once. The ensemble should be able to tell what the improviser is looking for based on that first line of dialogue. For example, if an improviser initiates by saying, "Gentlemen, we need to discuss these quarterly numbers," they have strongly suggested an All At Once response by dictating to the rest of the ensemble that they will be executives in a business meeting. If an improviser initiates by saying, "If you'll take a seat, Mr. Blackwell, we can go over the quarterly numbers," they have strongly suggested an Add On response by addressing just one other member of the ensemble.

When you initiate nonverbally, you are leaving the decision of how to Add On to your initiation up to your teammates. Whether the Group Game ends up being Add On or All At Once is left to the rest of the ensemble's discretion.

Let's look at some examples of each type of Group Game initiation and the responses that could follow:

EXAMPLE 1:

An improviser steps out onstage, puts out two chairs, and sits down in one. He says, "This is my first time eating at the Rainforest Café, Nancy."

This is verbal since we are starting with a line of dialogue. Because the improviser is addressing one other character, the appropriate response from the rest of the ensemble would be for one person from the back-line to sit down in the second chair. Because of this scene's placement in the Harold, the ensemble knows this is a Group Game. Therefore, each improviser on the back-line will be looking for the appropriate opportunity to Add On to the scene through support moves, such as walk-ons or tag-outs, until everyone (or nearly everyone) in the ensemble has participated in the scene.

EXAMPLE 2:

An improviser steps out onstage, facing the audience. He says, **"I am a bonobo. I am a gentle and intelligent primate."**

Since the ensemble should be looking to make patterns, the most likely response would be for another improviser to Add On by addressing the audience as another animal found in the rainforest.

EXAMPLE 3:

An improviser initiates by stepping out and facing the audience. They begin to narrate a story by saying, **"Once upon a time in the land of Slackerville, there was an underachieving boy named Bongo who wanted to procure a driver's license."** At this point, another member of the ensemble steps out to play Bongo.

This is a verbal initiation. The ensemble will continue to Add On, either by playing other characters set up in narration or by participating in the narration.

EXAMPLE 1:

An improviser steps out onstage, faces the audience, and mimes holding a protest sign. He says, **"We are protesting the destruction of this rainforest, and we are not moving until those machines are turned off!"**

This is verbal since we are starting with a line of dialogue. This time, the improviser initiating is indicating that he is part of a group. The appropriate response from the rest of the ensemble would be to join in All At Once.

EXAMPLE 2:

An improviser steps out onstage and holds his arms up in the air as if they are branches of a tree. He turns to his teammates and says, **"Trees of the rainforest, due to circumstances beyond our control, we are all going to have to support a few more organisms than we are used to."**

This improviser has established himself as a tree, and has indicated to the rest of the ensemble that they should join the scene All At Once, also playing trees.

EXAMPLE 3:

An improviser steps out and mimes holding a microphone. Addressing the audience directly, they say, **"Ladies and gentlemen, welcome to 'The Stupidest Person in America.' Let's meet our contestants."** Let's imagine that the rest of the ensemble joins in immediately. Three members play the contestants. Everyone else runs out into the seats to play the live studio audience.

This initiation let the ensemble know that they would be performing in the style of a game show. This initiation strongly suggested an All At Once response from the rest of the ensemble.

EXAMPLE 4:

An improviser steps out, mimes a podium, and addresses the audience by saying, **"Ladies and gentlemen, we are gathered here today to talk about our town's problem with cat overpopulation."**

The rest of the ensemble immediately plays residents of the town, either from the back-line or by taking places in the audience.

NONVERBAL INITIATIONS

Unlike verbal initiations, wherein the decision to Add On or join in All At Once is dictated by the initiating improviser, with nonverbal initiations, the decision to Add On or join in All At Once is left entirely to the back-line.

NONVERBAL, ADD ON

EXAMPLE 1:

An improviser steps out onstage and begins with nothing more than the physical action of pitching a tent.

At this point, we know that the initiation is nonverbal. One other improviser steps out and mimes rolling out a sleeping bag. Through the lines of dialogue that follow, we find out that they are members of the same Boy Scout troop on a camping trip. An ensemble that is paying close attention to the start of this scene can assume that they should continue to Add On by playing other members of the troop, the Boy Scout leader, etc.

EXAMPLE 2:

The Group Game starts with an improviser stepping out to silently mime swimming upstream as a salmon. One other improviser steps out to play another salmon. Then another improviser steps out to play waves. Another improviser then steps out to play a dam that the fish are jumping over. The salmon begin talking to each other. The ensemble has responded by Adding On one by one.

EXAMPLE 1:

An improviser steps out onstage and faces the audience. He mimes snapping a picture with a camera.

This time, the entire ensemble (except for one improviser who chooses to hang back) enters the scene and begins snapping pictures. After a few seconds of snapping pictures without dialogue, one improviser addresses an unseen celebrity on the red carpet.

EXAMPLE 2:

An improviser steps out onstage and faces the audience. He mimes putting on noise-canceling headphones and firing a gun.

The entire ensemble (except for one improviser who chooses to hang back) enters the scene and stands in a line as other people firing guns at this shooting range.

If any members of your ensemble have not had a chance to participate in one of the first-beat scenes, the rest of the ensemble should be sensitive to that and give their teammates a chance to initiate the Group Games. However, if after waiting a moment or two, one of these improvisers has not stepped out to initiate the Group Game, you can and should step out and offer an initiation, even if you initiated a scene in the first beat. You never want your show to lose momentum due to hesitation.

With their added emphasis on listening and reacting, Group Games reflect the ideals of team play and group mind in Long Form.

EXERCISE EXAMPLE: BUILD A MACHINE

- One member of the ensemble steps out and embodies a component of a machine by performing some sort of mechanical, repetitive motion along with a sound effect.

- While the first member of the ensemble continues their sound and motion, the next member will add a new component that complements what has already been established in some way.

- One by one, the rest of the ensemble will continue to add to the machine.

- Each member of the ensemble must maintain his or her sound and motion until the final member of the ensemble steps out.

- The final member of the ensemble will shut off the machine and explain what this machine does, by activating each component of the machine and describing it. When a component is "activated," that improviser will resume his or her sound and motion.

- The purpose of this exercise is to work together as a single unit.

- The goal of the improviser describing the machine should be to go into detail in describing every component, such that each member's contribution is acknowledged.

Variations on the Exercise

- Have the last member of the ensemble explain the machine while trying to "present" or "sell" it to the audience.

- Have your group build a "monster" instead of a machine. In this variation of the exercise, each member of the ensemble is creating a living, moving being, piece by piece. Each new improviser will form another part of the monster. Once the monster is completed, the ensemble will move around the stage, working together as one organism.

EXAMPLE: BUILD AN ENVIRONMENT

- This exercise starts with one person initiating a physical action (without talking) that suggests a specific environment. The environment should be one that you could reasonably imagine six to eight people in.

- The other improvisers will enter one at a time and add other physical actions in keeping with the environment established by the first improviser. (For example, if one person initiates by tossing pizza dough in the air, you could assume that you are in a pizzeria. The next member may enter and start rolling dough or man the oven or wait in line as a customer.)

- Improvisers are allowed to create sound effects, but these must be true-to-life sound effects (e.g., don't say "mop-mop-mop" while mopping; make the sound a mop would make).

- Once all members of the ensemble have entered the environment, sweep-edit and start over.

- This exercise teaches an ensemble to establish and agree on a location quickly at the start of a Group Game.

THE ROLE OF TAG-OUTS IN GROUP GAMES

Tag-outs can be used in Group Games, but you should hold off on using them until most or all of the ensemble has contributed to the scene. The goal of the Group Game is to allow the entire ensemble to improvise together. Using tag-outs too early can work against this.

Below are some exercises that will allow your ensemble to practice performing Group Games with specific, predetermined structures. Since you won't need to worry about finding the type of Group Game at the start, your ensemble will be able to focus on finding and creating comedic patterns, and playing Game together as a group.

EXERCISE: THE "I AM" GAME

INSTRUCTIONS

- Half of the group will take the stage and the other half of the group will act as an audience.

- One member of the ensemble steps off of the back-line and directly addresses the audience.

- This improviser makes a statement in the following format: "I am ___." This blank is filled in with an inanimate object.

- After this improviser declares their object, they should take a few lines to describe the object's actions, thoughts, feelings, beliefs, or opinions.

- The improviser embodies the object both verbally and physically.

- A second improviser will then step out to play a different inanimate object, adhering to the same "I am ___" format, followed by a few lines of further description. The second improviser will be looking to establish a pattern of some sort.

- A third improviser will step out to play a different inanimate object, speaking in the "I am ___" format once again. This third improviser will follow the pattern established by the second. If they do so, the pattern begun by the second improviser will be locked.

- Once the other improvisers on the back-line have established each of their inanimate objects, the ensemble will continue to describe their inanimate objects, adhering to the pattern that has been established.

EXAMPLE

- PLAYER 1: "I am a Hershey's chocolate bar. I'm the best candy bar because I'm a classic. I'm old-school."

- (PLAYER 2 finds it interesting that the Hershey bar is bragging about being the best. He establishes a pattern by playing another candy bar that is also bragging.)

- PLAYER 2: "I'm a Baby Ruth. I'm so good, they named me after the greatest baseball player who ever lived."

- (PLAYER 3 recognizes the pattern of bragging and locks it with the following move.)

- PLAYER 3: "I'm a Whatchamacallit. I'm so indescribably good that people can't even give me a name."

- (The ensemble continues this pattern until every member has Added On as another candy bar making a case for its superiority. The ensemble members then continue to make their cases for superiority through give-and-take.)

PURPOSE

- This exercise will force your ensemble to practice performing Verbal Add On Group Games.

EXERCISE: THE AD GAME

INSTRUCTIONS

- Four or more members of the ensemble take the stage.

- Another member of the ensemble comes up
  with an unusual product by taking an ordinary
  item and giving it an unusual trait (e.g., a car
  that changes color based on its surroundings,
  or a refrigerator that is also a radio).

- The ensemble will work together to create an
  advertising campaign for this product.

- They will work together to come up with a name
  for the product, a slogan, a target demographic,
  a celebrity spokesperson, a jingle, etc.

- All elements of the campaign should complement each
  other. For example, if Player 1 says, "We could call
  it 'The Chameleon,'" then Player 2 could say, "Yeah!
  We could have Meryl Streep be the spokesperson. She
  could talk about how she disappears into her roles
  just like this car disappears into its surroundings."

- No matter what idea is thrown out, the entire
  group must support and Yes And it.

- Now let's look at an example of a full
  improvised ad campaign for the car that
  changes color based on its surroundings:

- PLAYER 1: "We could call it 'The Chameleon.'"

- PLAYER 2: "Yeah! We could have Meryl Streep
  be the spokesperson. She could talk about how
  she disappears into her roles just like this
  car disappears into its surroundings."

- PLAYER 3: "Yeah, she could start off the commercial as Julia Child and then finish the spot as Margaret Thatcher."

- PLAYER 4: "We could sell it to criminals. If the police are chasing them, they can blend into their surroundings and hide."

- PLAYER 3: "We could take helicopter footage of a police chase and suddenly, the car disappears, blending into the highway!"

- PLAYER 2: "When you don't want to be seen, this is your machine."

- PLAYER 4: "Great slogan. [Singing] 'This car's named after a lizard that can hide, buy this car and camouflage your ride.'"

PURPOSE

- This exercise will force your ensemble to practice performing Verbal, All At Once Group Games.

- This exercise will help you strengthen your ability to listen, Yes And, and utilize give-and-take.

DON'T BE A STAGE HOG

Probably the most important thing to avoid during a Group Game is becoming a "stage hog." You should do a lot more listening and a lot less talking in Group Games than you would in most two-person scenes. In a two-person scene, you are responsible for half of what is said. In a Group Game, you are one of many improvisers. While there are exceptions to the rule, generally if there are eight people on your team, you are probably only going to have to do 1/8 of the talking in the scene.

BEWARE OF MOB MENTALITY

There is a tendency when more than two people get onstage to throw the basic rules of good improv out the window. However, the more people you have onstage, the greater the potential for chaos. Therefore, the more important it becomes to follow the rules of improv.

Some mob mentality pitfalls:

- Making independently funny moves instead of following a pattern

- Talking over each other

- Making patterns out of unintentional mistakes (a mispronounced word, not having enough chairs for the group, etc.)

- Cutting off the initiating improviser before they can fully express their idea

- Clinging to a preconceived choice that does not fit the initiation

These pitfalls can result in loud, sloppy scenes that devolve into a string of easy jokes that undermine the integrity of the Group Game. The way to avoid this is to adhere to the basic rules of good improv.

PRACTICE

The Harold, although seemingly very simple in structure, is actually quite challenging. If you want to perform Harolds that transcend funny and stand out as exciting pieces of art, you must be ready to dedicate a lot of time in rehearsal to the form, preferably with a steady cast and some sort of coach or director to help guide your progress. This time will be well spent, as the Harold encompasses all of the basics you will need to perform any longform. Becoming adept at the Harold will put you on the path to success in all longforms. For more information on practicing, see the section titled "Rehearsal & Performance" on page 351.

CHAPTER 12:

Other Longforms

n this chapter, we will introduce you to a few other longforms. If you have been working on the exercises described in the previous chapter and have a solid understanding of the Harold, you should be in a good position to learn and master the other longforms described in this chapter.

THE MOVIE

The Movie is a longform that involves six to nine improvisers performing a fully improvised 30-minute movie in a particular genre. Performers use the language and techniques of screenplays and filmmaking to present things onstage that would be impossible to present physically. Through description, you will be able to create everything from breathtakingly beautiful sunsets to battle scenes featuring thousands of people.

Structure

The Opening

The opening of the Movie starts with a single suggestion. From this single suggestion, the ensemble will set up three separate settings (by describing location, props, atmospheric sound, and lighting) and a character or characters (by describing age, gender, wardrobe, and demeanor) within those settings through narrative, third-person description. This third-person description is referred to as scene painting. Through this scenic and character description, the ensemble will also establish the genre of the movie. This scene painting is performed in a give-and-take fashion by the entire ensemble. Each improviser builds off of the image described by the previous improviser by adding an additional detail, then adding his or her own idea to the scene.

Once a character is mentioned, someone from the ensemble will step into the setting to become this character, remaining silent as the rest of the ensemble describes both the character and the setting. The improviser playing the character should, however, actively inhabit the space being described (e.g., typing in an office, pouring a cup of coffee in a kitchen, hammering boards at a construction site, etc.).

COMMON DESCRIPTION MISTAKES

Puppeting

Any time a character is described in the Movie, you must be careful not to "puppet" this character. Keep your descriptions as brief as possible. You don't want to do the work of the improviser playing the character. You only need to provide the essential information needed to get the improviser started. Do not describe every action from moment to moment. All that needs to be established are key character traits. You can, however, describe actions that help establish the specific type of character we are seeing.

Telling Not Showing

In the Movie, the ensemble should describe things about the characters that are nonvisual. They reveal backstory, what the character is thinking, or even what the character's Game will be throughout the Movie. An example of backstory would be to reveal the character's place of birth (e.g., an abusive father in a backwoods cabin brought him up). If you were to show what a character is thinking, you might say something like, "The character is thinking about how he can't wait to get home and relax in a hot tub." The following is an example of forcing a character Game: "This character seduces every woman he comes in contact with, regardless of her age or physical appearance." As is the case with puppeting, the danger of "telling and not showing" is that you are taking power away from the improviser by making too many decisions about their character for them.

The following is an example of a good character description that avoids "puppeting" and "telling not showing" (please note that this description would come from the collaboration of multiple members of the ensemble):

"We see a gruff-looking police officer. He isn't wearing an official uniform, but we know he's a cop because of the badge hanging around his neck. He is wearing a grimy-looking sleeveless T-shirt covered in stains. He has his feet up on his desk and is smoking a cigarette."

The ensemble has described a very specific character archetype: the "loose-cannon" police officer. The specificity of the character will help the entire ensemble focus in on the genre of their Movie. While this description gives a lot of specific information and provides an archetype character for the improviser, the improviser is still given the freedom to make all of the choices concerning his dialogue and behavior in the moment and later in the Movie. The description of physical actions such as "putting your feet up on a desk" and "smoking" are not considered to be puppeting because they give essential clues about what type of character this is.

Now let's look at an example of bad character description in which the ensemble resorts to "puppeting":

"We see a gruff-looking police officer. He puts his feet up on his desk. He crosses his right leg over his left leg. He reaches his arms back and folds his hands behind his head. He furrows his brow."

The mistake being made in this description is that the ensemble has overly focused on moment-to-moment actions that do not elucidate the character.

Now let's look at an example of bad character description in which the ensemble resorts to "telling not showing":

"We see a gruff-looking police officer. He looks around the precinct, thinking about how many of the rules he is going to break today. He's had a bad attitude ever since his partner was killed in a shoot-out. He also has a bad habit of using unnecessary force to deal with every criminal he encounters. He looks for every opportunity to tell the chief to 'shove it.'"

The primary mistake the ensemble has made in the above example is that they are describing things that are nonvisual. In a Movie, the characters should be revealed to an audience through dialogue and action. The above "description" is more like narration from a novel. Additionally, the ensemble has likely diminished the audience's enjoyment of the remainder of the Movie by revealing the character's "funny" behavior before it surfaces.

You don't have to know everything that is "funny" about a character by the end of the opening. By offering a few strong, specific, essential details of a character, you are giving the improviser playing the character a base reality to build from.

It is very important to identify a genre by the end of the opening, as this will provide you with a simple, generic plot outline to follow so that your primary focus can be on finding a Game in each scene. Note that the three settings of the opening should have no obvious connection outside of the genre.

Let's say the first setting of an opening establishes the sheriff at the jailhouse in a small town. The genre being hinted at after this first setting is a Western. Two settings that fit within this genre (without forcing an obvious connection) would be a setting with a singer in a saloon and a setting with a rancher on the outskirts of town. Two settings that would fit within the genre but force a connection would be a setting with a sheriff's deputy at the saloon and a setting with the sheriff's wife at her home. Forcing a connection between the settings established in the opening will cause the plot to collapse upon itself too early.

Once the third and final location is established, a member of the ensemble will step forward and offer a title. Try to avoid taking the title as an opportunity to just say something funny. The title is your last chance in the opening to try to lock in the genre for both your group and the audience. An audience that knows what genre you are working in is much more likely to understand and enjoy the show. Titling the Movie is also the cue that the opening has ended, and that it is time to start scene work.

Note: The opening of the Movie does not provide premises or half ideas. The function of a well-executed opening in the Movie is to provide a clear genre, which is essentially the base reality for your entire show.

SCENE WORK

Once the title has been established and the opening is finished, the improvisers who played characters in the first setting step out into the same established setting and start the first scene with dialogue. The ensemble will return to each of the three settings established in the opening, in order. These first three scenes are where the character and scenic Games that will be played throughout the rest of the Movie are discovered.

From this point on, you will add settings and characters as needed to service your plot and your Games. It is likely that you will end up with far more locations and characters than you would in a Harold. Also unlike the Harold, in which each Game is given equal weight, the genre of a Movie will cause certain characters or plotlines to return more often than others.

Your primary responsibility is to simply play the character Games and scenic Games that have been established. You will also look for connections appropriate to the genre. It is not your responsibility to come up with a clever plot. Instead, you will simply hit the archetypical plot points of the genre you are performing. The Movie ends when you come to an archetypical ending appropriate to your genre.

Creating spectacular and detailed scenes will require the involvement and attention of the entire ensemble. Compared to other forms, the Movie may be the most exhausting. It takes a lot of energy from the entire group to transcend simple scene work and present a vivid cinematic experience for the audience.

PAY TRIBUTE TO THE GENRE

As is the case with all Long Form scene work, the scene work in your Movie must have a base reality. You must first establish a base reality before you can find and play your Game. In a Movie, the base reality is provided by the genre. Every scene within your Movie will start with some bit of genre-specific base reality (i.e., something that would happen in the genre, played the way it would happen). From this point on, you will Yes And until you find the first unusual thing. The first unusual thing in any scene is anything that departs from the genre. In the Movie, playing at the "top of your intelligence" means that anything not tied to the Game of the scene will be played as you would expect it to be in this genre. Del Close referred to this as "paying tribute to the genre." (Note: Within the Movie, the Game of the scene will always be found organically. You will never enter a scene with a premise because the opening of the Movie does not provide premises or half ideas; it only provides a base reality.)

Genre alone does not equal Game. Genre provides a context within which to play your Game. Simply playing the genre is not enough. If you only play the genre instead of Games, you will only end up with jokes, references, and mere laughs of recognition from the audience.

For instance, if your genre is "George Romero zombie movies," a zombie bursting into a room is not going to count as a first unusual thing. Even though this would be very unusual if it happened in real life, in George Romero zombie movies, zombies bursting into rooms are part of the base reality. But if one of the characters in the scene then starts complaining about the property damage the zombie is doing to his home, this would count as a first unusual thing. That's because the expected response from a character like this in an actual zombie movie is panic, fear, or violence toward the zombie.

Returning to Games of the Movie

The structure of the Movie does not include a specific time or place wherein Games will return. There is no second-beat equivalent in the Movie. Still, the Games from previous scenes can return later on in the form of sub-Games. Sub-Games are secondary Games that can be played in addition to the new Game we find in each scene. While you will organically find a new Game in each new scene, the possibility to incorporate previously established Games as sub-Games is always available. Sub-Games are not the main focus, and they should not take priority over finding the Game of any scene.

Character Games are especially likely to recur as sub-Games. The behavior of a character in a Movie longform must remain consistent throughout the entire piece, just as the behavior of characters in real movies should remain consistent.

PLOT

As stated earlier, the plot of any Long Form Movie should closely mirror the plot of an archetypical movie within the genre being performed. This is not cheating! Remember, Long Form shows are never about the plot; they are always about the funny ideas or the Games. By following an expected or typical plot, your ensemble will know which scene or character to jump to next, freeing everyone to focus instead on finding, playing, and connecting Games.

There is one key distinction to be made between plot in actual movies and plot in Long Form Movies. It is important to realize that your ensemble will only have thirty minutes to accomplish what is normally done in ninety minutes or two hours. Put your focus on playing those moments and scenes that are the most essential and recognizable.

TERMINOLOGY

The Movie takes standard cinematic techniques and applies them to the stage. The ensemble uses cinematic terminology (close-ups, cut-aways, over-the-head shots, etc.) in their descriptions to help the members of the audience visualize what is happening onstage in a cinematic fashion.

TO GET THIS:

DO THIS:

CLOSE-UPS

Close-ups are used to focus the audience's attention on a character, an important action, or a significant detail in a scene. Close-ups are initiated verbally. At any time, any improviser can say, "Close-up on ____." The improviser initiating the close-up will also frame with his hands Who or What is being put in the close-up. At this point, the improviser can go on to describe details of the close-up (e.g., "We see a trickle of sweat running down his face," or "We close-up on her hand reaching for the gun"). The rest of the improvisers need to employ give-and-take, and hold their dialogue until the description is done. In order to end a close-up, any improviser from the ensemble can give the direction, "Cut back to the wide angle."

CUT-TOS

In the Movie, the cut-to is used as an edit to end one scene and start the next. Any improviser in the ensemble can call out, "Cut to ____." The blank will be filled in with a basic description of the next scene (e.g., "Cut to a boardroom, late at night, six men sit around a conference table..."). As opposed to simply editing and trusting that someone will step out and do something, the Movie requires the editor to specifically call out what location and/or characters they want to see next.

ANGLES

Low-angle or high-angle shots can be used to convey a more specific visual look for a scene. If you want to show a low-angle shot of a character in the Movie, first announce it (e.g., "Cut to a low-angle shot of the detective"). Then use your hands to create a frame low to the ground, pointed up, representing the perspective of the camera. For high-angle shots, you announce the shot (e.g., "Cut to a high-angle shot of the detective") and then use your hands to create a frame above the characters. You may even want to get up on a chair to establish a high-angle shot.

Low-angle and high-angle shots add to the aesthetic of the Movie and can help you further nail down your genre. These shots are often used in scenes of confrontation in films to illustrate which character holds the position of power. The subject of a high-angle shot will look vulnerable and insignificant on film. The subject of a low-angle shot will seem powerful and imposing (e.g., Darth Vader is usually shot at a low angle). Using these shots in the Movie is a way for the improvisers onstage to flesh out the characters and their relationships to each other.

PANS

The pan mimics the swinging horizontal or vertical movement of the camera in a film. You can use pans to reveal someone or something out of frame (e.g., "We pan to reveal a man lurking in the shadows") or to show more of the setting (e.g., "We pan across an elaborate child's birthday party to reveal children riding horses, a six-foot-high layer cake, a magician, etc."). Sometimes it will be appropriate for the characters in the scene to move offstage as the camera is panning off of them. Additionally, new characters may have to step into the scene in order to represent what is being focused on in the pan.

Sometimes pans are used to simply give the ensemble a chance to more fully describe the setting in a scene; they don't need to necessarily reveal a new character. In this situation, the character originally in the scene should still move offstage to ape the effect of the camera moving past them, but the environment should be included either through verbal descriptions from the back-line or by other members of the ensemble stepping out to play prominent or significant pieces of the environment.

TRACKING SHOTS

Tracking shots are used to follow a character as they move through their environment. In order to initiate a tracking shot, someone from the ensemble will step forward and say, "We cut to a tracking shot of ____," and then frame the person being tracked. The character will mime moving through space (while actually remaining in place) as the rest of the ensemble creates the effect of a changing background. They can do this through description or by moving through the frame as objects or other characters that the main character is moving past. You can also do tracking shots of objects.

POVs

POV shots are used to show the audience a specific character's point of view. A POV shot is initiated when a member of the ensemble says, "We cut to the ____'s POV." If what you are describing in the POV shot is small and specific, it may be necessary to frame it with your hands (e.g., "a spot of blood on a shirt"). The improviser initiating the POV will then describe what is happening in the shot. Since we are trying to show what a character is seeing, the character whose POV we are seeing will actually leave the stage when a POV shot is called. Other improvisers will enter the stage to become the characters, objects, or environment described in the POV.

RACK FOCUS

To rack-focus means to change the plane of focus from one character or object to another within a single shot. To initiate a rack focus, a member of the ensemble will say, "We rack-focus from ____ to ____." The initiating improviser will then create a frame around whatever they are rack-focusing to.

Let's say that we are watching a scene in which a hard-boiled detective is rummaging through a desk. An improviser from the back-line could step forward and say, "We rack-focus from the detective to a door that is opening slowly behind him." The improviser initiating this shot will create a frame around the door to focus the audience's attention on it.

REVERSE ANGLES

Reverse angles are used to show what is happening in the opposite direction from what we're currently seeing (180 degrees from the shot currently being depicted). To initiate a reverse angle, a member of the ensemble will say, "Cut to a reverse angle. We see ____." The improviser initiating the shot should establish the new information being revealed by the reverse angle. For example, in a scene about a doctor performing a surgery, a reverse angle could reveal a group of medical students watching the surgery being performed.

When a reverse angle is initiated, the scene will "flip" 180 degrees, with everyone currently in the scene maintaining his or her position relative to the other performers. Improvisers that were originally facing forward will now have to turn their backs to the audience. Other improvisers may need to join the scene to portray characters being revealed by the reverse angle.

SPLIT SCREENS

Split screens are used to show action occurring in two different locations simultaneously. To initiate a split screen, a member of the ensemble will say, "We split-screen to reveal ____." The improviser initiating the split screen will then step out to physically split the stage with their arms, while describing the new scene being added to the stage. New improvisers will step out as needed for this new scene. The improvisers in the two scenes will take their places on either side of the improviser who is "splitting" the screen. For example, in a scene where we see a girl getting ready for a date, a split scene could be called to reveal her date also getting ready.

CHYRONS

Chyrons are electronically generated captions superimposed on a television or movie screen. In the Movie, chyrons are a device used to establish information about a character or a setting through text on-screen. To initiate a chyron, a member of the ensemble from the back-line will say, "We see a chyron appear on-screen that reads ____" (e.g., "On the lower half of the screen a chyron appears: The Canary Islands, June 15th, 1944").

CRANE SHOTS

A crane shot is a shot taken by a camera on a crane to show action from above. To initiate a crane shot, a member of the ensemble will say, "We see a crane shot as the camera pulls away from this scene." The ensemble doesn't do anything physical to represent a crane shot; it is left up to the audience's imagination. Crane shots can add emotional weight to a key moment in your Movie. Since crane shots are commonly used to signify the end of a movie by moving up and away from the characters in the scene, they are an effective way to cue the rest of your ensemble that you have reached the end of the Movie.

SLOW MOTION

A slow-motion sequence is used to add dramatic emphasis to moments of action, high emotions, etc. To initiate a slow-motion sequence in the

Movie, a member of the ensemble simply says, "We see this sequence in slow motion." The improvisers in the scene will immediately slow down their movements. Characters in the scene modify their voices to mimic the effect of slowing down film.

GIMMICK SHOTS

These shots add relatively little to the improvisation in a scene. They are support-based moments that are funny because of their physical nature. Gimmick shots allow your ensemble to show off for the audience. While they are fun, they should be used sparingly.

OVER-THE-HEAD SHOT

An over-the-head shot in cinema occurs when the camera is looking down upon the action of the scene from directly above it. An over-the-head shot is initiated when a member of the ensemble says, "We cut to an over-the-head shot of this scene." To re-create an over-the-head shot onstage, the improvisers in the scene are picked up by improvisers from the back-line and held so that the tops of their heads are facing out to the audience.

MATRIX SHOT

A Matrix shot mimics the iconic scene in the movie *The Matrix* in which the camera revolved 360 degrees around a frozen moment. When someone from the ensemble initiates a Matrix shot, the entire scene, meaning everyone onstage, maintains their position relative to each other while rotating 360 degrees on an axis in the center of the stage.

DUTCH ANGLE

A Dutch angle is when a camera is tilted approximately 45 degrees. When a Dutch angle is initiated, everyone onstage will lean to the side to give the effect of the camera being tilted to the side.

These are only a few examples of innumerable gimmick shots. You may be able to come up with other gimmick shots by devising ways to physically represent actual cinematic techniques onstage. Remember to use gimmick shots sparingly. While gimmick shots are funny, they neither further the plot nor play the Game.

EXAMPLES

The following are some examples of Movie openings to give you a sense of how they are created.

Example One: Full Opening

Let's imagine that an ensemble asks for the suggestion of a song lyric:

SUGGESTION: "I was the king of the alley, Mama, I could talk some trash."

Taking inspiration from this song lyric, an improviser establishes the first setting of the opening by stepping forward to say:

PLAYER 1:   "We open on a shadowy back alley. We see a rat quickly scurry across in the foreground…"

Another improviser steps forward and takes over the scene painting by saying:

PLAYER 2:   "The camera pushes through the alley, landing on a man wearing a rumpled overcoat with an old fedora pulled down tightly on his head."

Once this is said, an improviser from the back-line will step out and play the man in the overcoat that is being described. Another improviser steps out and says:

PLAYER 3:   "Everything we're seeing is in black and white. The man lights a cigarette…"

At this point, the improviser portraying the man would mime lighting a cigarette. The improviser already speaking then says:

PLAYER 3:   "...when he lights up, we see that the man has a scar that runs from his forehead over his eye and down his cheek."

Given what has been established so far, the ensemble has strongly suggested that the genre of this movie is "film noir," and that the character being described is a private detective.

At this point an improviser might edit this setting entirely by saying:

PLAYER 4:   "Cut to, interior of a train. The car is filled with people dressed in 1940s clothes. Women are in knee-length skirts and high-heeled shoes. The men are in suit coats and hats."

Another improviser takes over and says:

PLAYER 5:   "We push in on a newspaper. The newspaper lowers, revealing a pair of suspicious eyes."

An improviser from the back-line steps out to play the man with the suspicious eyes. A new improviser takes over the scene painting:

PLAYER 6:   "The man is sweating. He folds the newspaper and places it on the seat next to him. He begins nervously clutching a briefcase."

Another improviser steps out and continues:

PLAYER 7:   "Close-up on the man opening the briefcase to reveal twenty fake passports, all with his face but different names."

The ensemble has further established the genre by adding another archetypical film noir setting and character.

Another improviser from the back-line edits out of this scene to the third and final setting of the opening by saying:

PLAYER 8:   "Cut to exterior, cemetery. A group of people dressed in black stand in a light drizzle."

Multiple members of the ensemble will step forward from the back-line to play this group of people. A new improviser takes over the scene painting, gestures toward one specific improviser in the group onstage, and says:

PLAYER 4:   **"We move in close on one woman wearing a black veil covering her eyes, with tears streaming down her face."**

A new improviser steps out and says:

PLAYER 6:   **"Dramatic music swells as the title fills the screen in big, white block letters: 'The False Identity.'"**

Example Two: Partial Opening

The inspiration for the Movie does not have to be a song lyric. This following example shows just the first setting of an opening inspired by nothing more than a single word.

SUGGESTION: **corn**

PLAYER 1:   **"We open on a cornfield and the sun is just peeking over the horizon. We can see workers in the field..."**

At this point, multiple improvisers can step out to play the workers.

PLAYER 2:   **"...the workers are covered in sweat and have leathery skin from long hours of hard labor. We angle on the foreman's cabin. Tough and confident-looking, the foreman stands outside of the cabin with a gun over his shoulder..."**

To angle on the cabin, this improviser would create a frame with his hands and physically angle the scene away from the workers toward where he imagined the cabin would be in this shot. Once the foreman is mentioned, a new improviser will step out and silently play this character.

PLAYER 3: "...the foreman is standing next to a spittoon. We see that he has a big wad of chew in between his gum and lip. He is looking out at the workers in the field..."

Note: While this is a very good character description, the improvisers have not yet nailed the foreman down as an archetypical character. In this case, his archetype will become apparent in relation to the other main characters described later on in the opening.

Notice that this improviser is only describing what he can see, not puppeting the improviser portraying the character. This allows the improviser playing the character to make choices about the character's behavior in the moment when this setting is returned to later in the Movie. Player 3 has only set up enough information about the character so that the other improvisers know the general direction of the scene and genre. The improviser playing the foreman will now be able to find his own actions, specific characteristics, and Game as the Movie unfolds.

PLAYER 4: "We cut to a POV shot of what the foreman is seeing. We see a ruggedly handsome worker supporting another weak, anemic-looking man who is down on his knees."

The above description establishes our first archetypical character in the Movie. By describing the worker in the field as "ruggedly handsome," and by having him do something benevolent, we are strongly suggesting that this is the hero or main character of the Movie. Now that we have identified this character as the hero, it is likely that the tough foreman described before is the villain.

PLAYER 5: "The weak man has a bloody handkerchief sticking out of a pocket in his overalls. The handsome worker shoots an angry look at the foreman."

PLAYER 6: "And we cut away from this scene to a steam locomotive pulling into an isolated train station..."

This improviser has started the description of the second setting in this Movie. Again, the ensemble will work together in describing this new setting and the characters that inhabit it. The genre is still being determined at this point, but we do have some clues as to what it may be: Key words like "spittoon" let us know that this movie is happening in the American past. Since steam locomotives were used from the start of the 19th century until the middle of the 20th century, the genre could be anything from a gold rush Western to a dust bowl *Grapes of Wrath*–style period drama. This second setting is in keeping with the first. The ensemble will work together in this new setting and a third to continue to get more specific about the genre of the Movie.

Example Three: Full Opening

Let's take a look at another Movie opening. This is a transcription of an actual performance of the Movie done by a class of UCB Training Center students. To inspire their Movie, they got the suggestion of someone's favorite song lyric.

SUGGESTION: **"Now we know how many holes it takes to fill the Albert Hall."**

PLAYER 1: **"We open on a computer-animated version of Albert Hall! We hear the sound of classical music playing as the camera pans over an orchestra playing onstage. The camera moves over the crowd and we see aristocrats in the seats. The camera begins to move up..."**

PLAYER 2: **"...and we move up, up, up into the very top of Albert Hall, where we see a tiny computer-animated cockroach."**

At this point, an improviser stepped out to play the cockroach.

PLAYER 3: **"This entire movie is animated. The cockroach is listening to the music intently and he has a miniature conductor's baton in his hand..."**

PLAYER 4: **"...he's got a giant smile on his face and his antennae are forming music notes as the music plays..."**

PLAYER 5: **"...and standing right next to him is a caterpillar trying with all his hands to keep the sheet music in front of the cockroach. As we see the sheet music flutter up** and fly around, we see a bead of sweat drip down the caterpillar's brow..."

Another improviser came forward at this point to play the caterpillar.

PLAYER 6:   "...and we cut away from this scene to a small house. Sitting on a chair next to a table is a small, sad-looking girl with blond hair swooped down all the way to
the floor..."

An improviser stepped out as the sad-looking girl.

PLAYER 7:   "...all the way down to the floor and in front of her on the table is a violin that is just in a horrible state of disrepair. It's got holes in it and the holes are covered with tape and patches..."

PLAYER 8:   "...and sitting next to her is an older man who is balding and who has a fat gigantic stomach..."

Again, someone from the back-line stepped forward as the older man.

PLAYER 5:   "...he's wearing a wifebeater that is stained all over the chest. He has a tattoo that says USMC on it, and he has a beard."

PLAYER 7:   "...and we cut away from this scene and we see a sign on a door in downtown London and it says 'The Royal Philharmonic Society' and the door opens, and we go past brilliantly dressed gentlemen and we see a man dressed in a very fine suit with a little thin moustache..."

As this shot was being described, the ensemble came forward as the brilliantly dressed gentlemen being described. When Player 7 described the man with the little thin moustache, a member of the ensemble from the back-line framed one improviser onstage with his arms, in order to indicate which member of the group was the man with the little thin moustache.

PLAYER 2:   "...a little thin moustache that extends out across his face, and his hair is very slicked-

> back and greasy, and standing next to him
> is a little girl with black ponytails that stick
> almost straight up from her head..."

Again, an improviser from the back-line came forward to play the girl with the black ponytails.

PLAYER 4: "...she's holding a violin but she has turned it upside down. Suddenly the music swells and we see fairylike dust appear across the screen as the title begins to appear..."

PLAYER 1: "...and the title begins to appear and in calligraphy. It reads 'Bugthoven's 2nd.'"

This group did a great job of setting up a clear genre in their opening. The moment this was labeled as an animated movie, we didn't need many clues in order to identify the genre. All of the players got on the same page about adding visuals and characters that you would expect to see in a computer-animated children's movie. Humans and anthropomorphic insects existing in the same world, the exaggerated visual appearance of the characters, details like "fairy dust," and the slightly corny title all support this genre.

In this opening, the players successfully set up the three opening scenes for their Movie. Each character is given some attributes through description, but the exact relationships between the characters are only hinted at. This group does a good job of using familiar archetypes from animated movies for kids: The "lead bug" has grand aspirations, he has a bumbling sidekick, and details like the thin moustache and greasy, slicked-back hair suggest that the gentleman in the third section is villain material.

ASSSSCAT

Asssscat is a made-up word that the Upright Citizens Brigade came up with for the free show that they started after moving to New York City. It is also a longform structure performed by six to nine improvisers in which the scenes are based on information culled from improvised personal monologues. The structure of Asssscat is intentionally very simple, the idea being that any skilled Long Form improviser could sit in and play at any given Asssscat.

An Asssscat begins by taking a suggestion from the audience. This suggestion inspires an initial monologue. The monologues can be provided by a guest performer or by one of the members of the ensemble. The monologist should not participate in scene work. Anyone capable of telling a detailed true story or anecdote could serve as a monologist for an Asssscat. In order to provide information for three to four scenes, an Asssscat monologue should generally be three to five minutes long. *(For a review on how to deliver monologues, please return to pg 254.)*

Following the initial monologue, the ensemble will perform three to four different longform scenes, each inspired by details, premises, and ideas generated by the monologue. When someone in the ensemble feels that the information in the initial monologue has been exhausted, they will cue the monologist to deliver a second monologue. This second monologue can follow up on the first, be inspired by the initial suggestion in a different way, or be inspired by something that happened in one of the scenes. When you start to run out of information from the second monologue, you want to look for your ending. You should try to end your show on a high point (a strong callback to another scene, an especially funny line, etc.). Please realize that if there is a paucity of information in the first or second monologue, you may require a third monologue to inspire further scenes.

Asssscat scenes tend to be premise-based, since comedic premises are relatively easy to identify and pull from monologues. As in all longforms, the improvisers in an Asssscat also have the option of starting scenes with a detail or a half idea from the monologue. However, starting with a strong premise is generally the preferred style of play in an Asssscat show. *(For a review on initiating scenes from monologues, please return to pg 264.)*

THE SIMPLICITY OF ASSSSCAT

Assssscat is one of the easiest structures because there are so few rules to follow. This is by design. Assssscat is meant to be a "drop-in" show that requires no rehearsal and can be performed by any group of improvisers well schooled in the basics of Long Form improvisation.

The simplicity of the Assssscat form makes it seem very appealing to new performers. It is important to realize that in other forms such as the Harold or the Movie, the audience will be impressed by callbacks and connections. The structures of those forms make them feel like a cohesive whole. While Assssscats can be very entertaining, they are only as good as each performer's individual scene work. You can't depend on the Assssscat form to elevate your scene work to a higher level.

MONOSCENE

The Monoscene is a longform that was perfected by the Swarm, a house team from UCBTNY. It is comprised of one long, continuous scene with no time dashes. Monoscenes should be of comparable length to a Harold or any other longform structure, meaning that this single scene will be sustained for about twenty-five to thirty minutes.

Like most longforms, the Monoscene is best performed by a group of six to nine improvisers. The structure of the Monoscene is, on the surface, very simple. The entire show will feature one location and uses no edits of any kind. Monoscenes do not include an opening. They begin with the ensemble taking an audience suggestion that directly inspires some members of the ensemble to establish a location and activity. A Monoscene can start with two improvisers, multiple improvisers, or the entire ensemble. The scene will unfold in this single location without jumping forward or backward through time. While this initial scene is technically never edited, the members of the ensemble can use entrances and exits to essentially split up the show into shorter "scenes." Within this single location, each improviser will establish a character that they will likely play for the duration of the show. However it is possible for one improviser to use entrances and exits to play multiple characters. The more improvisers there are in your ensemble, the less necessary it will be for any improviser to play multiple characters. As with any longform, ensembles performing the Monoscene will look to find and play Games. The Monoscene differs from most scenes in that you will intentionally find multiple Games within a single scene. A good Monoscene will end with a callback, connection, or heightened Game move.

As is the case with any scene, Monoscenes are more likely to succeed if improvisers establish a clear and simple base reality from the start.

Monoscenes typically start with the establishment of a location. A good Monoscene location will be a place where we are likely to see multiple characters (e.g., an office break room, an airport terminal, a dinner party, etc.).

You must also give yourself a strong What within this environment (e.g., "celebrating someone's birthday in the office break room," "being delayed due to weather in the airport," or "meeting someone's new girlfriend at the dinner party"). Why are these characters together? What are they doing? Giving your Monoscene a strong What makes all the Games seem like they are part of one scene. The What of your Monoscene also gives you something to return to as you and your teammates look for the next Game move.

Once you have your What and your Where, you can begin to make character choices. You can either establish a character choice for yourself or look to give gifts to your scene partners in order to help them find characters. (The approach you use could be predetermined in rehearsals or prior to performance.) Since you could be playing this single character for up to thirty minutes, it is important to make choices that create a grounded three-dimensional character. You want to avoid making "broad" or "big" choices that will quickly become tiresome. Silly or absurd choices can be hard to sustain over a thirty-minute longform. By establishing a strong point of view, you will make it easier for yourself to continually answer the questions, "What would my character say?" and "What would my character do?"

Game is an essential element for a successful Monoscene. As previously stated, your ensemble will intentionally find multiple Games within a single scene.

You should think of each individual character as having his or her own Game. For this reason, no one in a Monoscene will intentionally play a neutral straight man. Each character should have an interesting behavior or point of view that can be heightened and explored throughout the show. For example, let's imagine the Monoscene involving the birthday party in an office break room. You are playing a boss. In the first few minutes of the scene, you overshare about your weekend at home. This behavior can be followed as a character Game for the rest of the show. In every situation and conversation that follows, the boss should look to overshare some more.

While every character will have a Game, it is not possible to establish two different character Games simultaneously. You will need to use give-and-take. While an improviser is making choices that will lead to their character Game, the other improviser or improvisers in the scene with them at that time will remain relatively neutral. Once this improviser has established their character Game, they will pull back and remain relatively neutral, allowing another improviser to establish their Game. The ensemble will give and take in this manner until all of the improvisers have established individual character Games.

Give-and-take is also important for playing Game as the Monoscene progresses. Even though no character should be neutral, every character will at times play the straight man to someone else. Let's return to our break room birthday party and imagine another character: a temp who is trying too hard to impress everyone so that he will be hired as a full-time employee. Our boss could act as a straight man to this character, even though she has an established Game (oversharing personal information). When these two characters are together, the improviser playing the boss may rest the Game of oversharing in order to react to, question, and challenge the temp's Game of "trying too hard." Conversely, we could see an interaction wherein the temp rests his Game and plays the straight man to the boss's oversharing.

Finally, Monoscenes will sometimes have one or more "macro-Games" that can be played throughout the show. Often, these Games will be tied to the circumstances of the What and the Where. In our office birthday party example, a recurring macro-Game could be that everyone has brought terrible, clearly last-minute gifts to the party (a stapler off someone's desk, a salad from the cafeteria, a Post-it with "IOU a massage" written on it, etc.).

Entrances and exits in a Monoscene serve the same purpose that edits do in other longforms: helping with Game play, pacing, and give-and-take. If you start with two improvisers, the rest of the ensemble should look to take turns entering the scene to establish their characters. You don't want to wait too long to introduce a new character. Looking for an exit once you have introduced your own character will allow one of your teammates to introduce their own character. If you start with the entire ensemble onstage, you will find that exiting will give other improvisers onstage a chance to establish their character Games. Once you have clearly established your Game, it is a good idea to exit the scene so that you leave the audience wanting more, thereby setting you up to return to your character and Game later in the show. Having your character exit early on in the Monoscene has the same effect of a well-timed edit in the first beat of a Harold. It gets you offstage before you burn out your Game, and gives you something to come back to later in the longform. Once everyone has established their character Game, frequent entrances and exits can help you shift focus among the different Games of the Monoscene.

While entrances and exits can be very helpful, they are not required in a Monoscene. It is possible to perform a successful Monoscene with the entire ensemble onstage for the duration of the show. In this situation, the ensemble should be looking to give and take focus verbally such that the scene is easy to follow, and such that the different Games can be discovered, heightened, and explored.

As with all longforms, you want to end your Monoscene on a high note. Once you've passed the twenty- or twenty-five-minute mark, you should look to make a callback to something that happened earlier, whether you return to something you said or did, or you make a reference to something someone else said or did. It is also possible to set someone else up to make a callback to something from their Game.

Monoscenes differ from other longforms in that ending them on a plot point can be satisfying. A strategy that some ensembles use when performing a Monoscene is to hint at some significant future event early on in the show. The ensemble will then actively look to show that event by the end of the performance. Doing so can give the audience the sense that the entire show was building to this point. The plot that gets you there should not be your focus. Think of ending with this "payoff" as a sort of callback. You are simply returning to an idea established early on in the piece. For example, in the office birthday party, we could be anticipating the arrival of a party clown.

Ending with a callback or a "payoff" is not an absolute requirement. Simply ending with another heightened Game move can be enough to get you out of a Monoscene.

While their structures are obviously very different, you can draw parallels between a successful Monoscene and a successful Harold. Ideally, your Monoscene will start off with very disparate Games (in this case, the Games are tied to the different characters). Individual Games in a Monoscene will be returned to in the same way that Games from the first beat of a Harold are revisited in the second beat. The obvious difference is that there is no set order in which you will return to the Games of a Monoscene. Exiting and returning to a Game later in a Monoscene is equivalent to a time-dash second beat in a Harold. Finally, just like in a Harold, you should end your Monoscene with a strong callback.

The Monoscene is a great structure to focus on if your ensemble is interested in exploring character work.

DECONSTRUCTION

The Deconstruction is a longform that starts with a long, detailed, information-generating opening scene inspired by an audience suggestion. The name Deconstruction stems from the fact that this opening scene will be broken apart, its "pieces" used as the starting point for the other scenes. This opening scene serves as the opening for the piece, providing all of the information and ideas to inspire the rest of the scenes.

The first scene of a Deconstruction is normally a two-person scene that tends to be much longer than the average two-person scene. The performers in the scene should feel free to take their time, and the rest of the ensemble can be patient with editing the scene. The two improvisers performing this scene should look to establish strong characters, a clear relationship between these characters, and lots of information, opinions, and details about the world surrounding them. The improvisers on the back-line will be gathering this information from the opening scene to inspire later scenes.

Since this first scene will be the source of inspiration for all of the following scenes, filling it with details and information is extremely important. Whereas you normally stop Yes And–ing once you have found a first unusual thing and switch to If Then to play a Game, in the opening scene of a Deconstruction, you will continue to Yes And past any unusual things that arise so that you can generate more information. Remember, this is an opening, so the ensemble should note these unusual things such that they can be used later as premises and half ideas to start scenes. Instead of narrowing the focus of the scene by asking, "If this is true, then what else is true?," you should keep expanding, adding, and building in new information. Throwing in new observations, character beliefs, and other details will give you more ideas to choose from when starting new scenes. In other words, the opening scene of a Deconstruction can be less Game-focused and more like a meandering conversation.

In addition to continuing to Yes And after the discovery of unusual things, two other rules of good scene work can be broken in the opening scene of a Deconstruction. You will talk about characters that are not there so that these characters can appear in later scenes. Although you normally want to avoid talking about the past or the future, in an opening Deconstruction scene, doing so can provide useful information for later scenes. All of the other rules of good Long Form scene work apply to the opening scene of a Deconstruction (listening, playing at the top of your intelligence, starting in the middle, establishing a clear and specific relationship, etc.).

Since we are not following the rule of finding a Game after something unusual arises, the opening scene of a Deconstruction is not going to be as focused and funny as a scene built around a Game. Whereas these scenes do not have to be deathly serious, they will generally be closer in tone to a short play than a comedy sketch. You don't have to be concerned over the number of laughs you are getting in the opening scene, since your primary goal is generating information.

The rest of the form is like an Asssscat in that there is no set structure following the opening scene. All scenes that follow should be inspired by something that happened in the opening scene. These scenes will follow all the rules of Long Form comedy scene work. The improvisers should initiate ideas clearly, look for the first unusual thing, and make patterns of absurd or unusual behavior. The ensemble will edit all of the rest of the scenes in the piece normally.

There are two types of scenes in a Deconstruction: main character scenes and tangent scenes. Main character scenes are either time-dash scenes involving one or both of the characters from the opening scene, or scenes in which one or both of the characters from the opening scene are referenced. In time-dash main character scenes, you should try to put the main characters into new and different situations that will help you explore them further. Since we are deconstructing the two main characters, we may also see scenes that explore "personality-forming events" in their lives. These scenes show the audience how the characters became who they are and why they are unique to the Deconstruction.

Scenes that do not include one of the two original characters are called tangent scenes. Tangent scenes can be initiated with premises or half ideas that are analogous to funny ideas discovered in the opening scene. The second scene of the Deconstruction must be a tangent scene that has nothing to do with the two main characters. This helps you avoid any expectations from your audience that the show will be a sort of play about the two main characters. This will also ensure that the audience is not thrown when tangent scenes show up later in the longform.

Like most longforms, the Deconstruction should end on a callback or a high point of some sort. It is possible to end the show with one or both of the initial characters, but it is not mandatory that you do so.

Let's take a look at some examples from a Deconstruction performed by Reuben Williams, a house team at UCBTNY:

The first scene of the Deconstruction featured two older women, Carol and Charlene, who had gotten together to do some gardening over the weekend. The first information generated in the scene revolved around the fact that Charlene had recently spent some time in the hospital. It was established that Charlene was somewhat obsessed with mentioning her hospital stay—she constantly qualified whatever she was doing by describing it as the first time that she had done that thing since coming home from the hospital.

Other information generated in this scene included the following: Charlene expressed her frustration at her inability to stop her VCR from blinking "12:00 a.m.," in spite of her son's instructions on how to solve this problem. It was revealed that Charlene's injury and subsequent hospital stay were the result of falling off of a stationary motorcycle. Charlene also received a few text messages from her grandson. We found out that Carol was a librarian, and she talked about the recent rise in people stealing books from her library. Carol also mentioned that her husband had been in Cuba for weeks on business. Some of the information generated in this scene are premises and some are half ideas. Reuben Williams used the ideas in scenes as follows:

The second scene of the Deconstruction was a tangent scene inspired by the fact that books were being stolen from Carol's library. The scene started with the premise of a "gang" who stole books from a library instead of borrowing them for free. The Game of the scene ended up being that there was a gang that only stole "free stuff." Through support moves, we saw the gang terrorize a city by stealing pamphlets, McDonald's napkins, copies of *The Onion*, etc.

The third scene showed a main character scene that was inspired by Charlene's text messages from her grandson. The Game of the scene involved the grandson obsessively text messaging his grandmother instead of paying attention to his date.

From this point on, the scenes alternated between tangent scenes and main character scenes. These included (among others) a tangent scene about old people taking a class on "modern technology" (e.g., setting your VCR and recording answering machine messages) and a main character scene in which Charlene, on the stand as a witness in a murder trial, frustrated the judge by constantly referencing her hospital stay.

THE CHECK-IN DECONSTRUCTION

The Check-In is a variation of the Deconstruction. In the opening for the Check-In, one of the improvisers reenacts the most significant events of a particularly interesting day that he or she actually experienced. The performer reenacts these events through scenes in which we only hear their side of the dialogue. The opening should be as long and detailed as the opening scene for a standard Deconstruction. (Although you will usually perform one day of your life, you could perform the Check-In opening and cover a longer period of time: a week, a long weekend, the duration of a vacation getaway, etc.)

Ensembles should pick someone who has recently had an interesting day to perform the opening for the Check-In (e.g., "the day my sister backed out of her wedding," "the day I got arrested," etc.). It is important that the improviser performing the opening does not share any of the details of their interesting day with anyone else in the ensemble before the show.

During the opening of the Check-In, you are not telling the story of your day, but rather acting it out. Since the dialogue is going to be one-sided, you will need to fill in the other side of the conversation through repetition. For example, in real life you might have just said "yes" if someone asked to sit next to you. In the opening of the Check-In, you would say something like, "Excuse me? Yeah, you can sit here." Furthermore, when the audience needs to know what your inner thoughts or feelings were, you will need to "muse out loud" to yourself. For example, if part of the experience that you want to get across is that you met someone with a giant scar across their face that made you very uncomfortable, you might muse to yourself, "Whoa...look at that giant scar...no-no-no, please don't come over to me...okay, he's coming to talk to me," before breaking into your actual dialogue with the person: "—Hey! How are you doing?"

Let's take a look at an abbreviated example of an opening for the Check-In. *(The ellipses signify pauses that the performer would take in order to imply that they are being spoken to by another character.)*

(The improviser begins by putting his arm out to hail a taxi.) "Hey! Taxi!" (The improviser mimes getting into a cab with some bags and sits down.) "I'm going to JFK...American Airlines...Please step on it. I haven't gotten to eat anything yet today and I'm starving...What's that?...That's kind of crazy to say that all Americans are evil...Yeah, there's a whole aisle of snack foods in the supermarket—I don't see what that has to do with...So you think that Twinkies and cupcakes are evil?...It's an interesting theory, but I still don't agree with you. Thanks for the ride." (The improviser mimes getting out of the cab with his bags. He takes a few steps, implying his walk through the airport. He stands stationary for a few moments, looking weary and annoyed to imply waiting in line before stepping forward.) "Hi, I'd like to check these bags...My passport? Sure...Yeah, that's me...You don't think it looks like me?...Well, I guess I do look a lot fatter in that picture. I lost a lot of weight...I promise you, that's me!"

*(**Note:** This is a lot shorter than the opening for a Check-In would typically be.)*

The Check-In is similar to the Deconstruction in that the performers will deconstruct the one-sided dialogue for scene ideas, just as performers mine ideas from the opening scene of a standard Deconstruction.

It is different from the Deconstruction in that 95% of the scenes of the Check-In will be tangent scenes. Remember, these are initiated with premises and half ideas that are analogous to funny ideas discovered in the opening. Main character scenes are, for the most part, avoided to ensure that you don't merely reenact what the audience has already seen in the opening. Focusing on tangent scenes will also keep you from limiting one performer to only playing the role of the main character from the opening.

Here are a few sample premises that could be pulled from our truncated Check-In opening:

- A cupcake factory that is run by Satan. This is inspired by the cabdriver's claim that the snack food aisle in the supermarket is evil.

- A guy tries to get out of a speeding ticket with a cop by claiming that he was in a hurry because he was starving. This is inspired by the moment in the Check-In when the performer says, "Please step on it, I'm starving." "Please step on it" is a phrase that normally implies an emergency of some sort.

- A bartender checks the ID of a patron. Thinking the picture looks nothing like the patron and that the ID is a fake, he brutally insults the picture. This is inspired by the airport attendant from the opening.

There is no set structure to the Check-In beyond the opening. The ensemble will essentially perform a montage of scenes using ideas from the opening as inspiration. As in all longforms, you should be looking to vary your scenes between two-person and group scenes, and you should be looking to make callbacks and connections.

If your ensemble spends a lot of time together or you have lives that are very similar (e.g., you are all struggling actors), you may have to regularly elect one of the members of your group to go out and consciously have an interesting day (do something that you don't normally do) in order to avoid having repetitive shows.

A FINAL WORD ON LONGFORMS

The longforms described here are only a handful of those in existence. Even more are sure to be created by new and inventive performance groups. New ensembles should give themselves the freedom to try out many different forms until they find the one that best suits their strengths and weaknesses. Or you can use the basic components of the preexisting longforms to create something new that works for you.

At first, learning the structure and rules of a longform is going to make improvising more difficult than just doing isolated scenes. However, stick with it. Eventually, with practice, the structure will become second nature. Learning a structure will be worth it, since good scene work within a structure is always going to be more impressive than good scene work alone.

CHAPTER 13:

Rehearsal & Performance

Please remember what was said at the very beginning of this book:

"Just reading this book alone will not make you a great improviser, but should be a companion to constant practice and performance. Like any other art form, you will not become a competent improviser by just reading about how to do it. Experience will be your best teacher, so you must find the time to practice as much as possible."

It would take at least one to two years in classes to cover everything in this book, so don't expect to master it after one read. The only way to master Long Form is to practice.

REHEARSAL

It may seem odd to talk about rehearsal for an art form that is all about spontaneity and creating things in the moment. However, all great Long Form ensembles will undoubtedly attribute their success to the long hours they put into rehearsing.

Rehearsing is crucial to becoming amazing at Long Form improv. For many new improvisers, the only practice they get is at their weekly three-hour class. If you are really serious about becoming a great improviser, this is not nearly enough. The more time you devote to working on fundamentals, the better you will become as an individual performer. Set rehearsals are essential for working on the fundamentals of improv. The more you work on the fundamentals described in this book, the easier they will come to you when you need them most—on stage in front of an audience.

The simplest way to ensure success with rehearsals is to approach them with consistency. Make rehearsal with your team a priority.

Rehearsal isn't only about the time you put in; it's also about the effort you put forth and how you utilize this time. Do you have specific short-term and long-term goals that you hope to achieve through rehearsal? Are you taking your rehearsal time seriously? Is your energy level in rehearsal where it would need to be in a performance situation? This last question is extremely important. Even though you might be in a basement studio space or somebody's apartment, you need to resist the impulse to be casual or uncommitted.

WARM-UPS

A typical rehearsal should start with a few warm-ups. A warm-up is a short exercise your ensemble will do to establish group mind and/ or to get their energy up. Different warm-ups serve different functions and exercise different skills. All warm-ups can be put in one of two categories: energy or mental. A good energy warm-up should "wake you up" and get your energy up to performance level. Energy warm-ups also have the added benefit of helping you get out of your head and shed your inhibitions prior to rehearsal. Mental warm-ups are designed to get you thinking in terms of patterns and specifics. Good mental warm-ups will have you finding and continuing patterns as a group. Every rehearsal should start with at least one energy warm-up and at least one mental warm-up.

ENERGY WARM-UP EXAMPLES

The following are recommended energy warm-ups and descriptions of how they are played.

WARM-UP: CRAZY 8s

INSTRUCTIONS

- Your ensemble should form a circle.

- Everyone should loudly count to eight in unison. It is important to be very high-energy and committed.

- As you count to eight, everyone should also be shaking out their left hands and making eye contact with each other. (This movement should be reminiscent of "The Hokey Pokey.")

- Everyone should then count to eight while shaking out their right hands, then their left legs, and then their right legs to finish.

- At this point, your ensemble will start over by shaking out their left hands, this time counting to seven in unison.

- Continue to count to seven while shaking out each appendage in the same order.

- Continue this pattern for six, five, four, etc., until you get to "one."

- After you've counted out "one," everyone should let out a yell and go crazy.

WARM-UP: ENEMY, PROTECTOR

INSTRUCTIONS

- Your entire ensemble should take the stage.

- Without verbally or physically indicating so, each member of the ensemble should choose someone else to be their "enemy."

- Next, each member of the ensemble should choose someone else to be their protector. (Again, do not indicate your choice with words or actions.)

- The group should count down from three in unison.

- After you get to one, everyone should begin quickly moving around the space with the shared goal of getting your protector between you and your enemy.

- Since everyone is moving to get into position at the same time, the ensemble will be constantly moving around the space.

WARM-UP: CLAP/MOVE/SING

INSTRUCTIONS

- Your ensemble should form a circle.

- One member of the ensemble will begin the warm-up by facing the person to their immediate right.

- These two improvisers should then clap together once at the same time.

- The second improviser should then face the person to their immediate right.

- Now these two improvisers should clap together once at the same time.

- The clap should continue to be "passed" this way around the circle.

- When clapping, your goal should be synchronization, not speed. Make eye contact and try your best to clap at exactly the same time once, such that you only hear one clap.

- At any point, someone may pass the clap back in the direction it just came from. The clap should then continue in this new direction.

- After about a minute, someone in the ensemble will break out of the circle and begin moving around the space.

- The rest of the ensemble should follow so that everyone is moving around the space.

- As you move around the space, you should continue to pass the clap. Making eye contact will be key for successfully clapping at the same time as your partner.

- After another minute passes, someone in the ensemble should begin singing one of their favorite songs.

- The rest of the ensemble should join in as they continue to move around the space and pass the clap from improviser to improviser.

WARM-UP: FOLLOW THE FOLLOWER

This exercise can also serve as an effective warm-up. For instructions, please refer back to page 268.

MENTAL WARM-UP EXAMPLES

The following are recommended mental warm-ups with instructions.

WARM-UP: COUNT TO TWENTY

INSTRUCTIONS

- Your ensemble should form a huddle.

- Everyone should close their eyes.

- With only one improviser saying one number at a time, the group should start counting to twenty.

- If, at any point, two improvisers say the next number in the sequence at the same time, everyone must start over again at one.

- The game will end only once your team has counted to twenty without any two teammates speaking at the same time.

- In order to achieve this simple task, your ensemble must take their time, and give and take.

WARM-UP: POINTIES

INSTRUCTIONS

- Your ensemble should form a circle.

- Everyone should raise their right hand above their head.

- One member of the ensemble will point at someone else and say the first word in a category they have in mind. (At this point, the category will be unclear. Even though the improviser has a category in mind, that category will not necessarily play out.) For example, a member of the ensemble might point to someone else and say "orange."

- Throughout the exercise, once you say a word, you put your hand down.

- The person who was pointed to will point to someone else and say a new word. Their goal should be to add another word to the category that they believe the first improviser had in mind. In response to "orange," they might say "purple" if they think the category is colors, or "banana" if they think the category is "fruits."

- The second person who was pointed to should lock the category by pointing to someone else and saying a third word in the category. For example, if the first word was "orange," the second word was "purple," and the third word is "green," the category of "colors" has been locked.

- New words should be added until everyone has gone. The final person to add to the pattern should point to the person who started. Now we have established Category 1.

- Now this pattern of words (Category 1) can be repeated as a circuit, meaning that everyone will point to the same person and say the same word. Cycle through Category 1 a few times.

- Next, everyone raises their right hands again to begin a brand-new category. A different person will start a second category. This time around, each person should try their best to point to someone new. Once Category 2 is completed, cycle through it a few times.

- This process should then be repeated a third time.

- Now you can use this warm-up to test your ensemble's memory.

- Start over with Category 1, repeating the same words in the same order to the same people. Slowly, your ensemble should incorporate the second and third categories such that all three categories are being passed around the circle at the same time.

- You will need to be alert and ready to continue each category when you are called upon to do so.

- You may need to repeat your word or say it louder if someone does not respond, in order to keep that category alive.

WARM-UP: 7 THINGS

INSTRUCTIONS

- Your ensemble should form a circle.

- One member of the ensemble will name a category and then choose someone else to name seven items in this specific category. The category should not be totally obscure, but something that can be reasonably answered. ("Famous painters" would be a good category, while "professional lacrosse players" would be too obscure.)

- The ensemble will count off and clap once per item named.

- Once you reach seven, the ensemble should chant "These are seven things!" loudly, in unison, while punching the air.

- The person who just named seven items will choose a new category and assign it to another improviser.

- You must name seven items, whether you know seven "real" items that fit the category or not. If you know real items, use those first. It is always better to remember than to invent. If you do not know real items, or if you run out at some point, you must do your best to offer plausible-sounding items.

- Example: You are given the category of medicines. You name "Lipitor," "Zoloft," and "Claritin" before you run out. You should then give plausible-sounding items such as "Rejuvinor." Don't say fake, jokey-sounding items such as "Happy Pills."

- Repeat this process until everyone has named seven things.

WARM-UP: BA DA DA

INSTRUCTIONS

- Your ensemble should form a circle.

- Start by patting a steady rhythm on your thighs.

- You will work to build "compound words" together in pairs.

- Someone starts by saying the first half of the compound word (e.g., "shoe").

- The person standing to their immediate right says the second half of the compound word (e.g., "horn").

- The entire ensemble then says the newly formed compound word, followed by the nonsense phrase "ba da da" in unison (e.g., "shoehorn, ba da da").

- Everything said should be in sync with the rhythm you are patting on your thighs.

- After the person completes a compound word, they will offer up the first half of the next compound word.

- You should aspire to create compound words that make sense, such as "shoehorn." However, more important than making sense is staying on the rhythm. If a real compound word does not come to you, you can make up nonsense words such as "shoe-moon," as long as you stay on the rhythm.

WARM-UP: MIND MELD

INSTRUCTIONS

- Your ensemble should form a circle.

- Two improvisers volunteer to begin.

- They count to three and then say two different words simultaneously.

- Example: Improviser 1 says, "dog," and Improviser 2 says, "street."

- The entire ensemble will look for a word "in between" these words. Another way to think of this is to find a word that both of the initial words have in common.

- Once an improviser thinks they have the "definitive connecting word," they should raise their hand.

- The first two improvisers to raise their hands will count to three and then say their connecting words simultaneously.

- Let's says that the next two improvisers guess "walk" and "curb."

- The ensemble's goal is now to find the common word for these two new words.

- The same word cannot be guessed in two consecutive rounds.

- The ensemble continues this process until two improvisers say the same word simultaneously. For instance, after "walk" and "curb," two improvisers might say the word "leash," at which point the exercise would be complete.

Note: You do not have to say single words only. Terms that represent one thought, such as "ice cream cake" or "wedding reception," are acceptable.

- Additional Examples

  - Round 1: Gasoline & vegetable soup

  - Round 2: Liquid & oil spill

  - Round 3: Ocean & Katrina

  - Round 4: Hurricane

WARM-UP: ONE-WORD PATTERN GAME

This opening can also serve as an effective mental warm-up. For instructions, please refer back to page 223.

GETTING OUT OF YOUR HEAD

The benefit of rehearsal is that it will "get you out of your head." There are a lot of rules, guidelines, and theories that you are introduced to when you begin studying Long Form improv. If you are thinking about these rules, guidelines, and theories while performing, then you are bound to get stuck in your head. Being in your head is not optimal because if you are thinking of the rules, you can't fully listen to your scene partner.

While it is not optimal, being in your head in this way is inevitable at the beginning of the learning process, and is ultimately beneficial. Thinking about the rules means that you are consciously trying to follow them. With time, following the rules will become second nature, and you will no longer have to consciously think about them.

Here are some examples of being in your head that will ultimately lead to you being a better improviser:

- "I'm not letting my scene partner talk...I need to give and take."

- "Are my scene partner and I playing the same Game?"

- "We haven't made it clear who we are... we gotta get that into this scene."

- "I just said 'no' to my scene partner... was that a denial?"

The most worthless version of being in your head is worrying about "being funny." When you are in your head in this way, purposefully shift your attention to the rules, guidelines, and theories. You will still be in your head, but in a way that will ultimately benefit you.

Here are some examples of unproductively being in your head:

- "I'm not getting as many laughs as everyone else."

- "I haven't said anything in a while...I should just start talking."

- "I'm gonna pull out my Russian character that I know always goes well."

Being able to adhere to the rules, guidelines, and theories without consciously thinking about them is called being in the moment. Achieving this state is the primary goal of rehearsal. There is no magic shortcut to being in the moment. A performer's ability to do so comes as a result of lots of practice.

The concepts and rules that one person finds "easy" or "difficult" will vary wildly between any two improvisers. It is important that you do not allow those rules and concepts that you find difficult to overwhelm you. If you are struggling with many different concepts (which is bound to happen to you at some point), don't try to fix everything at once. Take each concept on one at a time. Let's say that listening is just one of many problems that you are struggling with. Focus on just that for a few rehearsals or shows. Once you feel that you've made some progress with listening, you can start focusing on something else you need to work on, such as pushing yourself to do more object work. If you try to fix everything at once, you will end up fixing nothing.

Let's revisit our earlier analogy of learning to ride a bike. You learn to ride over a period of time; the various skills and movements involved eventually becoming second nature to you. But if you remember back to the start of that process, it was probably very hard. When you first started riding a bike, you had to remember a lot of rules at once: keep balanced, keep pedaling, remember to steer, etc. Through constant practice and repetition, you eventually learned to follow all these rules without thinking about any of them. Following the rules has become "automatic," allowing you to just have fun riding the bike.

The same thing happens with Long Form. You will feel the same sort of struggle that you felt when learning to ride a bike. However, once you've put in the time, you should also find yourself thinking about each of these individual rules less and less. You will be "in the moment," allowing yourself to truly be present onstage with your fellow improvisers.

The transition from being in your head to being in the moment is not easy or predictable. In the early stages, the rules of improv will often seem to be making your improv worse. This is because you do not yet "own the rules." The time it takes for the rules of improv to become second nature will be different for every improviser. Learning the rules of improv isn't like checking items off of a list. There will be some rules that you will improve upon and then have to return to again.

Some you will own the rules from the first time you are introduced to them. There are some that you may think you will never understand until suddenly you do. Keep working hard and putting in the time, and eventually you will own all of the rules and be able to be in the moment.

WATCHING OTHERS

Watching other experienced improvisers perform is also an important part of the learning process. You will be able to learn the rules by watching others follow them. You will also learn from seeing improvisers make mistakes. Watching how different players approach scene work can help you to expand your range. When seeing shows, look for the concepts and techniques you are working on in class and/or rehearsal. If your ensemble is taking on a new form, try to find an accomplished troupe performing the same form, and use their shows to learn what works and what doesn't.

If you live in a place where you can't see live shows, you can find great Long Form improv online. A great source to check out is UCBComedy.com, but any good Long Form you can find will benefit you. If you want to get better at Long Form improv, see as much of it as you can.

GROUP MIND

In addition to your development as an individual player, rehearsal is also about developing ensemble or group mind. Long Form improvisation is a team activity. You can draw comparisons between improv rehearsal and practicing together as a sports team. How good would an NBA team be if they never practiced? Most professional sports teams work so well together because they practice with each other almost every day of the week.

It is crucial that all members of the group (or as many as possible) attend rehearsals. If you are constantly missing members, it will be very hard to develop group mind. Rehearsing is the simplest thing that you can do to become a great Long Form group. Meeting once a week for three hours is the bare minimum commitment to be expected from people calling themselves a Long Form group. For a group to get very good, they would need to rehearse a minimum of three times a week. While this might seem like a big time commitment, remember that for actors rehearsing a play, meeting every day of the week is the norm. The more you rehearse, the better your ensemble will become.

Rehearsal allows you and your group to get on the same page in terms of the structure of your show. Structural elements that can be decided upon in rehearsal include openings, editing techniques, and approaches to initiating.

Rehearsal is also where you will discover your ensemble's style. Are you a team who plays at a faster or slower pace? Are you especially adept at physicality, or are you more verbal? Do you keep the entire ensemble involved at all times through scene painting, sound effects, background work, etc.? Or perhaps characters are your ensemble's strength. Once you discover your style in rehearsal, you will know what strengths you can rely on in performance.

Rehearsal will allow individual players to discover their roles in the group. You will discover the aspects of Long Form at which you individually excel. Every member of the group doesn't have to be masterful at every single skill mentioned in this book. A great Long Form group is comprised of people who know when and where they need to step up, and when and where they can rely on others in a performance.

Rehearsal allows you to establish the trust in each other that you need in order to step out onstage in front of an audience with absolutely nothing planned in advance. Trust within an ensemble is what allows you to take the risks and play with the confidence and fearlessness that will make your performances memorable. Trust allows you to step out with any idea and know that you will be supported by everyone else standing onstage.

A team with a strong group mind will seem as if they are reading each other's thoughts and anticipating moves before they even happen. They will never seem to be lost or struggling for what to do next. The seamlessness of their performance will seem magical to an audience. In reality, a seemingly effortless performance is the result of all the hard work an ensemble has put in at rehearsals developing their group mind. Strong group mind will garner you the ultimate compliment in Long Form: that your improvisation had to have been scripted.

BEYOND REHEARSAL

While setting aside time for rehearsal is important, it is also good for your ensemble to simply hang out together. If you hang out with your fellow improvisers, you will most likely end up informally playing Game. You might end up joking around, pretending to be other people, creating fake conflict with each other for the fun of it, etc. Improvisers refer to this as "doing bits" with each other. In effect, this is just more practice. When you become friends with each other offstage, it will come across as chemistry onstage.

Finding the Right Balance in Chemistry

It is rare that the original cast of a Long Form group will stay the same for as long as that ensemble is active. Not all members of the original group will fit or belong forever.

As a group develops, certain players may no longer fit because they have not evolved in the same manner as the rest of the group. It is also possible for irreconcilable personal conflicts to arise between members of the group. In these cases—when a member or certain members choose to leave, or are asked to leave—the resulting group is usually the best scenario for all parties involved. The remaining members of the group can continue to pursue their goals while giving the improviser or improvisers who have left an opportunity to join a group for which they are a better fit. These changes often have nothing to do with a performer's competence as an improviser. They are made primarily with concerns about group dynamics in mind.

Furthermore, a performer who is a perfect fit may choose to leave a group due to personal or professional reasons.

You will want to replace members of the ensemble who leave with new improvisers who fit the chemistry of your ensemble.

Personnel changes have the potential to be awkward and challenging for any Long Form group. However, these changes are necessary. Along with rehearsal, having the right chemistry is one of the major keys to success for any Long Form improv ensemble.

COACHES & DIRECTORS

A coach is someone outside of the group who leads all rehearsals. Although they are not a member of the group, a coach should be another improviser or someone familiar with how Long Form works. It is their job to help a group work on the fundamentals of a longform structure with which the group is already familiar. It is the responsibility of the group to let the coach know what their specific needs are. (For example, a group working on the Harold may know that they want to work on openings and second beats.) A prepared coach comes into rehearsals with exercises in mind that will help a group achieve its goals. After working with a group for some time, a coach will shape rehearsals in order to reinforce good habits and help a group improve in areas of weakness. If possible, a coach should also attend performances in order to better know what their group needs to work on.

While it is possible to rehearse without a coach, it is highly recommended that your group hire one. The main reason for having a coach is to have an informed and objective source of criticism. Knowing your weaknesses is essential if you want to get better as a group.

We realize that some readers of this book who are far from New York, Chicago, Los Angeles, or other bigger cities with improv communities may have a hard time finding a qualified coach. If you find yourself in this situation, it is possible to conduct productive rehearsals by having one member of the ensemble serve as the coach for a given rehearsal. In order to remain objective, the person coaching does not improvise during the rehearsal. The improviser serving as the designated coach should change from rehearsal to rehearsal, rotating through each member of the ensemble. A coach from within the ensemble needs to be formally designated and agreed upon by all members of the ensemble. Having all members of an ensemble provide feedback during a rehearsal is not a viable substitute for a coach. That would require people to give notes on the improv that they were a part of. These notes will often end up feeling like unsolicited criticism and judgment from a peer, instead of an objective critique from an outside perspective.

If you are the designated coach, you must remember to act professionally when critiquing your fellow teammates. Remember to be objective and keep your feedback focused on the fundamentals of good improv without injecting your own personal opinions and philosophies. Present your notes with humility. Don't overstep your bounds. You need to constantly remind yourself that you are a part of this team. You are only giving suggestions to make your team stronger. When you are giving notes to your teammates, deliver them in the same way you would like them to be given to you.

If your ensemble wants to perform an existing longform that they are unfamiliar with, or wish to develop a brand-new form, they will want to hire a director. The director will have input on all elements of a performance: structure, style, and presentation.

Structure

- Teaching an existing longform

- Making modifications to an existing longform

- Developing a brand-new longform

Style

- Pacing (longer scenes with gradual heightening, shorter, fast-paced scenes with lots of tag-outs, etc.)

- Editing technique

- Emphasis on either character-based Games or premise-based Games

- Frequency of group scenes

- Types of support work (sound effects, physical support, playing objects, background characters, etc.)

Presentation

- Type of suggestion and how to elicit it

- Starting the show (Are you introduced? Do you take the stage with the lights up? Are you introduced individually or as a group?)

- Ending the show (Will you be "blacked out" by the tech booth, or will a member of the ensemble end the show from the stage?)

- Manner of dress (casual vs. formal)

- Use of the stage space

- Music (intro, outro, and scoring)

- Lighting for mood or emphasis

- Curtain call vs. no curtain call

A director is different from a coach who simply helps you hone fundamentals and address weaknesses within a form with which you are already familiar. In a coaching situation, the group is basically in control, since a coach serves the group's needs. A director, on the other hand, has far more control. Whereas the coach follows the group's lead, a group will follow the director's lead. Besides directing the group in the development of a longform, a director should also give feedback on basic scene work fundamentals, just as a coach would.

Becoming a Coach Yourself

Once you are consistently doing good work and feel as though you have a very strong understanding of the fundamentals, you may want to start coaching other groups. As stated earlier, a coach's primary goal is to address the needs of a group and help them reach their goals. You will also reinforce good habits and help them to rid themselves of any bad ones.

It will be your job as coach to run the rehearsal and keep the team on task. By coming up with an agenda of exercises and a focus for that day's rehearsal, you can ensure that rehearsal time is being used efficiently.

Be forewarned that some of the progress your group has made in rehearsal may go out the window once your group performs in front of an audience. The team is going to make mistakes and do things that they maybe wouldn't do in rehearsal in their attempt to entertain an audience. You should be mindful of how the change of environment can affect a team's performance. Do not become frustrated and hold it against them. Simply point out the strengths and weaknesses of the performance, just as you would in rehearsal. However, if you feel that your group has consciously abandoned the fundamentals of good scene work in an attempt to get quick laughs from the audience, you will have to point this out to them.

When coaching, you want to offer feedback in three major categories:

- Fundamentals of scene work

- Individual tendencies of each performer

- Group tendencies

While it is important to be honest when delivering notes, there isn't any need to be condescending or cruel. Criticism should always be constructive and provided in the most supportive way possible. Remember, you are not there to discourage them; you are there to help them learn from their mistakes.

Each group will need to devote a different amount of time to rehearsing and developing as an ensemble before they are ready to perform in front of an audience. How long it will take for your group depends on the level of talent and experience you have, as well as your goals as a group. Taking rehearsal and preparation seriously will ensure that your ensemble becomes the best that it can be.

SHOWMANSHIP

Once you are ready to perform in front of an audience, you should do so with a sense of professionalism. You should approach each performance with respect for your time onstage. Many people take an overly casual approach toward performing improv because of its unscripted and playful nature. However, performing Long Form should be considered a privilege, and getting the chance to perform for an audience should never be taken for granted. A paying audience that is watching you perform expects to be entertained. Treating the audience and your show with respect and professionalism will go a long way toward entertaining them.

RESPECT FOR THE SCENE

Respecting the scene means always committing to and remaining within the fiction of the scene. Therefore, when you get cheap laughs through postmodern commentary, you are disrespecting the scene and your scene partner. Postmodern commentary breaks from the established reality of the scene in a way that undermines it and interferes with the audience's suspension of disbelief. Some examples of postmodern commentary:

Example 1:   **A man with a beard is playing a woman in an improv scene. His scene partner says, "My, you're a little hirsute for a woman."**

In this case, the second improviser has undermined the reality of the scene by calling attention to the reality of the performance (e.g., that a man, out of necessity, was playing a woman).

Example 2:   **An improviser is having difficulty maintaining a German accent. His scene partner says, "Are you sure you're from Germany? Your accent sounds fake..."**

In this case, the second improviser has undermined the reality of the scene by calling attention to the imperfect accent, instead of supporting his scene partner by committing to the established reality.

Example 3:   **An ensemble is doing a group scene in which all of the characters are huge musical fans, sharing their favorites. One improviser with little knowledge of musicals is able to name the title of a musical. Another member of the ensemble, knowing his limited knowledge of musicals, asks him to sing a specific song from that musical.**

This type of postmodern commentary is referred to as "pimping." You are pimping your scene partner when you ask them to do something that you know will be difficult or embarrassing.

Example 4:   **An adult male improviser is called on to play a little girl. Instead of altering his voice and physicality slightly to commit to the character, the improviser talks and moves as he always does.**

In this case, the improviser is commenting on the fact that he is a man playing a little girl through a lack of commitment.

Example 5: **An ensemble is performing a scene taking place in a bar. The ensemble has already successfully found a Game in this scene. One of the improvisers accidentally walks through a space where the bar had been established. Another improviser stops the action of the scene to say, "Oh my God! Did you just see that? He has the ability to phase through solid objects!"**

In this instance, a new unusual thing has been introduced that will undermine and almost definitely trump the Game that was already being played.

Note that all of these instances of postmodern commentary would likely elicit laughs from an audience. However, these laughs are cheap laughs. You want your laughs to come from the content of the scene, not from commenting on its execution. Actively seeking cheap laughs from postmodern commentary will ultimately undermine your show and do more harm than good.

You can also look at "breaking" as a subtle form of postmodern commentary. Breaking is when an improviser breaks from the reality of the scene and begins laughing. This will sometimes happen unavoidably. However, it is unacceptable to pander to the audience by intentionally laughing at what happens in a scene. When you do this, you are causing the audience to see you as an improviser who is amused by what you are doing onstage, instead of allowing them to see you as a character within the fiction of the scene.

Having respect for the scene you are in is synonymous with having respect for your teammates. Notice that almost all of the examples we gave involved one improviser undercutting another. Postmodern commentary is always a selfish act, getting a laugh for oneself at the expense of the greater good of the scene. Playing with respect for the scene is as simple as stepping onstage with only one goal in mind: to make everyone else standing onstage with you look great.

STAGECRAFT

Stagecraft in improvisation is about being heard and being seen. If the audience can't hear or see you, they are going to have a hard time finding your show funny.

There are a few things to consider in order to make sure that you and your scene partners can be seen properly onstage. First, avoid blind spots on the stage from which the audience will not be able to see you. Second, make sure that the other performers are not blocking you. Third, make sure that you are at least partially facing out toward the audience. This is referred to as "cheating out." You want to remain turned out toward the audience so that they can see your face. Your facial expressions are one of your primary tools in comedy. Finally, be mindful of upstaging your scene partner. When you upstage another performer, you are standing behind them so that they are forced to turn their back to the audience to speak to you.

It is also important to be heard onstage. You will need to project. This means speaking loud enough so that the people in the back row of the audience can hear you. This is something that the director or coach will need to be on top of, since rehearsal will get improvisers used to playing to each other without considering being heard by an audience. Remember, even if your personal style is dry or understated, or you are playing a character that is shy or whispering, you still need to be heard.

Something else to consider with regard to being heard is "holding for laughs." If you say something that causes the audience to laugh, you may need to pause before offering your next line. Otherwise, it may be drowned out by the audience's laughter. This is a skill that comes with performance experience only. With enough time onstage, holding for laughs will become second nature, as will projecting and positioning yourself onstage so that you can be seen.

BEING READY TO PERFORM

You need to step onstage ready to perform. You can't start cold and find your groove ten minutes into your longform.

It is very important for you to greet your audience with energy and enthusiasm. If you are low energy or apathetic, you run the risk of losing the audience's attention and respect before you even begin. Your audience has come out to see a show. Your ensemble should give off the impression that you all are performing from the moment you step onstage.

Preshow warm-ups are the best way to get yourself physically and mentally ready to perform from the moment you step onstage. Just like in rehearsal, your ensemble should do one energy warm-up and at least one mental warm-up.

When you choose warm-ups to do before a show, choose the ones that your group has the most fun doing. Fun preshow warm-ups that get your ensemble laughing together and having a good time can be very valuable. You want to be in a positive mind-set before stepping onstage. A fun or silly preshow warm-up can help you do this.

WARM-UP: BEASTIE RAP

INSTRUCTIONS

- Your ensemble should form a circle.

- One improviser will throw out the first line of a rap (e.g., "I went to the pet store and I bought a cat!").

- The rest of the improvisers in the circle will respond by rapping, "DA-da-da-DA-da-DA-da-DA-DA!"

- The person to the immediate right of the first person who just rapped will offer a line in which the last word rhymes.

- Example: "It was cold outside so I put on my hat!"

- With each new line of the Beastie Rap, try to make the last word of the line fall on the final beat. The entire ensemble should attempt to say this word together, emulating the Beastie Boys.

- After each new line, the entire ensemble will repeat the "DA-da-da-DA-da-DA-da-DA-DA!"

- You will continue around the circle in the same direction until everyone has provided a new line for the rap, creating rhymes without repeating rhyming words.

- If a rhyme is repeated, the ensemble should shout, "Oh!" in unison and then start over.

- Additionally, if you simply run out of rhymes and hesitate or disrupt the rhythm, the ensemble should shout, "Oh!" in unison and then start over.

- If you make it all the way around the circle, the person who started the rhyme should add a final rhyme to that rap. The person to the immediate right will then offer a brand-new line to rhyme off of, beginning an entirely new rap.

WARM-UP: HOT SPOT

INSTRUCTIONS

- Your ensemble should form a circle.

- One improviser in the circle shouts out a suggestion.

- Someone else will step into the center of the circles and sing an existing song inspired by the suggestion.

- Example: The suggestion is "time." Someone steps into the center and sings, "Time Is on My Side" by the Rolling Stones.

- The improvisers in the circle will take turns tagging out the person in the middle to sing a new song. Each new song should be inspired by the last.

- Example: After hearing "Time Is on My Side," someone else might tag in and sing, "Rock Around the Clock" by Bill Haley and the Comets.

- You should confidently commit to singing the songs, even if you are not good at singing.

- The improvisers in the circle must support the singer by tagging them out and taking over. The goal is to never leave anyone in the center of the circle singing for too long.

- Further moves in this example could be "Feels Like the First" and "Parsley, Sage, Rosemary & Thyme."

The key to having high performance energy for the entire show is to start by hitting the ground running. If you start with the right energy, it shouldn't be hard to maintain it throughout the entire longform.

INTROS

A strong introduction at the top of your show is a great way to let your audience know right from the beginning that you have put some thought into your performance. A good intro tells the audience what it is they are about to see. Write your intro as though you are speaking to people who are attending your show for the first time. A good intro should avoid inside jokes or references to other shows at your theater, so that you don't alienate any newcomers. It is also important not to come off as "too cool for school" in your intro, seeming bored as if you've done this a million times.

Here is a good sample intro:

"Hello! We are the Upright Citizens Brigade and we are going to perform a Harold for you tonight. The Harold is a Long Form improvisational structure created by Del Close in Chicago."

"What you are about to see is completely improvised, and to begin, all we need is a suggestion of a single word. Everything that you see tonight is going to be inspired by the suggestion that you provide, and once we get this suggestion we won't need any other suggestions from you."

This introduction has explained the Harold clearly enough so that someone completely unfamiliar with it can have a sense of what they are about to see. Because the introduction is clear and concise, it will start the show with a sense of professionalism.

OUTROS

An outro is a short speech to the audience that follows the end of your show, given by one member of the ensemble. A strong outro thanks the audience for coming out and encourages them to come back again. If your show is one of many performed at a theater, the outro presents a great opportunity for you to inform your audience about other shows being performed there.

Here is a typical outro for the UCB Theatre:

"Thank you for coming out to Harold Night! If you enjoyed the show, please come again and tell your friends. We have other great shows here at the Upright Citizens Brigade Theatre seven nights a week. If you would like any information on other shows, please visit our website and sign our mailing list on your way out. Thank you and good night!"

SOBRIETY

Due to the cabaret atmosphere of most venues hosting improv shows, drinking is often considered to be part of the experience of performing improv. In fact, drinking is an activity commonly associated with comedians in general. In spite of this association, reckless or irresponsible drinking can have a very negative effect on the quality of your performances.

Performing sober is another way that you and your ensemble can show your audience that you respect them. Seeing improvisers performing in an inebriated state can be a painful experience. By performing drunk, you are essentially telling your teammates and the audience that the show means as little to you as playing video golf at a local bar.

DRESS

How you choose to dress for each performance is another way to show respect for your audience. The Upright Citizens Brigade believes that new, unproven ensembles should dress in a manner comparable to "business casual." This will lend an air of professionalism to your show. This suggestion is not an attempt by the UCB to alter or criticize anyone's personal style. The UCB believes that putting in some effort to look presentable will go a long way in making your audience take you seriously as performers. This is especially important for new performers whose success will be variable.

If you do choose to dress sloppily or without concern, your shows had better be amazing. An audience will forgive an ensemble's sloppy attire if their work is sharp and funny. However, if your show is subpar and your appearance is sloppy, the audience may feel disrespected. They are more likely to assume that your subpar performance was due to a lack of effort on your part.

Your manner of dress also shouldn't be distracting in any way. This applies to anything that is too slovenly, provocative, or likely to draw attention. You don't want the audience to be paying more attention to your ratty shorts, sexy clothing, or hilarious ironic T-shirt than they are to your scenes.

In a practical sense, it is important that you always dress so that you are ready to perform. If you are wearing a pair of pants that you're afraid of getting dirty onstage, you are going to be preoccupied thinking about your clothing and not invested in your scenes. If you are wearing a miniskirt that is liable to show off more than you want in certain positions, you may be unwilling to make physical choices that would best serve your scenes. Since you are going to want to be free of restraint, dress to be active. Dress to play.

FINAL THOUGHTS

For many writers and performers, Long Form improvisation remains one of the most rewarding performance experiences they can have. The connection a Long Form ensemble has with its audience is truly one of a kind. For many professional comedians, there is simply nothing else that compares to stepping onstage and creating a piece of comedy in the moment. This is why you see so many accomplished comedians returning to their improv roots on any stage that welcomes them. While becoming a great improviser is no easy task, any Long Form improviser that you ask will undoubtedly say that the hard work and time that they have put in to learning the craft was well worth it. Now that you have read this book, the next step in your pursuit of Long Form excellence is to see and do as much Long Form improv as possible.

Practice, practice, practice

It was mentioned in the very beginning of this book that reading it alone would not make you a great improviser. This book is only useful if it is read in conjunction with practice and performance. If you have read this book cover to cover without yet putting any of the information into practice, it is likely that you feel overwhelmed by all the rules and theories. It is important to realize that Long Form needs to be practiced for you to truly understand it. Long Form improvisation deserves the same respect and effort you would give to painting, acting, dancing, or any other art form. Putting in time watching, practicing, and doing is the step that no serious improviser can skip, no matter how naturally talented they may be. Much of the time you put in will be devoted to drilling the fundamentals, especially learning how to consistently Yes And and training yourself to play the patterns of If Then.

Constantly drilling the fundamentals so that you can react subconsciously in the moment will help you become truly comfortable onstage. The fundamentals, once they become second nature, will be the blueprint for your comedic genius. Mastering these fundamentals will allow you to react onstage in a way that both highlights your own talent and allows you to build successful comedic scenes and longforms with others.

NOTES

NOTES